The Way Women Are

The Way Women Are

Transformative Opinions and Dissents of Justice Ruth Bader Ginsburg

Edited with an Introduction by
Cathy Cambron

Welcome Rain Publishers
NEW YORK

The Way Women Are

Original content copyright © 2020 Welcome Rain Publishers LLC

Designed by Laura Smyth, Smythtype Design

10 9 8 7 6 5 4 3 2

Library of Congress Cataloging in Publication Data is available from the publisher.
Direct any inquiries to Welcome Rain LLC.

Printed in the USA

ISBN: 978-1-56649-404-5

Contents

The Way Women Are

INTRODUCTION

The Extraordinary Talent and Capacity of Ruth Bader Ginsburg

> Generalizations about "the way women are," estimates of what is appropriate for most women, no longer justify denying opportunity to women whose talent and capacity place them outside the average description.
>
> —U.S. Supreme Court Associate Justice Ruth Bader Ginsburg, majority opinion, *United States v. Virginia et al.* (1996)

Ruth Bader Ginsburg has become a cherished figure for many Americans, popular in a way no other Supreme Court justice has matched. For starters, no other justice, male or female, has been the subject of multiple biographies published during his or her lifetime.[1] But there's much more evidence of our affection for RBG: A documentary about her, *RBG*, became a surprise hit in movie theaters in 2018. The story of Ginsburg's early career was turned into a Hollywood biopic, *On the Basis of Sex*. A Tumblr feed in her honor became a best-selling book that made most of us familiar with the moniker "Notorious RBG."

Children's books celebrate her.[2] People wear Ruth Bader Ginsburg costumes on Halloween, in real life and on multiple television series.[3] The comedian Kate McKinnon has a recurring bit enacting a feisty RBG on *Saturday Night Live*. An abundance of Ruth Bader Ginsburg merchandise can be purchased online and in stores, from action figures to dissent collar jewelry to scented "Notorious RBG" candles. It's as though some of us can't get enough RBG in our day-to-day.

Those of us who applaud her physical and mental toughness, and her willingness to speak up in vigorous dissent when she believes the Court has made wrongheaded decisions, may consider her a role model. We may be grateful for the work she has done as a lawyer and a justice to break down stereotypes about "the way women (and men) are."[4] We may prize the keen sense she has of what real life might be like for real people in particular circumstances; we may value her understanding of how it can feel to be on the outside looking in. We are awed by her ability to virtually never miss work despite bereavement and illness. We gobble up articles about her taste in art, her relationships with other justices, the way her Brooklyn accent has gained strength over the years.[5]

We collect and share stories about her: The advice her mother-in-law gave when Ruth married ("Dear, in every good marriage, it helps sometimes to be a little deaf").[6] Her seriousness, which provoked Jane Ginsburg to track the times she and her brother succeeded in amusing their mother in a notebook Jane titled *Mommy Laughed*.[7] What exactly the justice does in that much-discussed regular workout of hers.[8] The deliberate way she talks, which inspired her clerks to come up with the "two-Mississippi" rule for counting how long to wait after it seems she is done speaking so as not to interrupt her.[9] Her passion for the opera. Her elegance in dress. The collar (or jabot) that she wears with her judicial robes; her decision to choose the famous one that appears on the cover of this book to signal a day on which she will be in dissent; and the fact that she wore a glittering, spiky jabot sent to her by a fan in her official Supreme Court group portrait for 2018, the first to include controversial justice Brett Kavanaugh.[10]

We have *feelings* about this justice. We admire her—fervently. We worry about her well-being. We want to continue to hear her voice.

Kiki Bader

Ruth Bader Ginsburg was born Joan Ruth Bader in Brooklyn, New York, on March 15, 1933, the second daughter, and the only child to survive to adulthood, of Nathan Bader, a Russian Jew who immigrated to New York when he was thirteen, and his wife, born Celia Amster, whose parents immigrated to New York from Poland shortly before Celia was born.[11] Ruth's older sister, Marilyn, gave the infant Ruth the nickname "Kiki," because she kicked so much; two years later, Marilyn contracted spinal meningitis and died at the age of six. Ginsburg has said that she grew up with a "smell of death" hovering around the household.[12]

Celia, who loved literature and the arts, had cut short her own schooling to help pay for her older brother's university attendance. As Ruth grew up, Celia somehow carefully saved $8,000 for Ruth's education. In high school, Ruth was a "model American teenager"—attractive, popular, smart.[13] At home, however, her mother had become ill with cervical cancer. Ruth told none of her classmates and studied by her mother's bedside in the afternoons. Celia died just two days before Ruth was due to give a speech at her high school graduation. Justice Ginsburg often repeats the advice her mother gave as Ruth was growing up: Always be independent, and be a lady.[14]

Ruth went to college at Cornell University, where in 1950 she met Martin Ginsburg, who was a year ahead of her. She thought he was smart and funny, and he was smitten at once. He loved that she was smart. She loved that he loved that about her. She later said, "He was the only guy I ever dated who cared whether I had a brain."[15] They knew that unlike many women at the time, Ruth would work after their marriage; together they chose the field of law for their careers so that they could bounce ideas off each other. The wedding took place soon after Ruth graduated, in June 1954.

The Ginsburg Family

Marty had finished one year at Harvard Law School when he was called to service in the U.S. Army, teaching artillery in Lawton, Oklahoma. There, Ruth had her first experience with pregnancy discrimination: she took the civil service exam, made a score that qualified her for the rank of claims adjuster (GS-5), made the mistake of informing the Social Security office where she worked that she was pregnant, and was then immediately demoted to the lowest rank (GS-2).[16]

After the birth of their daughter, Jane, and the conclusion of Marty's service, the couple returned to Harvard Law School, where Ruth had also been accepted. A nanny took care of Jane until four in the afternoon, when Ruth took over; after Jane's bedtime, Ruth would resume studying. Ruth was near the top of her class by the end of the first year and was selected for *Harvard Law Review*, a significant accomplishment.

Then Marty was diagnosed with testicular cancer. Ruth stoically handled his illness. She managed all the household chores, which the couple normally split equitably. She recruited other students in Marty's classes to make carbon copies of their class notes, and she typed his papers after she had completed her own schoolwork. The other students on the *Harvard Law Review* knew only that Ruth never missed class, was always perfectly prepared, and turned all her assignments in promptly.[17] This may have been when Ruth discovered one of her seemingly magical powers: her ability routinely to function well on very little sleep.

Marty recovered and graduated. He had a job offer in New York that was better than any he received in Boston. Ruth made the difficult decision to transfer to Columbia Law School from Harvard to keep the family together. She graduated tied for first in her class but could not find a job as a lawyer; many law firms at the time still hired only the occasional token woman associate. At last, one of her Columbia professors made heroic efforts to help Ruth land a two-year clerkship with a federal judge. Next, she learned Swedish and spent time with Jane in Sweden in order to write a book about the Swedish legal system. Around this time Ruth manifested another power in her life: the physical and mental discipline of a rigorous regular workout. She says she started doing daily calisthenics based on the Royal Canadian Air Force exercise plan when she was twenty-nine years old.[18]

Ruth then took a tenure-track position at Rutgers Law School in Newark. She became pregnant with her second child but resolved this time to keep her pregnancy secret and was back to teaching within a month of delivering her son, James, in September 1965. She managed to care for her father while he recovered from an automobile accident around this time in the family's life as well.[19]

Professor Ginsburg, Advocate

By 1970, urged by her students, Ruth agreed to teach the first class at Rutgers on women and the law. She had signed up to work as a volunteer lawyer with the American Civil Liberties Union (ACLU)—where letters pouring in from women complaining about gender discrimination were routed to Ruth—and also helped the other female professors at Rutgers file a pay discrimination claim against the university.[20] Meanwhile, Marty, urged by the couple's children, had taken over the family's cooking and had become an accomplished chef while carrying on a very successful tax law practice. Supporting Ruth's career had become second nature to him.

Marty discovered a case that he thought would interest Ruth and perhaps the ACLU. The case that became *Moritz v. Commission of Internal Revenue Service*, 469 F.2d 466 (10th Circuit 1972), involved a traveling salesman whose elderly mother lived with him; he wanted to take a tax deduction for the money he spent on a caregiver when he was away from home. The IRS allowed that deduction only for taxpayers who were women, widowers, or the husbands of incapacitated women; but Charles Moritz had never been married.

Ruth contacted Melvin Wulf, a friend from her days at Jewish summer camp, who was national director of the ACLU. Ruth knew that the ACLU had taken on the appeal to the U.S. Supreme Court in a case called *Reed v. Reed*, involving an Idaho law that preferred men over women when more

4

than one person applied to administer the estate of a decedent. Together the Ginsburgs wrote a brief in support of Moritz's claim and sent it to Wulf, and Ruth appended a note suggesting that some of what the couple had written could be useful for *Reed v. Reed*. Then she asked whether Wulf had ever considered hiring a woman as co-counsel in that case.[21]

Reed v. Reed would become the first case that Ruth briefed before the U.S. Supreme Court and the first-ever Supreme Court decision invalidating a law that discriminated by gender; Ginsburg's brief is included in this book. The ACLU's Women's Rights Project, which Ruth co-founded, went on to litigate a series of cases before the U.S. Supreme Court in the 1970s that transformed the legal landscape for women.

Times had changed. By 1971, universities trying to avoid the appearance of sexism or charges of sex discrimination were now more eager to hire the qualified women who a decade earlier had had trouble finding work in the law. Ruth became a professor at Columbia Law School after deciding not to pursue an opportunity at Harvard Law School. Soon after she was hired, she admonished the university's vice president that Columbia had violated Title VII of the Civil Rights Act of 1964 and possibly the Equal Pay Act when, in workforce cutbacks, the university laid off twenty-five maids but not a single janitor.[22] Ginsburg went on to help file a class action lawsuit on behalf of female administrators and teachers at the university who were paid less than men.

In the arguments she made before the U.S. Supreme Court for the ACLU, Ginsburg manifested yet another of her awe-inspiring powers: her extraordinary boldness in advocacy. The brief she wrote in *Reed v. Reed* presents a sweeping survey of the ways women had been disparaged and disadvantaged on the basis of sex. Ginsburg compared women's treatment to racial or national origin discrimination and argued that courts should view sex discrimination in the same way, as suspect, in view of the U.S. Constitution's guarantee of equal protection of the laws.

In advance of her first oral argument before the U.S. Supreme Court, in *Frontiero v. Richardson* in 1973, Ginsburg skipped lunch so that she wouldn't vomit from the stress. She then proceeded to tell the nine silent male justices arrayed in front of her, in the words of nineteenth-century abolitionist Sarah Grimké: "I ask no favor for my sex. All I ask of our brethren is that they take their feet off our necks." This book includes a transcript of the oral argument in *Frontiero*, as well as portions of Ginsburg's brief.

Tempering her boldness, however, Ginsburg has long been pragmatic. She did not hesitate to change her approach over the years as she witnessed how the Court responded to her arguments. She has advised others, "Fight for the things you care about, but do it in a way that will lead others to join you."[23]

Judge Ginsburg of the U.S. Court of Appeals for the District of Columbia Circuit

When President Jimmy Carter took office in 1977, only one woman served as a federal appeals court judge. Ginsburg decided to try to become a judge herself and hear cases rather than advocate for causes. She knew she was not interested in the grind of federal district (trial) court work and instead applied to two intermediate appeals courts (U.S. Courts of Appeals): the Second Circuit (which sits in New York City) and the District of Columbia Circuit. She was disappointed to learn that the Second Circuit would not consider her application because she had applied to the D.C. Circuit as well.

Ginsburg's application to the D.C. appeals court summarized what everyone who knew her had long understood: that she had a "high capacity for sustained work . . . long hours, homework, extending day as long as necessary to accomplish task needed to be done."[24] Only Senator Strom Thurmond of North Carolina voted against her nomination in the Senate Judiciary Committee, and in the full Senate, Ginsburg was confirmed unanimously in 1980. Ever the supportive spouse, Marty left his highly successful tax law practice in New York to follow Ruth to D.C. There, he made sure she ate and slept, as she had a habit of working through mealtimes and late into the night.

After the boldness of her advocacy with the ACLU, her thirteen years on the circuit court bench proved Ginsburg an even-handed judge who did not alarm conservatives: "She became known as a consensus builder who adhered closely to precedent, wrote narrowly tailored decisions, and refused to join intemperately written opinions. A 1987 study showed that she voted more often with Republican appointees than with Democratic appointees."[25]

Marty was always on the lookout for ways that Ruth could reach her full potential. The more convivial half of the couple, when he became aware that President Bill Clinton was looking for a woman to nominate to the Supreme Court in 1993, Marty worked his network to urge consideration of Ruth. Her nomination to the Supreme Court was not very controversial; in the end, the vote in the Senate was 96–3 in favor of her confirmation.

At the conclusion of her warm, well-received remarks accepting the nomination in the White House Rose Garden, Ruth said, "I have a last thank-you. It is to my mother, Celia Amster Bader, the bravest and strongest person I have known, who was taken from me much too soon. I pray that I may be all that she would have been had she lived in an age when women could aspire and achieve and daughters are cherished as much as sons."[26]

U.S. Supreme Court Justice Ruth Bader Ginsburg

At the U.S. Supreme Court, Ginsburg was the second woman Supreme Court justice on a bench led by conservative Chief Justice William Rehnquist. Justice Sandra Day O'Connor, the first woman on the Supreme Court, had been appointed by President Ronald Reagan in 1981. In spite of the two justices' very different appearances and points of view, others often confused them. Ginsburg called O'Connor her "big sister."[27]

Justice O'Connor had spent twelve years having to use a bathroom in her chambers, as the bathroom in the Court's Robing Room was for men only. Now that a second woman had joined the Court, a renovation was at last undertaken to fix that. By the time Justices Sonia Sotomayor, in 2009, and Elena Kagan, in 2010, were appointed to the Court by President Barack Obama, Justice O'Connor had retired (in 2006), but it no longer seemed unusual for a woman to serve as a justice.

Ginsburg saw the retirement of O'Connor (who was succeeded by Justice Samuel Alito, appointed by President George W. Bush) as a turning point for the Court. "If you look at the term when she was not with us," Ginsburg said, "every five-to-four decision when I was with the four, I would have been with the five if she had stayed."[28] Ginsburg now often votes with the other two female justices and Justice Stephen Breyer, appointed by Clinton in 1994.

When she was appointed, Ginsburg also joined Justice Antonin Scalia, who had served with her on the U.S. Court of Appeals for the D.C. Circuit. While liberal Ginsburg and deeply conservative Scalia disagreed on many issues, they shared a love of opera, and Ginsburg appreciated Scalia's humor. Their families spent New Year's Eve together many years, and a photograph Ginsburg keeps in her chambers features tiny RBG riding an elephant behind the rotund Scalia, from a 1994 trip to India.[29]

Justice Scalia died in February 2016. The Republican Senate refused to consider President Obama's nominee to succeed Scalia, Chief Judge Merrick

Garland of the D.C. Circuit, leaving the Court short a member for more than a year, until President Donald Trump's nominee, Neil Gorsuch, was confirmed in April 2017.

Ginsburg's relationships with all the justices have always been cordial. "I was very fond of the old Chief," she said of Chief Justice Rehnquist, whose chair is now occupied by Chief Justice John Roberts, who was appointed by President George W. Bush in 2005 after Rehnquist's death. Of Roberts, Ginsburg said, "For the public, I think the current Chief is very good at meeting and greeting people, always saying the right thing for the remarks he makes for five or ten minutes at various gatherings."[30] Of Justice Brett Kavanaugh—whose nomination by Trump in 2018 stirred controversy when Professor Christine Blasey Ford testified before the Senate that as a teenager Kavanaugh had sexually assaulted her—Ginsburg noted that he "made history by bringing on board an all-female law clerk crew."[31]

Ginsburg's work on the Court has often drawn on the superpower she has always had: overcoming every difficulty to get her work done. She survived a bout with colorectal cancer in 1999 while missing virtually no Court days.[32] After being diagnosed with pancreatic cancer in January 2009, she managed to recover from surgery so rapidly that she did not miss a single oral argument of the Court's spring term.[33] She was back at work for the last week of the Court's term the day after Marty died, in June 2010.[34] About to be treated again for pancreatic cancer in August 2019, she said: "'There was a senator, I think it was after my pancreatic cancer, who announced with great glee that I was going to be dead within six months. That senator, whose name I have forgotten, is now himself dead, and I,' she added with a smile, 'am very much alive.'"[35]

The Writings in This Book

The writings included in this book give a perspective on a broad range of Ginsburg's legal reasoning, from her early work on women's rights with the ACLU to her thoughts about abortion to her view of what the First Amendment requires. These writings begin with the brief in *Reed v. Reed*, filed in 1971. Ginsburg's opinions and dissents are sampled from the years she has served on the Supreme Court, including the term that began in October 2018 (the Court's yearly term begins the first Monday in October and generally continues until the following June or July).

Ginsburg chooses to read a simplified, shortened version of many of her opinions and dissents from the bench when the decision in the case is announced. Transcripts of these bench announcements have been included when available.

How these writings have been edited is indicated at the beginning of each brief, opinion, or dissent. Lawyers and judges must back up every proposition they make with a citation to a case, statute, or other authority; in this book, many of these citations have been omitted to make reading easier.

Unedited versions of U.S. Supreme Court opinions are available at a website maintained by the Court (supremecourt.gov). Oyez, a joint project of Cornell University's Legal Information Institute, Justia, and Chicago-Kent College of Law, offers public access to recordings and transcripts of oral arguments and bench announcements at the Court (oyez.org).

"All I Ask": Briefs and Oral Argument from *Reed v. Reed* to *Craig v. Boren*

> In 1971, for the first time in our Nation's history, this Court ruled in favor of a woman who complained that her State had denied her the equal protection of its laws. *Reed v. Reed*, 404 U.S. 71, 73 (holding unconstitutional Idaho Code prescription that, among "several persons claiming and equally entitled to administer [a decedent's estate], males must be preferred to females").
>
> —U.S. Supreme Court Justice Ruth Bader Ginsburg's majority opinion in *United States v. Virginia*, 518 U.S. 515 (1996)

When Ruth Bader Ginsburg wrote her U.S. Supreme Court brief in *Reed v. Reed* (1971), it was permissible and routine for the law to draw sometimes dramatic distinctions—"a sharp line"—between women and men in virtually every aspect of life. Over the course of the following decade, Ginsburg changed all that, in her characteristically bold but pragmatic style, while carefully crediting others for the parts they played every step of the way.

As co-founder of the American Civil Liberties Union's Women's Rights Project, Ginsburg was "the leading Supreme Court litigator"[1] on more than two dozen cases in the Supreme Court during the 1970s, while also teaching and publishing academic articles as a professor at Columbia Law School. On the side, she helped file a class-action lawsuit against Columbia on behalf of women teachers and administrators who were being paid less than men.

As a result of her and others' work, by the end of the decade, gender had become a "disfavored classification" for legislation. Laws that discriminated on the basis of sex were subject to a heightened level of scrutiny from courts to ensure that the laws did not violate the equal protection of the laws promised to all persons by the Fourteenth Amendment to the U.S. Constitution (and by extension the Fifth Amendment as well).[2]

Reed v. Reed (1971)

Marking a turning point in constitutional interpretation of laws that treated men and women differently, the case of *Reed v. Reed* involved the estate of the adoptive son of Sally Reed and Cecil Reed, who were divorced. The boy, Skip, had lived with Sally as a young child; when Skip became a teenager, Cecil asserted custodial rights. One weekend, when Skip was at the home of Cecil and his second family, Skip called Sally begging to come home; she told him he was legally required to stay for the entire weekend. Skip then went to Cecil's basement and killed himself with one of Cecil's guns.

Sally took charge of Skip's personal belongings—clothing, a savings account she had started for him, a guitar, a clarinet—and applied to be his administrator. Cecil then decided his former wife was "too dumb" to deal with this responsibility and also applied.[3] Because an Idaho statute provided that men were to be preferred over women in administering the estate of a dead person, Cecil was appointed as administrator.

At the time, a law that drew distinctions on the basis of sex did not violate equal protection under the Fourteenth Amendment of the U.S. Constitution as long as the law had a "rational basis." All that was required was some reason—virtually any reason—for legislators to make a distinction between different persons (in her 1976 brief in *Craig v. Boren*, Ginsburg called this the "anything goes" standard).

After Sally Reed appealed Cecil's appointment as administrator, the Idaho Supreme Court rejected the argument that the Idaho statute violated the constitutional guarantee of equal protection of the laws. The court ruled that the preference for men over women avoided some disputes about who could serve as an estate administrator and made administration more convenient, so the statute had a rational basis and should be enforced in the case.

In her classes at Columbia, Ginsburg had been teaching using articles by Pauli Murray, an African American civil rights attorney, who argued that this interpretation of what equal protection required should change and that laws discriminating by sex should be subject to the same strict scrutiny for constitutionality that racially discriminatory laws received. Strict scrutiny in such cases required that a compelling governmental interest supported a challenged law's racial classification and that the least restrictive means were chosen to further that interest. The *Reed* case offered a good opportunity to make the argument for strict scrutiny in gender discrimination cases to the nine justices of the U.S. Supreme Court.

As Ginsburg later recounted:

Sally Reed thought she had experienced an injustice...and that the laws of the United States would protect her from injustice. She went through three levels of the Idaho court system, on her own dime.... Hers was the turning-point case in the Supreme Court—nothing that the National Organization for Women or the ACLU had generated as a test case. Sally Reed was among the women across the country waking up to the inequality to which they had been exposed, for which there was no rhyme or reason.[4]

Ginsburg took over writing the brief for the ACLU team, headed by Melvin Wulf, that was handling Sally Reed's appeal. As a way of acknowledging that Ginsburg stood on the shoulders of others, on the cover of the brief she credited Pauli Murray; Dorothy Kenyon, who had challenged laws automatically excluding women from jury service; and Allen Derr, Sally Reed's Idaho attorney. The brief surveyed virtually all the extant literature on equality between the sexes and gave a historical perspective on attitudes about gender discrimination, drawing from sources as diverse as Sojourner Truth and Alfred, Lord Tennyson. Ginsburg argued that the U.S. Supreme Court should declare sex a "suspect classification" like race, triggering courts' strict scrutiny of laws based on the classification to ensure that no one was denied equal protection.

The Court ruled in favor of Sally Reed, finding that the Idaho statute at issue did not pass the test that it must be "reasonable, not arbitrary, and must rest upon some ground of difference having a fair and substantial relation to the object of the legislation, so that all persons similarly circumstanced shall be treated alike." This formulation was from a 1920 tax case cited in Ginsburg's brief for her fallback position, in case the Court did not wish to declare that gender was a suspect classification.

The Supreme Court had never before invalidated a statute drawing distinctions between men and women. But the Court declined to rule that women constituted a suspect class. In agreeing with Ginsburg's fallback argument that the Idaho statute was too arbitrary to pass the "rational basis" test, the Court invalidated the discriminatory statute but did not signal a clear change in the constitutional validity of sex-based legal discrimination.

Frontiero v. Richardson (1973)

Ginsburg's next U.S. Supreme Court brief, for the ACLU as amicus curiae (friend of the court) in *Frontiero v. Richardson* (1973), highlighted the uncertainty left by the *Reed* ruling in a review of cases that reached lower courts after the decision in *Reed*. *Frontiero* involved laws that extended housing and medical benefits automatically to the spouse of a male member of the uniformed services (in this case, the U.S. Air Force), but not to the spouse of a woman service member unless the woman provided her spouse with more than half of his support. The brief gave Ginsburg the opportunity to try to open the all-male Supreme Court justices' eyes to the economic realities of women in the work force.

For a reader today, the briefs in *Reed* and *Frontiero* are still eye-opening, revealing how much has changed for American women in the nearly fifty years since the briefs were written as well as how much remains the same. For example, in *Reed*, Ginsburg pointed out the scarcity of women in her own profession, the law: in 1971, women constituted only 3 percent of all Americans employed as lawyers. Today, that number is 38 percent.[5]

On the other hand, the *Frontiero* brief discussed the Equal Rights Amendment (ERA), approved by Congress and submitted to the states for ratification in 1972, which promised a clear path to equal treatment for women in the economy and under the law. Having been ratified by thirty-five of the thirty-eight state legislatures required, by 1977 the ERA was most of the way toward becoming part of the U.S. Constitution.[6] After Phyllis Schlafly mobilized a conservative backlash against the ERA, however, its progress in state legislatures stalled, and the ratification deadline came and went. The effectiveness of current efforts to revive the ERA's ratification process in state legislatures without further Congressional action remains in doubt.

As co-counsel in *Frontiero*, Ginsburg made her first oral argument before the Supreme Court justices. At the end, she quoted nineteenth-century feminist abolitionist Sarah Grimké: "I ask no favor for my sex. All I ask of our brethren is that they take their feet off our necks." The bench of male justices was unusually silent, not interrupting Ginsburg's argument once.

Having made the "suspect classification" argument for a second time, Ginsburg won over four of the nine justices on the Court. Her fallback argument that the discriminatory statutes failed an intermediate level of scrutiny (something more than the "rational basis" test and less than strict scrutiny) carried the vote of another justice who concluded that the statutes challenged in the case worked an "invidious discrimination" impermissible after *Reed v. Reed*. Three justices concluded that because the ERA had been submitted to the states for ratification, it was inappropriate to decide at the time whether sex was a suspect classification.

Weinberger v. Wiesenfeld (1975)

Ginsburg liked to choose cases in which gender discrimination worked against men, as she believed that the male justices of the Supreme Court might more easily identify with a man complaining about gender discrimination. *Weinberger v. Wiesenfeld* was such a case. The brief is also notable for reflecting Ginsburg's decision to favor use of the term "gender discrimination" rather than "sex discrimination"—on the advice of her secretary, who after typing a brief said, "I look at these pages and all I see is sex, sex, sex. The judges are men, and when they read that they're not going to be thinking about what you want them to think about."[7]

Paula Wiesenfeld, a schoolteacher and the primary wage earner for her family, died in childbirth, and her widower, Stephen, sought a Social Security benefit (a "mother's insurance benefit") given to mothers whose husbands had died, to help the mothers care for their children themselves. He was denied the benefit even though he wished to care for his baby himself; after his request for review went in his favor, the U.S. government ultimately appealed to the U.S. Supreme Court.

Ginsburg's brief explained for the justices the multiple, layered ways women's efforts in the economic sector were devalued and highlighted how discrimination against women could operate to harm men as well. As she later said, "We were confronting the justices with real-life situations so they could understand that what they once thought was a system operating benignly in women's favor in fact disadvantaged them. . . . The aim was to break down the stereotypical view of men's roles and women's roles."[8] She argued that the rigid sex-role "pigeonholing" that was written into the law did not reflect the realities of many people's lives. (It certainly did not reflect her own career or personal life.)

In the end, all justices voting that day agreed to strike down the statute that created the discrimination. Justice Rehnquist agreed to do so because the statute treated the Wiesenfelds' baby son unfairly. Ginsburg called this her favorite case and has remained close with the Wiesenfelds over the years, officiating first at the son's wedding and then years later at the father's second wedding.[9]

Craig v. Boren (1976)

Ginsburg's career has made clear that she is both a fighter and a pragmatist. By 1976, when she wrote the brief in *Craig v. Boren*, she focused on arguing that, at minimum, an intermediate standard—something more than the rational basis test, if less than strict scrutiny—applied in cases challenging laws that discriminated by gender.

In what became known as "the beer case," a male university student over eighteen but under twenty-one years of age wished to buy, and a vendor wished to sell him, 3.2 percent beer; however, Oklahoma statutes prohibited the sale of 3.2 percent beer to minors, whom the statutes defined as females under the age of eighteen and males under the age of twenty-one. Ginsburg had again picked a successful case featuring a male plaintiff disadvantaged by a law based on stereotypes about the genders.

In invalidating the Oklahoma statutes, the U.S. Supreme Court at last stated clearly that laws that discriminate by gender triggered a more substantial review than the simple "rational basis" test, even as that was elaborated in *Reed v. Reed*. While gender was not explicitly deemed a suspect classification and did not trigger the strict scrutiny that racial and national origin classifications did, the Court adopted Ginsburg's proposed intermediate standard: to withstand constitutional challenge, classifications by gender must serve important governmental objectives and must be substantially related to achievement of those objectives.

Some years later, in the 1996 Virginia Military Institute case, as author of the majority opinion, Justice Ginsburg had the opportunity to tweak that standard further upward. Justice Antonin Scalia complained in his dissent that her opinion effectively made something very like strict scrutiny the standard for reviewing laws that classify people by gender.

SALLY M. REED, APPELLANT, V. CECIL R. REED, ADMINISTRATOR, IN THE MATTER OF THE ESTATE OF RICHARD LYNN REED, DECEASED
ON APPEAL FROM THE SUPREME COURT OF THE STATE OF IDAHO
404 U.S. 71 (November 22, 1971)

BRIEF FOR APPELLANT

Filed June 25, 1971

Most citations and footnotes have been omitted for ease of reading, as well as some punctuation (including brackets and internal quotation marks). Also omitted are the text of the statutes involved, table of authorities, statement of opinion below, statement of jurisdiction, and appendix of U.S. laws discriminating against women.

Question Presented
Whether Idaho Code, Sec. 15–314, which provides that as between persons equally entitled to administer an estate, males must be preferred to females, denies appellant, a woman, the equal protection of the laws.

SUMMARY OF ARGUMENT
I
Idaho Code, Sec. 15–314, which provides that as between persons "equally entitled to administer [a decedent's estate], males must be preferred to females," denies appellant, an "equally entitled" woman, the equal protection of the laws.

The sex line drawn by Sec. 15–314, mandating subordination of women to men without regard to individual capacity, creates a "suspect classification" requiring close judicial scrutiny. Although the legislature may distinguish between individuals on the basis of their need or ability, it is presumptively impermissible to distinguish on the basis of an unalterable identifying trait over which the individual has no control and for which he or she should not be disadvantaged by the law. Legislative discrimination grounded on sex, for purposes unrelated to any biological difference between the sexes, ranks with legislative discrimination based on race, another congenital, unalterable trait of birth, and merits no greater judicial deference.

17

The distance to equal opportunity for women in the United States remains considerable in face of the pervasive social, cultural and legal roots of sex-based discrimination. As other groups that have been assisted toward full equality before the law via the "suspect classification" doctrine, women are sparsely represented in legislative and policy-making chambers and lack political power to remedy the discriminatory treatment they are accorded in the law and in society generally. Absent firm constitutional foundation for equal treatment of men and women by the law, women seeking to be judged on their individual merits will continue to encounter law-sanctioned obstacles.

Prior decisions of this Court have contributed to the separate and unequal status of women in the United States. But the national conscience has been awakened to the sometimes subtle assignment of inferior status to women by the dominant male culture. In very recent years, both federal and state courts have expressed sharp criticism of lines drawn or sanctioned by governmental authority on the basis of sex. With some notable exceptions, for example, the case at bar, these lines have not survived judicial scrutiny. The time is ripe for this Court to repudiate the premise that, with minimal justification, the legislature may draw "a sharp line between the sexes," just as this Court has repudiated once settled law that differential treatment of the races is constitutionally permissible. At the very least the Court should reverse the presumption of rationality when sex-based discrimination is implicated and, rather than requiring the party attacking a statute to show that the classification is irrational, should require the statute's proponent to prove it rational.

Biological differences between the sexes bear no relationship to the duties performed by an administrator. Idaho's interest in administrative convenience, served by excluding women who would compete with men for appointment as an administrator, falls far short of a compelling state interest when appraised in light of the interest of the class against which the statute discriminates—an interest in treatment by the law as full human personalities. If sex is a "suspect classification," a state interest in avoiding a hearing cannot justify rank discrimination against a person solely on the ground that she is a female.

II

The sex line drawn by sec. 15-314, arbitrarily ranking the woman as inferior to the man by directing that the probate court take no account of the respective qualifications of the individuals involved, lacks a fair and substantial relation to a permissible legislative purpose. The judgment that "in general men are better qualified to act as an administrator than are women" rests on totally unfounded assumptions of differences in mental capacity or experience relevant to the office of administrator. To eliminate a woman who shares an eligibility category with a man when there is no basis in fact to assume that women are less competent to administer than are men, is patently unreasonable and constitutionally impermissible.

ARGUMENT

Introduction

By the explicit terms of Sec. 15-314 of the Idaho Code, appellant was denied the right to qualify as the administrator of her son's estate solely because of her sex. The issue in this case is whether, as appellant contends, mandatory disqualification of a woman for appointment as an administrator, whenever a man "equally entitled to administer" applies for appointment, constitutes arbitrary and unequal treatment proscribed by the fourteenth amendment to the United States Constitution.

In determining whether a state statute establishes a classification violative of the fourteenth amendment guarantee that those similarly situated shall be similarly treated, this Court has developed two standards of review.

In the generality of cases a test of reasonable classification has been applied: Does the classification established by the legislature bear a reasonable and just relation to the permissible objective of the legislation? Under this general test, if the purpose of the statute is a permissible one and if the statutory classification bears the required fair relationship to that purpose, the constitutional mandate will be held satisfied.

In two circumstances, however, a more stringent test is applied. When the legislative product affects "fundamental rights or interests," or when the statute classifies on a basis "inherently suspect," this Court will subject the legislation to "the most rigid scrutiny."* Thus, a statute distinguishing on the

* *Korematsu v. United States*, 323 U.S. 214, 216 (1944). Although the first case to develop the concept that classifications based on race are "suspect," *Korematsu* justified the detention of men and women solely because of their Japanese ancestry, on the basis of an espionage threat, when imminent foreign invasion was feared. With the glaring exception of *Korematsu*, "suspect" classifications have not survived this Court's rigid scrutiny. In retrospect, the extreme personal deprivation countenanced wholesale in *Korematsu* is recognized generally as having been grossly disproportionate to the national security interest at stake.

basis of race or ancestry embodies a "suspect" or "invidious" classification and, unless supported by the most compelling affirmative justification, will not pass constitutional muster.

It is appellant's principal position that the sex line drawn by Sec. 15-314 of the Idaho Code, mandating subordination of women to men without regard to individual capacity, creates a "suspect classification" for which no compelling justification can be shown. It is appellant's alternate position that, without regard to the suspect or invidious nature of the classification, the line drawn by the Idaho legislature, arbitrarily ranking the woman as inferior to the man by directing the probate court to take no account of the respective qualifications of the individuals involved, lacks the constitutionally required fair and reasonable relation to any legitimate state interest in providing for the efficient administration of decedents' estates.

In very recent years, a new appreciation of women's place has been generated in the United States. Activated by feminists of both sexes, courts and legislatures have begun to recognize the claim of women to full membership in the class "persons" entitled to due process guarantees of life and liberty and the equal protection of the laws. But the distance to equal opportunity for women—in the face of the pervasive social, cultural and legal roots of sex-based discrimination—remains considerable. In the absence of a firm constitutional foundation for equal treatment of men and women by the law, women seeking to be judged on their individual merits will continue to encounter law-sanctioned obstacles.

Currently, federal and state measures are beginning to offer relief from discriminatory employment practices. Principal measures on the national level are the Equal Pay Act of 1963/Title VII of the Civil Rights Act of 1964 and Executive Orders designed to eliminate discrimination against women in federal jobs and jobs under federal contracts. These developments promise some protection of the equal right of men and women to pursue the employment for which individual talent and capacity best equip them. But important as these federal measures are, their coverage is limited. Even in the employment area they cover only a small percentage of the nation's employers and less than half of the labor force. They provide no assistance at all in the many areas apart from employment, as in the case at bar for example, where women are relegated to second class status.

The experience of trying to root out racial discrimination in the United States has demonstrated that even when the arsenal of legislative and judicial remedies is well stocked, social and cultural institutions shaped by centuries of law-sanctioned bias do not crumble under the weight of legal pronouncements proscribing discrimination. Thus, just as the Equal Pay Act and Title VII have not ended discrimination against women even in the employment spheres to which they apply, sex-based discrimination will not disintegrate upon this Court's recognition that sex is a suspect classification. But without this recognition, the struggle for an end to sex-based discrimination will extend well beyond the current period in time, a period in which any functional justification for difference in treatment has ceased to exist.

Very recent history has taught us that, where racial discrimination is concerned, this Court's refusal in *Plessy v. Ferguson*, 163 U.S. 537 (1896), to declare the practice unconstitutional, reinforced the institutional and political foundations of racism, made it more difficult eventually to extirpate, and postponed for fifty-eight years the inevitable inauguration of a national commitment to abolish racial discrimination.

As an example of the slow awakening of the national conscience to the more subtle assignment of inferior status to women, this Court a generation ago came close to repeating the mistake of *Plessy v. Ferguson*. See *Goesaert v. Cleary*, 335 U.S. 464 (1948). Fortunately, the Court already has acknowledged a new direction, see *United States v. Dege*, 364 U.S. 51, 54 (1960), and the case at bar provides the opportunity clearly and affirmatively to inaugurate judicial recognition of the constitutionally imperative claim made by women for the equal rights before the law guaranteed to all persons.

In sum, appellant urges in Point I of this brief that designation of sex as a suspect classification is overdue, is the only wholly satisfactory standard for dealing with the claim in this case, and should be the starting point for assessing that claim. Nonetheless, as developed in Point II of this brief, it should be apparent that the reasonable relation test also must yield a conclusion in favor of the appellant. Surely this Court cannot give its approval to a fiduciary statute that demands preference for an idler, because he is a man, and rejects a potentially diligent administrator solely because she is a woman. In addition to the argument based on the traditional reasonable relation test, Point II formulates a modification of that test, appropriate in the event this Court, contrary to appellant's primary position, would delay recognition of sex as a suspect classification. The proposed modification would reverse the presumption of rationality when sex is implicated and, rather than requiring the party attacking a statute to show that the classification is irrational, would require the statute's proponent to prove it rational.

I. The sex-based classification in Section 15-314 of the Idaho Code, established for a purpose unrelated to any biological difference between the sexes, is a "suspect classification" proscribed by the fourteenth amendment to the United States Constitution.

A. Sex as a Suspect Classification.

Commanding a preference for men and the subordination of women, Section 15-134 of the Idaho code reflects a view, prevalent in the law a generation ago that, with minimal justification, the legislature could draw "a sharp line between the sexes." *Goesaert v. Cleary*, 335 U.S. 464, 466 (1948). Similarly, it was once settled law that differential treatment of the races was constitutionally permissible. *Plessy v. Ferguson*, 163 U.S. 537 (1896). Today, of course, a classification based on race, nationality or alienage is inherently "suspect" or "invidious" and this Court has required "close judicial scrutiny" of a statute or governmental action based upon such a classification. *Graham v. Richardson*, ___U.S.___ (June 14, 1971). The proponent of a measure creating "classifications constitutionally suspect" must establish an "overriding statutory purpose," *McLaughlin v. Florida*, 379 U.S. 184, 192 (1964), and bears "a very heavy burden of justification." *Loving v. Virginia*, 388 U.S. 1, 9 (1967).

It is only within the last half-dozen years that the light of constitutional inquiry has focused upon sex discrimination. Emerging from this fresh examination, in the context of the significant changes that have occurred in society's attitudes, is a deeper appreciation of the premise underlying the "suspect classification" doctrine: although the legislature may distinguish between individuals on the basis of their ability or need, it is presumptively impermissible to distinguish on the basis of congenital and unalterable biological traits of birth over which the individual has no control and for which he or she should not be penalized. Such conditions include not only race, a matter clearly within the "suspect classification" doctrine, but include as well the sex of the individual.

The kinship between race and sex discrimination has attracted increasing attention. A capsule description of the close relationship between the two appears in Sex Discrimination and Equal Protection: Do We Need a Constitutional Amendment?, 84 Harv. L. Rev. 1499, 1507-1508 (1971):

The similarities between race and sex discrimination are indeed striking. Both classifications create large, natural classes, membership in which is beyond the individual's control; both are highly visible characteristics on which legislators have found it easy to draw gross, stereotypical distinctions. Historically, the legal position of black slaves was justified by analogy to the legal status of women. Both slaves and wives were once subject to the all-encompassing paternalistic power of the male head of the house. Arguments justifying different treatment for the sexes on the grounds of female inferiority, need for male protection, and happiness in their assigned roles bear a striking resemblance to the half-truths surrounding the myth of the "happy slave." The historical patterns of race and sex discrimination have, in many instances, produced similar present day results. Women and blacks, for example, hold the lowest paying jobs in industry, with black men doing slightly better than white women. . . .

The factual similarities between race and sex discrimination are reinforced by broader concerns. Through a process of social evolution, racial distinctions have become unacceptable. The old social consensus that race was a clear indication of inferiority has yielded to the notion that race is unrelated to ability or performance. Even allegedly rational attempts at racial classification are now generally rejected outright. The burden of showing that these attempts are based on something other than prejudice is enormous.

There are indications that sex classifications may be undergoing a similar metamorphosis in the public mind. Once thought normal, proper, and ordained in the "very nature of things," sex discrimination may soon be seen as a sham, not unlike that perpetrated in the name of racial superiority. Whatever differences may exist between the sexes, legislative judgments have frequently been based on inaccurate stereotypes of the capacities and sensibilities of women. In view of the damage that has been inflicted on individuals in the name of these "differences," any continuing distinctions should, like race, bear a heavy burden of proof. One function of the fourteenth amendment ought to be to put such broad-ranging concerns into the fundamental law of the land.

Dr. Pauli Murray recently synopsized scholarly commentary on the same point in The Negro Woman's Stake in the Equal Rights Amendment, 6 Harv. Civ. Rts. Civ. Lib. Law Rev. 253, 257 (1971):

> The relationship between sexual and racial prejudice is confirmed by contemporary scholarship. The history of western culture, and particularly of ecclesiastical and English common law, suggests that the traditionally subordinate status of women provided models for the oppression of other groups. The treatment of a woman as her husband's property, as subject to his corporal punishment, as incompetent to testify under canon law, and as subject to numerous legal and social restrictions based upon sex, were precedents for the later treatment of slaves. In 1850, George Fitzhugh, one of the foremost defenders of slavery in the United States, analogized it to the position of women and children. And in 1944, a justice of the North Carolina Supreme Court noted "the barbarous view of the inferiority of women which manifested itself in civil and political oppression so akin to slavery that we can find no adequate word to describe her present status with men except emancipation."
>
> Race and sex are comparable classes, defined by physiological characteristics, through which status is fixed from birth. Legal and social proscriptions based upon race and sex have often been identical, and have generally implied the inherent inferiority of the proscribed class to a dominant group. Both classes have been defined by, and subordinated to, the same power group—white males.

When biological differences are not related to the activity in question, sex-based discrimination clashes with contemporary notions of fair and equal treatment. No longer shackled by decisions reflecting social and economic conditions or legal and political theories of an earlier era, see *Harper v. Virginia Board of Elections*, 383 U.S. 663, 669-70 (1966), both federal and state courts have been intensely skeptical of lines drawn or sanctioned by governmental authority on the basis of sex. Absent strong affirmative justification, these lines have not survived constitutional scrutiny.

A recent decision of the California Supreme Court, *Sail'er Inn, Inc. et al. v. Edward J. Kirby, Director, et al.*, 3 CCH Employment Practices Decisions

¶8222 (May 27, 1971), explicitly denominated sex a suspect classification and, consequently, held unconstitutional a California statute similar to the Michigan statute upheld by this Court in *Goesaert v. Cleary*, 335 U.S. 464 (1948). The California Supreme Court described the factors upon which its conclusion rested in the following terms:

> Sex, like race and lineage, is an immutable trait, a status into which the class members are locked by the accident of birth. What differentiates sex from nonsuspect statuses, such as intelligence or physical disability, and aligns it with the recognized suspect classifications is that the characteristic frequently bears no relation to ability to perform or contribute to society. The result is that the whole class is relegated to an inferior legal status without regard to the capabilities or characteristics of its individual members. Where the relation between characteristic and evil to be prevented is so tenuous, courts must look closely at classifications based on that characteristic lest outdated social stereotypes result in invidious laws or practices.
>
> Another characteristic which underlies all suspect classifications is the stigma of inferiority and second class citizenship associated with them. Women, like Negroes, aliens, and the poor have historically labored under severe legal and social disabilities. Like black citizens, they were, for many years, denied the right to vote and, until recently, the right to serve on juries in many states. They are excluded from or discriminated against in employment and educational opportunities. Married women in particular have been treated as inferior persons in numerous laws relating to property and independent business ownership and the right to make contracts.
>
> Laws which disable women from full participation in the political, business and economic arenas are often characterized as "protective" and beneficial. Those same laws applied to racial or ethnic minorities would readily be recognized as invidious and impermissible. The pedestal upon which women have been placed has all too often, upon closer inspection, been revealed as a cage. We conclude that the sexual classifications are properly treated as suspect, particularly when those classifications are made with respect to a fundamental interest such as employment.

[*Here the brief cites two pages' worth of cases finding unequal treatment of women to violate equal protection and the Fourteenth Amendment.*]

The trend is clearly discernible. Legislative discrimination grounded on sex, for purposes unrelated to any biological difference between the sexes, ranks with legislative discrimination based on race, another condition of birth, and merits no greater judicial deference. Each exemplifies a "suspect" or "invidious" classification.

B. Women as a Disadvantaged Second Sex.

While the characteristics that make a classification "suspect" have not been defined explicitly by this Court, a series of cases delineates as the principal factor the presence of an unalterable identifying trait which the dominant culture views as a badge of inferiority justifying disadvantaged treatment in social, legal, economic and political contexts. Although the paradigm suspect classification is, of course, one based on race, this Court has made it plain that the doctrine is not confined to a "two-class theory." Rather, interpretation has been dynamic, as is appropriate to fundamental constitutional principle.

American women have been stigmatized historically as an inferior class and are today subject to pervasive discrimination. As other groups that have been assisted toward full equality via the suspect classification doctrine, women lack political power to remedy the discriminatory treatment they are accorded in the law and in society generally. This section synopsizes attitudes toward women traditional in the United States and the principal areas in which the law limits the opportunities available to women for participation as full and equal members of society.

"'Man's world' and 'women's place' have confronted each other since Scylla first faced Charybdis." A person born female continues to be branded inferior for this congenital and unalterable condition of birth. Her position in this country, at its inception, is reflected in the expression of the author of the declaration that "all men are created equal." According to Thomas Jefferson, women should be neither seen nor heard in society's decision-making councils:

Were our state a pure democracy there would still be excluded from our deliberations women, who, to prevent deprivation of morals and ambiguity of issues, should not mix promiscuously in gatherings of men.

Alexis de Tocqueville, some years later, included this observation among his commentaries on life in the young United States:

> In no country has such constant care been taken as in America to trace two clearly distinct lines of action for the two sexes, and to make them keep pace one with the other, but in two pathways which are always different. American women never manage the outward concerns of the family, or conduct a business, or take a part in political life.... *Democracy in America*, pt. 2.*

During the long debate over women's suffrage the prevailing view of the partition thought ordained by the Creator was rehearsed frequently in the press and in legislative chambers. For example, an editorial in the *New York Herald* in 1852 asked:

> How did women first become subject to man as she now is all over the world? By her nature, her sex, just as the negro, is and always will be, to the end of time, inferior to the white race, and, therefore, doomed to subjection; but happier than she would be in any other condition, just because it is the law of her nature. The women themselves would not have this law reversed....

And a legislator commented during an 1866 debate in Congress:

> It seems to me as if the God of our race has stamped upon [the women of America] a milder, gentler nature, which not only makes them shrink from, but disqualifies them for the turmoil and battle of public life. They have a higher and holier mission. It is in retiracy [sic] to make the character of coming men. Their mission is at home, by their blandishments and their love to as-suage the passions of men as they come in from the battle of life, and not themselves by joining in the contest to add fuel to the

---

* Cf. Ibsen's observation on the society of his day:
  A woman cannot be herself in a modern society. It is an exclusively male society with laws made by men, and with prosecutors and judges who assess female conduct from a male standpoint. Quoted in Meyer, Introduction to H. Ibsen, *A Doll's House*.

very flames.... It will be a sorry day for this country when those vestal fires of love and piety are put out.

The common law heritage, a source of pride for men, marked the wife as her husband's chattel, "something better than his dog, a little dearer than his horse."* Blackstone explained:

> By marriage, the husband and wife are one person in law: that is, the very being or legal existence of the woman is suspended during the marriage, or at least is incorporated and consolidated into that of the husband; under whose wing, protection, and cover, she performs everything; and is therefore called in our law-french a *feme-covert*...under the protection and influence of her husband, her *baron*, or lord; and her condition during her marriage is called her coverture. 1 Blackstone's Commentaries on the Law of England 442 (3d ed. 1768).

Prior to the Civil War, the legal status of women in the United States was comparable to that of blacks under the slave codes, albeit the white woman ranked as "chief slave of the harem."† Neither slaves nor married women had the legal capacity to hold property or to serve as guardians of their own children. Neither blacks nor women could hold office, serve on juries, or bring suit in their own names. Men controlled the behavior of both their slaves and their wives and had legally enforceable rights to their services without compensation. As Gunnar Myrdal remarked, the parallel was not accidental, for the legal status of women and children served as the model for the legal status assigned to black slaves:

> In the earlier common law, women and children were placed under the jurisdiction of the paternal power. When a legal status had to be found for the imported Negro servants in the seventeenth century, the nearest and most natural analogy was the status of women and children. The ninth commandment—linking together women, servants, mules and other property—could be invoked,

---

* Alfred, Lord Tennyson, *Locksley Hall* (1842).
† Comment attributed to Dolly Madison, in H. Martineau, *Society in America*, Vol. 2, (1837).

as well as a great number of other passages of Holy Scripture. *An American Dilemma* 1073 (2d ed. 1962).

In answer to feminist protests, the legal disabilities imposed on women were rationalized at the turn of the century much as they were at an earlier age. Blackstone set the pattern:

> Even the disabilities which the wife lies under are for the most part intended for her protection and benefit: so great a favourite is the female sex of the laws of England. 1 Blackstone's Commentaries on the Laws of England 445 (3d ed. 1768).

Grover Cleveland echoed this rationale, arguing that although women were denied the vote, the statute books were full of proof of the chivalrous concern of male legislators for the rights of women. Would Woman Suffrage Be Unwise?, 22 *Ladies' Home Journal* 7–8 (October 1905).

American women assessed their situation from a different perspective. At the Women's Rights Convention in Seneca Falls, New York, in 1848, a declaration of women's rights was drafted which included the following sentiments:

> The history of mankind is a history of repeated injuries and usurpations on the part of man toward woman, having in direct object the establishment of an absolute tyranny over her....
>
> He has compelled her to submit to laws, in the formation of which she had no voice.
> ★★★★★
> He has taken from her all right in property, even to the wages she earns.
> ★★★★★
> ...In the covenant of marriage,...the law gives him power to deprive her of her liberty and to administer chastisement.
> ★★★★★
> ... He closes against her all the avenues to wealth and distinction which he considers most honorable to himself....
> ★★★★★

He has endeavored, in every way that he could, to destroy her confidence in her own powers, to lessen her self-respect, and to make her willing to lead a dependent and abject life. *History of Woman Suffrage*, Vol. I, at 70-75 (E. C. Stanton, S. D. Anthony & N. J. Gage eds. 1881).

Men viewing their world without rose-colored glasses would have noticed in the last century, as those who look will observe today, that no pedestal marks the place occupied by most women. At a women's rights convention in Akron, Ohio, in 1851, Sojourner Truth, an abolitionist and former slave, responded poignantly to the taunts of clergymen who maintained that women held a favored position and were too weak to vote:

The man over there says women need to be helped into carriages and lifted over ditches, and to have the best place everywhere. Nobody ever helps me into carriages or over puddles, or gives me the best place—and ain't I a woman?

Look at my arm! I have ploughed and planted and gathered into barns, and no man could head me—and ain't I a woman? I could work as much and eat as much as a man—when I could get it—and bear the lash as well! And ain't I a woman? I have born thirteen children, and seen most of 'em sold into slavery, and when I cried out with my mother's grief, none but Jesus heard me—and ain't I a woman?

Of course, the legal status of women has improved since the nineteenth century. The Married Women's Property Acts, passed in the middle of the nineteenth century, opened the door to a measure of economic independence for married women. The nineteenth amendment gave women the vote in 1920, after almost three-quarters of a century of struggle. But woman's place as subordinate to man is still reflected in many statutes regulating diverse aspects of life. Some of the areas in which women receive less favored treatment than men are summarized below.

1. Male as head of household

It remains the general rule that a wife's domicile follows that of her husband. The Idaho provision is typical:

The husband is the head of the family. He may choose any reasonable place or mode of living and the wife must conform thereto.
Idaho Code sec. 32-902 (1947).

Thus the law subordinates a woman's work and home preference to
her husband's. If the two are in fact living apart, the attribution of husband's domicile to wife may nullify her right to vote, to run for public office, or to serve as administrator of an estate. A 1968 survey of the laws of
all of the states revealed only five that permit a married woman to establish
a separate domicile for all purposes, eight that permit a separate domicile
for eligibility for public office, six that permit a separate domicile for jury
service, eight that recognize a separate domicile for probate, nine that permit a separate domicile for taxation, and eighteen that permit a separate
domicile for voting.

The social custom in the United States that upon marriage a woman
takes her husband's surname, and ceases to be known by her maiden name,
is supported by laws and decisions that deal harshly with a woman who
seeks to retain her separate identity. For example, in *Bacon v. Boston Elevated
Ry.*, 256 Mass. 30 (1926), a married woman who retained her car registration in her maiden name was declared a "nuisance on the highway" and
therefore barred from maintaining an action for injuries occasioned when
her car was struck by a train. A federal decision of the same order is *In re
Kayaloff*, 9 F. Supp. 176 (S.D.N.Y. 1934), holding that a married woman
should not be granted a naturalization certificate in her maiden name, although in her career as a musician she was well-known by that name. For
voting purposes the married woman, but not the married man, may be
required to indicate marital status.

The common law system of separate ownership of property by each
spouse, effective in most states, fails to accord adequate recognition to the
contribution to the family made by a wife who works only in the home. By
accepting a "woman's place" and relieving her husband of the burdens of
child and home care, she forgoes the opportunity to acquire earnings and
property of her own. In community property states, in which marriage is
regarded in theory as an economic partnership, management and control
generally vest exclusively in the husband. And although Married Women's
Property Acts were passed over a century ago, numerous anachronistic limitations on the contractual capacity of women survive.

2. Women and the role of motherhood

The traditional division within the home—father decides, mother nurtures—is reinforced by diverse provisions of state law. For example, several retain general statutes reflecting the common law rule that father is sole guardian of the children. More particularized provisions include the Washington rule that father, not mother, is qualified to sue for the wrongful death of a legitimate child. In Idaho, the father presumptively may make a testamentary guardianship appointment for a child, while the mother may do so only if the father is dead or incapable of consent.

If the parents separate, mother generally gets custody preference when the child is of tender years. But if the child is older, and needs preparation for the world, preference may go to father.

Most states permit girls to marry without parental consent at an earlier age than boys. The differential, generally three years, reflects two presumptions: (1) the married state is the only proper goal of womanhood; (2) men need more time to prepare for bigger, better and more useful pursuits.

3. Women and criminal law

As of 1970, women served on juries on the same basis as men in only 28 states. Differential treatment for women in the remaining states takes a variety of forms. Some states automatically exempt women on the basis of their sex alone; others exempt women, but not men, who have child care responsibilities; and some exempt women based on the nature of the proceeding or inadequate courthouse facilities.

In most states, only a woman can be prosecuted as a "prostitute" and only her conduct, not her male partner's, is criminal.

Special treatment of female juvenile offenders is another example of the double standard in operation. In New York, for example, a child can be declared a "person in need of supervision"* for acts that would be non-criminal if committed by an adult. While there may be sound reasons for this special category for juveniles, there can be no constitutional justification for New York's treatment of young women as "persons in need of supervision" until age 18, while boys are subject to the statute only until age 16. In addition to the age differential, the statute discriminates against girls in a manner

---

* A person who is a "habitual truant...incorrigible, ungovernable or habitually disobedient and beyond the lawful control of parent or other lawful authority."

less apparent but no less real. A charge of ungovernability against a girl occurs most frequently as a promiscuity-control device. A study of 1500 cases decided by a New York juvenile court judge revealed that he "refused to treat any form of sexual behavior on the part of boys, even the most bizarre forms, as warranting more than probationary status. The Judge, however, regarded girls as the cause of sexual deviation in boys in all cases of coition involving an adolescent couple and refused to hear the complaints of the girl and her family; the girl was regarded as a prostitute." Reiss, Sex Offenses: The Marginal Status of the Adolescent, 25 Law and Contemporary Problems 310, 316 (1960).

While a very young woman is considered dangerous for her sexuality, in adult life she is considered far less passionate than the adult man. At least this appears to be the view of states that allow the defense of "passion killing" only to the wronged husband.

4. Women and employment

Current tax law presents a significant disincentive to the woman who contemplates combining a career with marriage and a family. If a wife's earnings approach those of her husband, the Internal Revenue Code counsels divorce, for the couple will retain more if they live together without benefit of a marriage license. And if a father or mother goes off to work as a divorcee, he or she may be entitled to a child care deduction regardless of income. For a married pair, both working, however, the deduction is available only if joint adjusted gross income of the couple remains close to the subsistence level. Moreover, the size of the deduction ($600) renders it of scant assistance even to the few who qualify for it.

Despite the tax disincentive, married women are entering the labor force in increasing numbers. In the two decades between 1947 and 1967, the percentage of women in the labor force increased by 70%, from an average of 24% to an average of 41%. Married women constitute a majority of full-time women workers. Report of the Task Force on Labor Standards to the Citizens' Advisory Council on the Status of Women 6-7 (1968). This development is particularly remarkable in view of the deplorable shortage of child care facilities. During World War II, when women workers were essential to the economy, provision was made for the care of some 1,600,000 children. By 1967, although more women were in the labor force, only 200,000 children were accommodated. Although the dire need for commitment of substantial resources to development of child care facilities is beginning to be appreciated, progress has been slow. For example, in New York City, day care services may not be provided for children under the age of two. New York City Health Code, sec. 47.07(a)(1). Moreover, an explanatory note to this section states:

> It is recognized that as an ultimate goal, it is not desirable to permit children under three years of age in a day care service, and many services now have a policy of not admitting such children....

In April 1971, 42.7% of all women sixteen years of age or older were in the labor force as compared to 28.9% in March 1940. But wage statistics are indicative of the pervasive sex discrimination still characteristic of the labor market. The wage or salary income for full-time year-round women workers dropped from 63.9% of male workers' salaries in 1956 to 58.2% in 1968.

The disparity in earnings is often discounted by men who accept the myth that women are secondary workers seeking employment only to enjoy some consumer luxuries. But in fact, almost 60% of all employed women work in order to provide primary support of themselves or others or to supplement the incomes of husbands who earn under $5,915 a year.

Within occupational categories, women are paid less for the same jobs. For example, in 1968 the median salary for all scientists was $13,200. For women scientists, the median salary was $10,000. The median wage for a full-time male factory worker in 1968 was $6,738. His female counterpart earned only $3,991. Differences in work experience, job tenure and training do not account for these large gaps.

Women at work remain heavily concentrated in a small number of sex-stereotyped occupations. In 1968, about one-quarter of all employed women worked in only five occupations: secretary-stenographer, household worker, bookkeeper, elementary school teacher, and waitress. Over a third of all employed women held clerical jobs; 70% of all clerical positions were filled by women. Two-thirds of the female labor force would have to change jobs to achieve an occupational distribution corresponding to that of men. Indeed, the index of occupational segregation by sex is approximately the same now as it was in 1900.

Beyond doubt, the status of women in the labor force is separate and unequal. The consequence for the nation is severe: almost two-thirds of this country's adult poor are women. *See* A Matter of Simple Justice: Report of the President's Task Force on Women's Rights and Responsibilities 21 (1970):

> Without any question the growing number of families on Aid to Families with Dependent Children is related to the increase in unemployed young women. For many…the inability to find a job means…having a child to get on welfare. Potential husbands do not earn enough to support an unemployed wife.
>
> The stability of the low-income family depends as much on training women for employment as it does on training men.…
>
> The task force expects welfare rolls will continue to rise unless society takes more seriously the needs of disadvantaged girls and young women.

While this brief survey offers merely a sample of the legal and economic realities of woman's inferior status, it should suffice to indicate a compelling need for correction. Strict scrutiny of classifications disadvantaging the "submissive majority," the "majority" so sparsely represented in legislative and policy-making chambers, should speed the day when emancipated men accept Mill's thesis:

> That the principle which regulates the existing social relations between the two sexes—the legal subordination of one sex to other—is wrong in itself, and now one of the chief hindrances to human improvement; and that it ought to be replaced by a principle of perfect equality, admitting no power or privilege on the one side, nor disability on the other. John Stuart Mill, *The Subjection of Women* (1869).

C. *Muller, Goesaert* and *Hoyt*

Three decisions of this Court bear particularly close examination for the support they appear to give those who urge perpetuation of the treatment of women as less than full persons within the meaning of the Constitution: *Muller v. Oregon*, 208 U.S. 412 (1908); *Goesaert v. Cleary*, 335 U.S. 464 (1948); *Hoyt v. Florida*, 368 U.S. 57 (1961).

A landmark decision of this Court responding to turn of the century conditions when women labored long into the night in sweatshop operations,

Muller v. Oregon has been misinterpreted by some as an impediment to appellant's position. Recently, in a perceptive opinion, the Court of Appeals for the Ninth Circuit focused on the different societal climate and legal setting in which Muller was decided, and demonstrated that the equal protection issue presented here was not at all involved in that case. *Mengelkoch v. Industrial Welfare Commission*, 437 F.2d 563 (9th Cir. 1971).

The issue in *Muller* was the constitutionality of a state statute prohibiting employment of women "in any mechanical establishment, factory, or laundry" for more than ten hours a day. Muller, a laundry owner, was prosecuted for violating the statute and was convicted. Muller contended in this Court that the statute abridged freedom of contract in violation of the fourteenth amendment, that it was class legislation, and that it was an invalid exercise of the police power because it lacked a reasonable relation to public health, safety or welfare. He relied principally upon *Lochner v. New York*, 198 U.S. 45 (1905), which had struck down only three years earlier a state statute limiting employment (of men as well as women) in bakeries to ten hours each day and sixty hours each week.

To distinguish *Lochner*, the Court was required to rely upon differences in the station occupied by men and women in the society of that day. Interwoven in the opinion are two themes: (1) recognition of the intolerable exploitation of women workers ("in the struggle for subsistence she is not an equal competitor with her brother"); (2) concern for the health of the sex believed to be weaker in physical structure but assigned the role of bearing the future generation ("the physical well-being of woman becomes an object of public interest and care in order to preserve the strength and vigor of the race"). Accepting as historic fact man's domination of woman, the Court stressed that women must "rest upon and look to [man] for protection" and, somewhat inconsistently, that she requires aid of the law "to protect her from the greed as well as the passion of man."

Putting *Muller* in its proper place, the Ninth Circuit, in *Mengelkoch v. Industrial Welfare Commission*, presented three reasons for its lack of precedential value in a case such as the one at bar.

First, it was the *Muller* Court's task to determine "whether the state, in exerting its police power to the end of establishing maximum hours of labor for women, acted with the wisdom which, in those days, it was thought was required by the Due Process Clause. That kind of inquiry is no longer made by the federal courts."

Second, in *Mengelkoch*, as in *Muller*, a state statute limiting hours of work for women only was challenged on constitutional grounds, but the basis of the challenge and the identity of the challenger put the two cases at opposite poles. As the Ninth Circuit explained:

> In our case, the constitutional attack against a state statute is mounted, not by an employer, but by an employee. The employee, Velma Mengelkoch, unlike the employer in *Muller*, does not question the state's police power to legislate in the field of hours of labor. Unlike Muller, she invokes the Equal Protection Clause, and she does so not to preserve the right of employers to employ women for long hours, but to overcome what she regards as a system which discriminates in favor of male employees and against female employees. In *Muller*, the statute was upheld in part because it was thought to be a necessary way of safeguarding women's competitive position. Here the statute is attacked on the ground that it gives male employees an unfair economic advantage over females.

Here, as in *Mengelkoch*, the challenger is a woman and she invokes the equal protection clause to shield her against discrimination. Of course, the second point made by the Ninth Circuit in *Mengelkoch* applies with even greater force to the case at bar. Perhaps the California legislature, decades ago when it originally enacted the legislation at issue in *Mengelkoch*, was motivated by an intent to protect women against "the greed as well as the passion of man." The Idaho statute here at issue lacks even that ostensible justification. It was not designed to protect women. On the contrary, it is explicit in its deliberate subordination of women to men for expediency's sake.

Third, the *Muller* Court, unprepared to overrule Lochner barely three years after it was decided, had to place men and women in different categories in order to escape its prior holding. As the Ninth Circuit pointed out, "the right of states to prescribe maximum hours of labor by employees, including male employees, has been recognized since at least *Bunting v. Oregon*, 243 U.S. 426 (1917)." And in 1940, in *United States v. Darby*, 312 U.S. 100, this Court completely repudiated the reasoning responsible for the Lochner decision. Thus, the critical issue in *Muller*—whether half a loaf would be allowed to state legislatures after the full loaf was denied by the Court—long ago lost all vitality.

In sum, *Muller* was a product of social conditions and constitutional theory peculiar to an earlier era in this nation's history. It is entirely irrelevant to the issue presented here, whether sex-based classifications are "suspect." The wholly different constitutional perspective, the difference in the nature of the claims, and the magnitude of the disparity between present day social and cultural norms and those prevailing at the time of *Muller*, require the conclusion that *Muller* has no bearing at all on the issue at bar.

While *Muller* reflects the law in mid-passage from *Lochner* to *Darby*, *Goesaert v. Cleary*, 335 U.S. 464 (1948), hardly exemplifies a first step toward enlightened change. It was retrogressive in its day and is intolerable a generation later. Unlike *Muller*, *Goesaert* was not intended to assist women "in the struggle for subsistence" or to safeguard women's competitive position. The statute at issue in *Goesaert*, although it allowed women to serve as waitresses in taverns, barred them from the more lucrative employment of bartender. In contrast to the protective motive apparently present in *Muller*, the actual motivation behind the statute in *Goesaert* was said by the appellant to be "an unchivalrous desire of male bartenders to try to monopolize the calling."

The majority opinion in *Goesaert* reflects an antiquarian male attitude towards women—man as provider, man as protector, man as guardian of female morality. While the attitude is antiquarian, unfortunately it is still indulged even by persons who would regard as anathema attribution of inferiority to racial or religious groups. But however much some men may wish to preserve Victorian notions about woman's relation to man, and the "proper" role of women in society, the law cannot provide support for obsolete male prejudices or translate them into statutes that enforce sex-based discrimination.

Although recognizing that society had advanced beyond the Victorian age, Mr. Justice Frankfurter stated for the *Goesaert* majority, "The Constitution does not require legislatures to reflect sociological insight, or shifting social standards, any more than it requires them to keep abreast of the latest scientific standards." But only six years later, this Court explicitly relied upon "sociological insight" and contemporary "social standards" in declaring racial segregation unconstitutional. *Brown v. Board of Education*, 347 U.S. 483 (1954).

Perhaps the *Brown* decision led Mr. Justice Frankfurter to reconsider the position he expressed in *Goesaert*. In any event, in 1960, he refused to rely on "ancient doctrine" concerning the status of women. In *United States v. Dege*, 364 U.S. 51 (1960), he buried the historic common law notion that husband and wife are legally one person. Writing for the Court, he declared, "we...do not allow ourselves to be obfuscated by medieval views regarding the legal status of women and the common law's reflection of them." Precedent from an earlier age was appraised by Mr. Justice Frankfurter as expressing a view of womanhood "offensive to the ethos of our society." Sounding the death-knell as well of *Goesaert*'s disregard of "sociological insight or shifting social standards," he quoted Mr. Justice Holmes and applied the quoted wisdom to the case before him:

> "It is revolting to have no better reason for a rule of law than that so it was laid down in the time of Henry IV. It is still more revolting if the grounds upon which it was laid down have vanished long since, and the rule simply persists from blind imitation of the past." Holmes, The Path of the Law, 10 Harv. L. Rev. 457, 469 (1897).
>
> For this Court now to act on Hawkins's formulation of the medieval view that husband and wife "are esteemed but as one Person in Law, and are presumed to have but one Will" would indeed be "blind imitation of the past." It would require us to disregard the vast changes in the status of woman—the extension of her rights and correlative duties—whereby a wife's legal submission to her husband has been wholly wiped out, not only in the English-speaking world generally but emphatically so in this country.

Unfortunately, Mr. Justice Frankfurter's observation in *Dege* does not correspond to contemporary reality. As this case and the statutes set out in the Appendix illustrate, the law-sanctioned subordination of wife to husband, mother to father, woman to man, is not yet extinguished in this country.

A federal court deciding a closely related issue, and two state courts deciding the identical issue, found scant difficulty in dispatching *Goesaert*.

In *Seidenberg v. McSorleys' Old Ale House*, 317 F. Supp. 593 (S.D.N.Y. 1970), Judge Mansfield declared a tavern owner's exclusion of women patrons inconsistent with the fourteenth amendment. In answer to the argument that *Goesaert* was controlling, he stated:

> Nor do we find any merit in the argument that the presence of women in bars gives rise to "moral and social problems" against

which McSorleys' can reasonably protect itself by excluding women from the premises. Social mores have not stood still since that argument was used in 1948 to convince a 6–3 majority of the Supreme Court that women might rationally be prohibited from working as bartenders unless they were wives or daughters of male owners of the premises.

In *Paterson Tavern & Grill Owners Ass'n v. Borough of Hawthorne*, 57 N.J. 180 (1970), the New Jersey Supreme Court considered a local ordinance which, like the statute in *Goesaert*, denied women the right to tavern employment behind the bar. Indicative of the change in social norms to which Judge Mansfield referred in *Seidenberg v. McSorleys' Old Ale House*, the New Jersey case presented this interesting difference in party line-up: The plaintiffs were a male tavern owner who wished the freedom to select a woman bartender, and an association of tavern owners. The New Jersey Supreme Court ruled that in the light of current customs and mores, "the municipal restriction against female bartending may no longer fairly be viewed as a necessary and reasonable exercise of the police power." It concluded, reminiscent of this Court's expressions in *United States v. Dege*:

> While the law may look to the past for the lessons it teaches, it must be geared to the present and towards the future if it is to serve the people in just and proper fashion. In the current climate the law may not tolerate blanket municipal bartending exclusions grounded solely on sex.

Finally, the California Supreme Court in *Sail'er Inn Inc. v. Kirby* said of *Goesaert*: "Although *Goesaert* has not been overruled, its holding has been the subject of academic criticism...and its sweeping statement that the states are not constitutionally precluded from 'drawing a sharp line between the sexes' has come under increasing limitation."

In sum, *Goesaert's* sanction of "a sharp line between the sexes" and its "blind imitation of the past" have rendered it a burden and an embarrassment to state and federal courts; enlightened jurists politely discard it as precedent, refusing "to be obfuscated by medieval views regarding the legal status of women." It should be plain that no one would now mourn its formal burial.

Hoyt v. Florida, 368 U.S. 57 (1961), completes the trilogy of cases invoked most frequently to justify second class status for women. In *Hoyt*, this Court sustained a Florida statute limiting jury service by women to those who registered with the court a desire to be placed on the jury list. That case, although it harks back to the stereotyped view of women rejected in *United States v. Dege*, is readily distinguishable. Unlike the situation now before the Court, in which a woman's disqualification is mandated whenever a male contender appears, in *Hoyt*, the Court "found no substantial evidence whatever in this record that Florida has arbitrarily undertaken to exclude women from jury service." Underscoring the point, the three concurring Justices stated their inability to find "from this record that Florida is not making a good faith effort to have women perform jury duty without discrimination on the ground of sex."

While the *Hoyt* holding offers no support at all for a statute of the Idaho Code sec. 15-314 genre, in which discrimination on the ground of sex is undisguised, this Court included language in the opinion that has been turned against women who seek to realize their full potential as individual human beings:

> Despite the enlightened emancipation of women from the restrictions and protections of bygone years, and their entry into many parts of community life formerly considered to be reserved to men, *woman is still regarded as the center of home and family life.* We cannot say that it is constitutionally impermissible for a State, acting in pursuit of the general welfare, to conclude that a woman should be relieved from the civic duty of jury service unless she herself determines that such service is consistent with her own special responsibilities.

While an image of woman, first and predominantly as keeper of the hearth, might have been expected from jurists writing at the turn of the century, it is disquieting to find the antiquated stereotype repeated so late in the day. Even in times past, when the absence of family planning and effective birth-control devices restricted options for most women, many by choice or fortune did not play the role of mother-wife. Today, of course, scientific developments have placed the choice and timing of parenthood within the realm of individual decision. Even for those who suspend or curtail economic activity to care for offspring, the period devoted to child-rearing is limited.

In these days of longevity, most women, for the larger part of their lives, are not preoccupied with child care functions.

The brief reversion to stereotype in the *Hoyt* opinion has had unfortunate consequences. For example, in a 1970 decision a New York trial court rejected the challenge of a female plaintiff to a jury system with automatic exemption for women. As a result of this exemption, women constituted less than twenty percent of the available jury pool. In his published opinion, the judge relied on *Hoyt* to explain to the complainant that she was "in the wrong forum." Less chivalrous than this Court, but more accurately reflecting the impact of the stereotype, the judge stated that plaintiff's "lament" should be addressed to her sisters who prefer "cleaning and cooking, rearing of children and television soap operas, bridge and canasta, the beauty parlor and shopping, to becoming embroiled in plaintiff's problems...." *DeKosenko v. Brandt*, 313 N.Y.S. 2d 827, 830 (Sup. Ct. 1970). Nothing was said of the likelihood that many men would find other pursuits preferable to jury service were they offered automatic exemption.

Although *Hoyt* no doubt has impeded full recognition throughout the country that jury duty is a responsibility shared equally by all citizens, male and female alike, the majority of states either treat women and men on the same basis, or relieve women only when family duties in the particular case require exemption. For example recognizing the contemporary reality that among today's young parents, child care functions are often shared, the New Jersey statute provides exemption for any "person" who has the actual physical care and custody of a minor child.

D. The Discrimination Against Women Mandated by Sec. 15-314 Is Not Justified by Any Compelling State Interest.

If, as appellant urges, sex-based classification is declared "suspect," this Court must next consider whether a compelling state interest justifies the discrimination embodied in Sec. 15-314 of the Idaho Code.

Section 15-314 is the direct descendant of Sec. 52 of the Idaho Probate Practice Act adopted by the First Territorial Legislature in 1864. The current provision incorporates the language of its 1864 predecessor without change. Idaho does not publish legislative committee reports or debate proceedings; consequently, no legislative history is available. Indeed, no source for discovering legislative intent exists apart from the decisions by the courts below in this case, the only Idaho case directly in point.

The Supreme Court of Idaho justified the statute in these terms:

By I.C. §15-314, the legislature eliminated [an area] of controversy, i.e., if both a man and woman of the same class seek letters of administration, the male would be entitled over the female.... This provision of the statute is neither an illogical nor arbitrary method devised by the legislature to resolve an issue that would otherwise require a hearing as to the relative merits as to which of the two or more petitioning relatives should be appointed.

Philosophically it can be argued with some degree of logic that the provisions of I.C. §15-314 do discriminate against women on the basis of sex. However nature itself has established the distinction and this statute is not designed to discriminate but is only designed to alleviate the problem of holding hearings by the court to determine eligibility to administer.

It is our opinion that the state has a legitimate interest in promoting the prompt administration of states and that the statute in question promotes this interest by curtailing litigation over the appointment of administrators.

Thus, the Idaho Supreme Court explained as a time and decision saving device its tolerance of a patent legislative discrimination against women. The decision below contrasts dramatically with decisions on kindred matters rendered by the West German Federal Constitutional Court, a high court created with the model of the United States Supreme Court in close view. In a leading case, several wives and mothers challenged under the equal protection principle of the post–World War II West German Constitution, provisions of the German Civil Code declaring "if parents are unable to agree, father decides," and mandating preference to the father as representative of the child. Both Code provisions were declared unconstitutional (July 29, 1959). While the Idaho Supreme Court was content to rely on considerations of expediency and the legislature's evident conclusion "that in general men are better qualified to act as administrators than are women," the West German Federal Constitutional Court focused on the superior norm. The differences in life styles alleged to exist, and the interest in saving time and sparing court facilities, it declared, are hardly so decisive as to override the fundamental constitutional guarantee of equal protection. The Court expressly rejected the notion that the legislature may introduce discriminations "of women, Jews, members of some political party or religious association" under "reasonable" circumstances. In a subsequent case concerning preference to sons over daughters in agrarian inheritance law, the West German Federal Constitutional Court relegated to the scrap heap of history legal distinctions based on the assumption that men are better equipped than women to manage property (March 20, 1963).*

No doubt promotion of expeditious administration of estates and curtailment of litigation are bona fide state interests. But it is equally plain that the end of expediency cannot be served by unconstitutional means. Surely this Court would find offensive to the Constitution, to "the ethos of our society," and to common sense a fiduciary selection statute that preferred whites to blacks or Christians to Jews. A statute preferring men to women should fare no better. If sex is a "suspect classification," a state interest in avoiding a hearing cannot justify rank discrimination against a person, solely on the ground that she is a female.

Convenience, simplicity and curtailment of litigation, while grand virtues in the administration of public affairs, do not supersede the fundamental right of individuals to even-handed application of governmental action. Thus, such obviously convenient state measures as restricting the ballot to "two old, established parties" (*Williams v. Rhodes*, 393 U.S. 23 (1968)), and denying welfare payments to persons with less than a year's residency in the state (*Shapiro v. Thompson*, 394 U.S. 618 (1969)), did not survive this Court's scrutiny under the equal protection clause.

Williams v. Rhodes and *Shapiro v. Thompson* involved justifications more substantial than expedition. Yet the several reasons offered by the states in those cases, even in combination, were found insufficient to overcome the heavy burden required by this Court.

---

* Cf. United Nations Charter preamble, Art. 1, para. 3 (calling for respect for human rights and fundamental freedoms for all persons without distinction as to race, sex, language or religion). For a progress report indicating a pace more rapid than that of the United States, see The Status of Women in Sweden: Report to the United Nations (1968). See also The Emancipation of Man, address by Mr. Olof Palme, Swedish Prime Minister, at the Women's National Democratic Club, Washington, D.C., June 8, 1970: "The public opinion is nowadays so well informed that if a politician should declare that the woman ought to have a different role than the man and that it is natural that she devotes more time to the children he would be regarded to be of the Stone Age."

In *Shapiro v. Thompson*, the state sought to justify its one-year waiting period on seven grounds: (1) as a protective device to preserve the fiscal integrity of the state public assistance programs; (2) to discourage the influx of poor families in need of assistance; (3) to discourage the influx of indigents who would enter the state solely to obtain larger benefits; (4) to facilitate planning of the welfare budget; (5) to provide an objective test of residency; (6) to minimize the opportunity for recipients fraudulently to receive payments from more than one jurisdiction; (7) to encourage early entry of new residents into the labor force.

In *Williams v. Rhodes*, the state asserted that its restrictive election legislation (1) promoted a two-party system in order to encourage compromise and political stability, (2) avoided election of plurality candidates, (3) allowed those who disagree with the major parties and their policies "a choice of leadership as well as issues," and (4) avoided confronting voters with a choice so confusing that the popular will could be frustrated.

While any of these reasons might be considered "rational," this Court concluded that, even taken together, they were not "compelling." In contrast to the relatively serious reason asserted to save the Connecticut, Pennsylvania and District of Columbia statutes in *Shapiro v. Thompson*, and the Ohio law in *Williams v. Rhodes*, the justification advanced here by the Idaho Supreme Court—administrative convenience—falls far short of a "compelling" state interest when appraised in light of the interest of the class against which the statute discriminates—an interest in treatment as full human personalities. As this Court said in *Williams v. Illinois*, 399 U.S. 235, 245 (1970), "the constitutional imperatives of the Equal Protection Clause must have priority over the comfortable convenience of the status quo."

Moreover, even the vaunted convenience afforded by Idaho Code sec. 15-314 is largely illusory. Hearings are avoided only in those cases where an eligible female applicant is challenged by an equally eligible male applicant. But if, for example, four sisters individually sought letters of administration, the court would have to hold a hearing to select an administrator; if three brothers and one sister each sought appointment, the court would have to hold a hearing—even though the female applicant would be eliminated from the competition. In any situation in which two or more applicants of the same sex from a class of equal eligibles separately seek letters of administration, a hearing must be held so that the court may issue letters of administration "to the party best entitled thereto." Idaho Code sec. 15-323.

The fact that not all women are denied the right to a hearing or presumed less than competent to administer an estate highlights the invidious discrimination inherent in the statute. A woman may compete on terms of equality whenever her challenger is another woman. If no male equally eligible opposes, the woman will be appointed. Through this device of law-mandated subordination of "equally entitled" women to men, the dominant male society, exercising its political power,* has secured women's place as the second sex.

II. The statutory classification based on the sex of the applicant established in Section 15-314 of the Idaho Code is arbitrary and capricious and bears no rational relationship to a legitimate legislative purpose.

If the Court concludes that sex is not a suspect classification, appellant urges application of an intermediate test. Attributable in part to decisions of this Court, women continue to receive disadvantaged treatment by the law. In answer to the compelling claim of women for recognition by the law as full human personalities, this Court, at the very least, should reverse the presumption of a statute's rationality when the statute accords a preference to males. Rather than require the party attacking the statute to show that the classification is irrational, the Court should require the statute's proponent to prove it rational.

Yet, the discrimination embodied in section 15-314 of the Idaho Code is so patently visible that the statute is readily assailable under the less stringent

---

* Although women were granted the vote over fifty years ago, the legacy of their disenfranchisement is still apparent. Elected or appointed office in this country remains, with sparse exceptions, a male preserve.

For the levity with which even the judiciary treats women's lack of representation, see *State v. Hunter*, 208 Ore 282, 287–88 (1956):

> We believe that we are justified in taking judicial notice of the fact that the membership of the legislative assembly which enacted this statute was predominantly masculine. That fact is important in determining what the legislature might have had in mind with respect to this particular statute.... It seems to us that its purpose, although somewhat selfish in nature, stands out in the statute like a sore thumb.... Is it any wonder that the legislative assembly took advantage of the police power of the state in its decision to halt this ever-increasing feminine encroachment upon what for ages had been considered strictly as manly arts and privileges?

At the time Idaho Code section 15-314 was originally enacted, 1864, women in Idaho lacked the right to vote for members of the legislature.

reasonable-relationship test. The mandatory preference to males lacks the constitutionally required fair and substantial relation to a permissible legislative purpose and therefore must be held to violate the equal protection clause.

The Idaho Supreme Court held the sex-based classification of section 15-314 reasonable on the ground that "the legislature when it enacted this statute evidently concluded that in general men are better qualified to act as an administrator than are women." Conceding that "there are doubtless particular instances in which [the legislature's evident conclusion] is incorrect," the Idaho Supreme Court was "not prepared to say that [the conclusion] is so completely without a basis in fact as to be irrational and arbitrary."

Declaring that "nature itself has established the distinction," the Idaho Supreme Court seemingly justified the discrimination challenged here by finding it "rational" to assume the mental inferiority of women to men. This assumption, particularized in the judgment that "men are better qualified to act as an administrator than are women" demands swift condemnation of this Court. In the Idaho District Court, where the argument was made in terms of the supposed greater "business experience" of men, Judge Donaldson responded, "The Court feels that this statement has no basis in fact in this modern age and society," and promptly declared section 15-314 unconstitutional. At a time when assumptions concerning the physical inferiority of women no longer go unquestioned, the Court surely cannot countenance distinctions based on totally unfounded assumptions of differences in mental capacity, or "experience" relevant to the office of administrator.

Despite the massive discrimination that women still face in the job market, their participation in the business world is increasing dramatically. In 1969, 30,512,000 women over the age of sixteen were at work, and comprised 37.8% of all workers. The comparable figures thirty years ago were 13,783,000 and 25.4%. About 42% of all women over the age of sixteen work full-time the year round. In 1969, 58.9% of all married women living with husbands worked. The Department of Labor has projected that by 1980 there will be 37,000,000 working women, twice as many as there were in 1950, and that for the first time there will be as many female professionals and technical workers as female blue-collar workers.

A similar trend is apparent in education. In 1967, women comprised 40.5% of the undergraduate student population in four-year institutions of higher learning and 29.7% of the graduate population. In the same year, women earned 40.3% of the bachelor's degrees, 34.7% of the master's degrees, and 11.9% of the doctorate degrees. Close to 3,000,000 women were enrolled in institutions of higher learning in 1967, representing a 10% increase over 1966 and a 53% increase over 1963.

In April, 1971, 4,500,000 women were employed as professional or technical workers compared to 6,706,000 men; 1,440,000 women were employed as managers, officials or proprietors, compared to 7,150,000 men. In 1968, 10,000 women worked as accountants, 20% of the total; 12,500 were employed as bank officers, 10% of the total; 8,100 were employed as lawyers, 3% of the total; 6,500 worked as mathematicians, 10% of the total; and 7,560 were engaged as statisticians, 33% of the total.

In 1970, 2,226 women passed the federal service management intern examination, 38% of the total. Women employed by the federal government as category III employees in 1969 included 5,481 in accounting and budget, 12% of the total; 5,621 in legal and law-related areas, 23% of the total; 6,686 in business and industry, 14% of the total. As of April 1971, 13,000 women were serving as officers in the Armed Forces.

Any legislative judgment that "men are better qualified to act as an administrator than are women" is simply untenable in view of these statistics, revealing what the Department of Labor describes as "a major change in American life style." Moreover, although the Idaho Supreme Court did not provide any enlightenment on the specific functions an administrator performs for which "men are better qualified," the standard responsibilities are evident: receiving payments from creditors, paying out debts, paying state and federal taxes if any, preserving the assets of the estate, and finally paying out the net estate to the lawful heirs. Except for the occasional millionaire who dies intestate, the responsibilities are hardly onerous. They can be handled satisfactorily by most people who have completed secondary school education.

Moreover, the extent to which "business experience" is needed for performance of the duties of an administrator is questionable. The Idaho Code, like most statutes relating to administration, confers very limited authority upon the administrator and empowers the court to supervise the estate closely during the entire period of administration. Thus the administrator must hire an appraiser for the estate. No claims can be allowed without court approval. Distribution of the estate is strictly prescribed. Furthermore, the criteria for disqualification of an administrator set out in Idaho Code sec. 15-317 provide no support whatever for treating "business experience" as a characteristic of the competent executor. Any resident above the age of majority who has not been convicted of an infamous crime, and who is not mentally defective, a drunk, a wastrel, a spendthrift, or a cheat, is presumptively competent.

In any event, it is not unlikely that more women than men have the kind of "business experience" most relevant to the duties of an administrator. Women who do not work outside the home often handle most if not all the financial affairs of their family unit. Managerial responsibility, including the settlement of accounts and the preservation of property, is a central part of their daily occupation. As preparation for the duties of an administrator experience in household management surely is not inferior to experience in such typically male occupations as truck driver, construction worker, factory worker, or farm laborer.

Finally, as developed in the preceding section, Idaho's interest in prompt administration of estates and curtailment of litigation is barely served by section 15-314. The male preference system operates in relatively few cases. In most situations in which more than one applicant from a class of equal eligibles separately seek letters of administration, hearings must be held. Indeed, and quite appropriately, the Idaho Code invites hearings by providing that "any person interested" may challenge the competency of the administrator.

To eliminate women who share an eligibility category with a man, when there is no basis in fact to assume that women are less competent to administer than are men, is patently unreasonable and constitutionally impermissible. A woman's right to equal treatment may not be sacrificed to expediency.

CONCLUSION

For the reasons stated above, the decision of the Idaho Supreme Court should be reversed and Sec. 15-314 should be declared unconstitutional.

SHARRON A. FRONTIERO AND JOSEPH FRONTIERO, APPELLANTS, V. MELVIN R. LAIRD AS SECRETARY OF DEFENSE, HIS SUCCESSORS AND ASSIGNS; DR. ROBERT C. SEAMANS, JR., AS SECRETARY OF THE AIR FORCE, HIS SUCCESSORS AND ASSIGNS; AND COL. CHARLES G. WEBER, AS COMMANDING OFFICER, MAXWELL AIR FORCE BASE, ALABAMA, HIS SUCCESSORS AND ASSIGNS, APPELLEES

ON APPEAL FROM THE UNITED STATES DISTRICT COURT FOR THE MIDDLE DISTRICT OF ALABAMA, NORTHERN DIVISION

411 U.S. 677 (May 14, 1973)

Oral Argument

January 17, 1973

Warren E. Burger: Mrs. Ginsburg.

Ruth Bader Ginsburg: Mr. Chief Justice and may it please the Court.

Amicus views this case as kin to *Reed v. Reed*, 404 U.S. The legislative judgment in both derives from the same stereotype: The man is or should be the independent partner in a marital unit. The woman with an occasional exception is dependent, sheltered from breadwinning experience.

Appellees stated in answer to interrogatories in this case that they remained totally uninformed on the application of this stereotype to service families—that is, they do not know whether the proportion of wage-earning wives of servicemen is small, large, or middle size.

What is known is that by employing the sex criterion, identically situated persons are treated differently.

The married serviceman gets benefits for himself, as well as his spouse, regardless of her income.

The married servicewoman is denied medical care for her spouse and quarters' allowance for herself as well as her spouse even if, as in this case, she supplies over two-thirds the support of the marital unit.

For these reasons, amicus believes that the sex-related means employed by Congress fails to meet the rationality standard.

It does not have a fair and substantial relationship to the legislative objective so that all similarly circumstanced persons shall be treated alike.

Nonetheless, amicus urges the Court to recognize in this case what it has in others, that it writes not only for this case and this day alone, but for this type of case.

As is apparent from the decisions cited at pages 27 to 34 of our brief, in lower federal as well as state courts, the standard of review in sex discrimination cases is, to say the least, confused.

A few courts have ranked sex as a suspect criterion.

Others, including apparently the court below in this case, seem to regard the *Reed* decision as a direction to apply minimal scrutiny, and there are various shades between.

The result is that in many instances, the same or similar issues are decided differently depending upon the court's view of the stringency of review appropriate.

To provide the guidance so badly needed and because recognition is long overdue, amicus urges the Court to declare sex a suspect criterion.

This would not be quite the giant step appellee suggests.

As Professor Gunther observed in an analysis of last term's equal protection decisions published in the November 1972 *Harvard Law Review*, it appears that in *Reed*, some special suspicion of sex as a classifying factor entered into the Court's analysis.

Appellees concede that the principal ingredient involving strict scrutiny is present in the sex criterion: Sex, like race, is a visible, immutable characteristic bearing no necessary relationship to ability.

Sex, like race, has been made the basis for unjustified or at least unproved assumptions concerning an individual's potential to perform or to contribute to society.

But appellees point out that although the essential ingredient rendering a classification suspect is present, sex-based distinctions, unlike racial distinctions, do not have an especially disfavored constitutional history.

It is clear that the core purpose of the Fourteenth Amendment was to eliminate invidious racial discrimination.

But why did the framers of the Fourteenth Amendment regard racial discrimination as odious?

Because a person's skin color bears no necessary relationship to ability. Similarly, as appellees concede, a person's sex bears no necessary relationship to ability.

Moreover, national origin and alienage have been recognized as suspect classifications, although the newcomer to our shores was not the paramount concern of the nation when the Fourteenth Amendment was adopted.

But the main thrust of the argument against recognition of sex as a suspect criterion centers on two points.

First, women are a majority.

Second, legislative classification by sex does not, it is asserted, imply the inferiority of women.

With respect to the numbers argument, the numerical majority was denied even the right to vote until 1920.

Women today face discrimination in employment as pervasive and more subtle than discrimination encountered by minority groups.

In vocational and higher education, women continue to face restrictive quotas no longer operative with respect to other population groups.

Their absence is conspicuous in federal and state legislative, executive, and judicial chambers; in higher civil service positions; and in appointed posts in federal, state, and local government.

Surely, no one would suggest that race is not a suspect criterion in the District of Columbia because the black population here outnumbers the white.

Moreover, as Mr. Justice Douglas has pointed out most recently in *Hadley against Alabama*, 41 Law Week 3205, equal protection and due process of law apply to the majority as well as to the minorities.

Do the sex classifications listed by appellees imply a judgment of inferiority?

Even the court below suggested that they do.

That court said it would be remiss if it failed to notice lurking in the background the subtle injury inflicted on servicewomen—the indignity of being treated differently so many of them feel.

Sex classifications do stigmatize when, as in *Goesaert against Cleary* 235 U.S., they exclude women from an occupation thought more appropriate to men.

The sex criterion stigmatizes when it is used to limit hours of work for women only.

Hours regulations of the kind involved in *Muller against Oregon*, though perhaps reasonable under turn-of-the-century conditions, today protect women from competing for extra remuneration, higher paying jobs, promotions.

The sex criterion stigmatizes when, as in *Hoyt against Florida*, 368 U.S., it assumes that all women are preoccupied with home and children and therefore should be spared the basic civic responsibility of serving on a jury.

These distinctions have a common effect.

They help keep woman in her place, a place inferior to that occupied by men in our society.

Appellees recognize that there is doubt as to the contemporary validity of the theory that sex classifications do not brand the female sex as inferior.

But they advocate a hold-the-line position by this Court unless and until the Equal Rights Amendment comes into force.

Absent the Equal Rights Amendment, appellees assert, no close scrutiny of sex-based classifications is warranted. This Court should stand pat on legislation of the kind involved in this case: legislation making a distinction, servicewomen regard as the most gross equity, the greatest irritant and the most discriminatory provision relating to women in the military service.

But this Court has recognized that the notion of what constitutes equal protection does change.

Proponents as well as opponents of the Equal Rights Amendment believe that clarification of the application of equal protection to the sex criterion is needed and should come from this Court.

Proponents believe that appropriate interpretation of the Fifth and Fourteenth Amendments would secure equal rights and responsibilities for men and women.

But they also stressed that such interpretation was not yet discernible and in any event the amendment would serve an important function in removing even the slightest doubt that equal rights for men and women is fundamental constitutional principle.

In asking the Court to declare sex a suspect criterion, amicus urges a position forcibly stated in 1837 by Sarah Grimké, noted abolitionist and advocate of equal rights for men and women.

She spoke not elegantly, but with unmistakable clarity.

She said, "I ask no favor for my sex. All I ask of our brethren is that they take their feet off our necks."

In conclusion, amicus joins appellants in requesting that this Court reverse the judgment entered below and remand the case with instructions to grant the relief requested in appellant's complaint.

Thank you.

Chief Justice Warren E. Burger: Thank you, Mrs. Ginsburg.

BRIEF OF AMERICAN CIVIL LIBERTIES UNION
AMICUS CURIAE

Filed December 8, 1972

Most citations and footnotes have been omitted, as well as some punctuation (including brackets and internal quotation marks). Also omitted are the table of authorities and statements of opinion below, statutes involved, and jurisdiction.

Question Presented

Whether the classification according to sex made by 37 U.S.C. Sections 401 and 403, and 10 U.S.C. Sections 1072 and 1076, which provide "dependency" allowances automatically for the spouse of male members of the uniformed services, whether or not the spouse is in fact dependent on the member for any of her support, but which provide such allowances for the spouse of female members of the uniformed services only upon a showing that the spouse is in fact dependent on the member for more than one-half of his support, violates the due process clause of the fifth amendment to the United States Constitution.

Statement of the Case

Appellant Sharron Frontiero joined the Air Force on October 1, 1968, for an obligated period of service of four years. On December 17, 1969, she married appellant Joseph Frontiero, who was and remains a full-time student at Huntington College, Montgomery, Alabama. As stated in the agreed stipulation of fact on the basis of which this action was heard and determined, appellant Joseph Frontiero's total expenses are approximately $354.00 per month. With the exception of $205.00 per month which appellant Joseph Frontiero receives under the educational provisions of the G.I. Bill and $30.00 per month income from a part-time job, appellant Sharron Frontiero provides the sole support for both appellants.

The provisions of 37 U.S.C. Sections 401 and 403 grant a supplemental housing allowance to armed forces members living off-base (Basic Allowance for Quarters—BAQ), the allowance varying with the number of dependents claimed by the armed forces member. Male members are allowed to claim their spouses as dependents, and hence to gain extra benefits, regardless of the wives' actual financial dependency. The statute sets up a different definition of dependency for female armed forces members, allowing the females to claim their spouses as dependents, and hence gain supplemental benefits, only if the husband is in fact dependent upon the female service member for over one-half of his support.*

In the fall of 1970, after consulting with her commanding officer and a representative of the Base Legal Office, appellant Sharron Frontiero advised Col. George Jernigan, MAFB Hospital Commander, that she wanted to secure BAQ which would include the additional housing allowance that would have been granted automatically to males with spouses. Col. Jernigan informed her that the regulations prohibited such allowances. In November, 1970, pursuant to the advice of a member of the Inspector General's staff, MAFB, appellant Sharron Frontiero submitted a formal complaint. Approximately one week thereafter, appellant Sharron Frontiero was informed that the complaint had been reviewed and that she was ineligible for any housing allowance.

Under 10 U.S.C. Sections 1072 and 1076, the wife and children of military personnel are entitled to comprehensive medical benefits, regardless of their potential or actual income. However, the husband of a female member of the armed forces is not entitled to any medical benefits unless he is "in fact dependent upon" the female member for more than one-half of his support. Appellant Sharron Frontiero seeks extension of these medical benefits to her spouse, appellant Joseph Frontiero.

On December 23, 1970, appellants filed a complaint in the United States District Court for the Middle District of Alabama, Northern Division, asserting that the distinctions drawn by these statutes and regulations, insofar as they required different treatment for female and male members of the uniformed services, arbitrarily and unreasonably discriminate against appellants and therefore violate the due process clause of the fifth amendment to the United States Constitution.

Over the dissent of Judge Johnson, the district court held that "the challenged statutes are not in conflict with the Due Process Clause of the Fifth Amendment and...are in all respects constitutional." 341 F. Supp. at 209.

---

* Maxwell Air Force Base (MAFB) does not provide any base housing for the families of married female members of the Air Force. Complaint, para. III (2).

SUMMARY OF ARGUMENT

I.

37 U.S.C. Sections 401 and 403 and 10 U.S.C. Sections 1072 and 1076, providing that all wives of servicemen are eligible for housing allowances and medical benefits but only husbands of servicewomen who actually receive more than half their support from their wives are eligible for these allowances and benefits, denies appellants the equal protection of the law guaranteed by the due process clause of the fifth amendment.

Historically, women have been treated as subordinate and inferior to men. Although some progress toward erasing sex discrimination has been made, the distance to equal opportunity for women in the United States remains considerable. Like other groups that have been assisted toward full equality before the law via the "suspect classification" doctrine, women are sparsely represented in legislative and policy-making chambers and lack political power to remedy the discriminatory treatment they are accorded in the law and in society generally. Absent firm constitutional foundation for equal treatment of men and women by the law, women seeking to be judged on their individual merits will continue to encounter law-sanctioned obstacles.

II.

The distinctions between male and female members of the armed forces established by 37 U.S.C. Sections 401 and 403 and 10 U.S.C. Sections 1072 and 1076 create a "suspect classification" requiring close judicial scrutiny.

The challenged classification, based solely on sex, rests upon a foundation of myth and custom which assumes that the male is the dominant partner in marriage and which reinforces restrictive and outdated sex role stereotypes about married women and their participation in the work force. In recent years the national conscience has been awakened to the sometimes subtle injury inflicted on women by these stereotypes. Enlightened courts have begun to strike down discriminatory sex-based classifications as inconsistent with the equal protection guarantees of the Constitution. Nevertheless there is still substantial judicial confusion as to the standard of review appropriate to these challenges.

Recent changes in society's attitudes toward equal opportunity for men and women have made the underlying premise of the "suspect classification" clear: although the legislature may distinguish between individuals on the basis of their need or ability, it is presumptively impermissible to distinguish on the basis of an unalterable identifying trait over which the individual has no control and for which he or she should not be disadvantaged by the law. Legislative discrimination grounded on sex, for purposes unrelated to any biological difference between the sexes, ranks with legislative discrimination based on race, another congenital, unalterable trait of birth, and merits no greater judicial deference. The time is now ripe for this Court to repudiate the premise that, with minimal justification, the legislature may draw "a sharp line between the sexes," just as this Court has repudiated once settled law that differential treatment of the races is constitutionally permissible. Amicus is asking this Court to add legislative distinctions based on sex to the category of "suspect" classifications.

III.

The challenged classification is not justified by administrative convenience, the primary rationale relied on by the court below. There is every indication, given the fact that almost 60% of married women work, that the increased cost of administration, if the test of actual dependency were applied to servicemen and their spouses, would be more than offset by the resultant reduction in benefits paid out. Apart from the question of whether the challenged classification actually results in financial savings, the administrative convenience rationale has been rejected by this Court, lower federal courts and, with regard to benefits payable to veterans and non-military federal employees, by the Congress, as a justification for discriminatory sex-based classifications. Finally, federal law prohibits private and state employers from engaging in practices like those challenged in the case at bar.

IV.

The discrimination against women mandated by the challenged classification is neither supported by a compelling state interest, necessary to the accomplishment of legitimate legislative objectives nor reasonably related to a permissible legislative objective. It is well established that convenience and simplicity, while admirable virtues in the administration of public affairs, do not constitute a compelling state interest. If the Court concludes that sex is not a suspect classification, or defers determination of this issue, amicus urges that it apply an intermediate test, developed in previous decisions of the Court: the challenged classification should be "closely scrutinized" to determine whether it is "necessary to the accomplishment of legitimate legislative objectives." Even if the "rational relationship" test is applied, the challenged classifications do not pass constitutional muster: it is doubtful that the goal of administrative convenience is in fact served by the challenged classification; in any event, administrative convenience has been rejected by this Court under the rational relationship test as a justification for sex-based classifications.

V.

Upon finding that the challenged provisions violate the fifth amendment, the Court should remedy the defect by extending to female members of the armed forces the same benefits now available to male members. The dominant purpose of the statutes in which the challenged provisions appear, to attract and retain competent men and women in the armed forces, impels the remedy of extension. This remedy has been employed in numerous comparable cases by the Court. Recent action of the Congress to equalize fringe benefits available to male and female veterans and non-military federal employees by extending the benefits to the sex suffering discrimination, provides a clear indication of its remedial preference.

ARGUMENT

...The central question raised in this case is whether Congress, consistent with the equal protection principle inherent in the due process clause of the fifth amendment, may legislate that married female members of the armed forces must meet a "dependent spouse" requirement in order to receive fringe benefits granted automatically to similarly situated male members. The statutes at issue classify married male members of the armed forces as dominant partners in their marriage, but assign to married female members a subordinate status, absent proof that they supply more than half of their husbands' support. It is the position of amicus that this sex-based classification, established for a purpose unrelated to any biological difference between the sexes, cannot survive constitutional review.

[*"Historical Perspective" section is largely repeated from Reed v. Reed brief.*]

The overwhelming approval of the Equal Rights Amendment to the United States Constitution confirms the dominant intent of Congress to terminate sex-based discrimination by law. In the course of the debate on the Amendment, however, Congress made plain its view that appropriate construction and application of the fifth and fourteenth amendments would amply secure equality of rights and responsibilities between the sexes. Nonetheless, Congress wishes to provide further assurances so there would not be the slightest doubt that the right of men and women to equal treatment under the law would be recognized as a fundamental constitutional principle.

In 1963, the President's Commission on the Status of Women concluded that "equality of rights under the law for all persons, male or female, is so basic to democracy and its commitment to the ultimate value of the individual that it must be reflected in the fundamental law of the land." The Commission believed that this principle was embodied in the fifth and fourteenth amendments, and looked to this Court for "imperative" clarification to eliminate "remaining ambiguities with respect to the constitutional protection of women's rights." The case at bar presents an opportunity for definitive pronouncement providing this overdue clarification.

II. The statutes at issue discriminate against female members of the uniformed services and constitute a denial of equal protection of the laws, guaranteed by the due process clause of the fifth amendment.

A. The fifth amendment due process clause encompasses guarantees of security from arbitrary treatment and of equal protection of the laws; appellants' case rests upon these fundamental guarantees. . . .

B. The classification at issue in this case is based solely on sex. . . .

C. Equal protection standards of review.

In determining whether legislation violates the concept of equal protection, the courts have applied standards of review ranging from lenient to stringent. Two standards are generally contrasted: (1) the lenient or "rational relationship" test applicable in the generality of cases; (2) the "rigid scrutiny" test met only by demonstration of a "compelling state interest," applicable when the legislation relates to a "fundamental right or interest" or invokes a "suspect" criterion.

To survive the "rational relationship" test, a classification "must be reasonable, not arbitrary, and must rest upon some ground of difference having a fair and substantial relation to the object of the legislation so that all persons similarly circumstanced shall be treated alike." The more stringent test is exemplified in cases dealing with the right to vote, and the right to travel, and in cases involving classification based on race, ancestry or national origin.

In addition to the two commonly articulated review standards, some of the decisions of this Court suggest an intermediate standard: the legislation is "closely scrutinized," and the proponent of the challenged classification is required to show that it is "necessary to the accomplishment of legitimate [legislative] objectives."

With respect to the standard of review in this case, our position is three-fold: (1) 37 U.S.C. Sections 401 and 403 and 10 U.S.C. Sections 1072 and 1076 establish a suspect classification for which no compelling justification can be shown; alternatively, (2) the classification at issue, closely scrutinized, is not reasonably necessary to the accomplishment of any legitimate legislative objective; and, finally, (3) without regard to the suspect or invidious nature of the classification, the line drawn by Congress, distinguishing between married servicemen and married servicewomen for purposes of fringe benefits, lacks the constitutionally required fair and reasonable relation to a permissible legislative objective.

D. Rather than assigning a "heavy burden" to appellants and applying a "lenient" standard of review, the court below should have subjected 10 U.S.C. Sections 1072 and 1076 and 37 U.S.C. Sections 401 and 403 to close scrutiny, identifying sex as a "suspect" criterion for legislative distinctions.

1. The challenged classification rests upon a view of the married woman which does not accord with present day reality.

The challenged classification, which assumes that the man is the dominant partner in a marriage and that the woman occupies a subordinate position, rests upon a foundation of myth and custom still reflected in myriad laws, but out of tune with conditions of life in this second half of the Twentieth Century. Such classifications once appeared to jurists as "benign," benefiting women who occupied the traditional role of mother and homemaker, or "neutral," accurately describing social reality. Examined from a contemporary perspective, however, these classifications reinforce restrictive and outdated sex-role stereotypes and penalize married women who do not conform to the assumed general pattern.

National statistics relegate to myth the notions that relatively few married women work, and that when they do, their earnings are "pin money" rather than an essential part of the family's finances. In April, 1971, 42.7% of all women 16 years of age or older were in the labor force, compared with 28.9% in March, 1940. Of these women, 18.5 million, or 58.5% of working women, were married and living with their husbands. This is almost twice the rate of 1940. From 1960 to 1970, nearly half of the increase in the labor force was accounted for by married women. And for the last four years, married women have made up the largest portion of the annual increase in the civilian labor force. Married women of all ages are increasing their rate of labor force participation while other groups are not.

Nor are these largely families where the husband is unemployed. In 42% of families where both spouses were present, both were employed. Of women who work, the number of wives in the labor force with working husbands has been increasing at a faster rate than the number of working wives with husbands who are not employed. Thus, at present, the husband's unemployment is not a prime indicator of the wife's labor force status.

Neither the dramatic increase in women's labor market participation, nor statutory remedies against sex discrimination in employment, however, has halted discrimination against working women. The median annual income in 1970 for full-time work was $8,966 for men and $5,323 for women; i.e., women earned 59.4% of the male median income. This differential is in large part the product of multiple discrimination: in base pay; in fringe benefits; and in tracking women into lower paying and less responsible jobs and keeping them there. The most frequently offered justification for these practices is that women are merely secondary earners; as "pin money" workers, they want less responsibility and thus deserve lower pay even for the same job. But in fact, the financial contribution of the "assistant breadwinner" frequently means the difference between poverty and a decent standard of living for her family. In 23.4% (or 7.4 million) of families with both spouses working, the husbands earned less than $7,000 ($6,960 is estimated by the Bureau of Labor Statistics as sufficient to provide only a low standard of living for an urban family of four).

Sharron and Joseph Frontiero fall into this last mentioned income category. Both are financial contributors; Joseph Frontiero's G.I. bill stipend amounts to $205 per month. His income totals approximately $2,820 per year, hardly enough by any realistic standard to warrant the conclusion that he is financially independent of his wife. In this marriage, the wife is presently the primary wage earner; the husband, the "assistant breadwinner." The benefits appellants have been denied would significantly supplement a very moderate family income. These benefits are an integral part of the compensation men in Lt. Frontiero's situation receive automatically. Appellants Sharron and Joseph Frontiero do not receive them, because her labor, by congressional mandate, is worth less than the labor of a similarly situated man in terms of the benefits it brings to the family unit.

2. Enlightened courts have begun to strike down discriminatory sex-based classifications as inconsistent with the equal protection guarantees of the United States Constitution; but there is substantial confusion as to the standard of review appropriate to these challenges.

The significant changes that have occurred in society's attitudes toward equal opportunity for men and women should yield a deeper appreciation of the premise underlying the "suspect classification" doctrine: although the legislature may distinguish between individuals on the basis of their ability or need, it is presumptively impermissible to distinguish on the basis of congenital and unalterable traits of birth over which the individual has no control and for which he or she should not be penalized. Such conditions include not only race, lineage and alienage, criteria already declared "suspect" by this Court, but include as well the sex of the individual.

No longer shackled by decisions reflecting social and economic conditions of an earlier era,* enlightened judges in both federal and state courts are becoming increasingly skeptical of lines drawn or sanctioned by governmental authority on the basis of sex. A recent decision of the California Supreme Court, *Sail'er Inn v. Kirby*, exemplifies the new understanding and explicitly denominates sex a suspect classification [quoting *Sail'er Inn, Inc. v. Kirby*, 5 Cal. 3d 1 (1971)].

---

*See *Harper v. Virginia Bd. of Elections*, 383 U.S. 663, 669–70 (1966): "In determining what lines are unconstitutionally discriminatory, we have never been confined to historic notions of equality.... Notions of what constitutes equal treatment for purposes of the Equal Protection Clause *do* change."; *White v. Crook*, 251 F. Supp. 401, 408 (M.D. Ala. 1966) (three-judge court): "The Constitution of the United States must be read as embodying general principles meant to govern society and the institutions of government as they evolve through time. It is therefore this Court's function to apply the Constitution as a living document to the legal cases and controversies of contemporary society." *See also* L. Hand, *The Spirit of Liberty* 160 (Dillard ed. 1952).

In numerous other cases, sex lines unsupported by strong affirmative justification have failed to survive constitutional review. [*Here the brief cites two pages' worth of cases finding unequal treatment of women to violate equal protection and the Fourteenth Amendment.*]

This Court's decision in *Reed v. Reed* has heightened the debate concerning the degree of scrutiny appropriately accorded sex-based classifications. In *Reed*, the question of the stringency of review was left open because the Idaho statute there at issue "failed to satisfy even the more lenient equal protection standard." Significantly, the majority below overlooked the explanation in *Eisenstadt v. Baird* of the approach taken in *Reed*, and instead understood *Reed* as requiring application of a "lenient" review standard in sex discrimination cases.

Some courts regard *Reed* as a major precedent marking a new direction in judicial review of sex-based classifications [*citing numerous cases from 1972*].

On the other hand, "lenient" review of sex-based discrimination is evident in [*other cases from 1972 cited*]. Significantly, in the cases appraising *Reed* as a decision marking a new direction, the challenged classifications succumbed to judicial review; in those assigning minimal precedential value to *Reed*, including the case at bar, the classifications survived.

Some courts have even seen in *Reed* implicit rejection of a strict standard of review in cases challenging sex-based classifications.* *See*, e.g., *Buchas v. Illinois High School Ass'n*, 41 U.S.L.W. 2277 (N.D. Ill. Nov. 15, 1972) ("implicit in [the *Reed*] holding is the proposition that sex is not an inherently suspect classification"). And the majority below concluded, on the basis of *Reed*, "in this case we would be remiss in applying the compelling interest test." Then, in making the judgment "whether the classification established in the legislation is reasonable and not arbitrary and whether there is a rational connection between the classification and a legitimate governmental end," the court concluded that "the statute must be upheld if any state of facts rationally justifying it is demonstrated to or perceived by the courts."

---

* This interpretation of *Reed* is urged in a petition for certiorari now before the Court:
... The decision below is in conflict with the decision of this Court in
Reed v. Reed.... This Court [in *Reed*] did not adopt nor comment upon,
although urged to do so by 'Women's Liberation' groups, the standards by
which discriminations based on race are judged for Fourteenth Amendment
purposes, i.e., the 'strict scrutiny' test.

3. Precedent in need of revaluation: "benign" classifications that provide a "place" for woman in man's world.*

Decisions of this Court that span a century, none of them revaluated in *Reed*, have contributed to this anomaly: presumably well-meaning exaltation of woman's unique role as wife and mother has, in effect, denied women equal opportunity to develop their individual talents and capacities and has impelled them to accept a dependent, subordinate status in society.

This Court's assessment of women's claims to full participation in society outside the home began with *Bradwell v. Illinois*, 83 U.S. (16 Wall.) 130 (1873), in which the majority, in a brief, dispassionate opinion explained that neither the privileges and immunities clause of article IV, section 2 of the Constitution, nor the privileges and immunities clause of the fourteenth amendment, secured to Myra Bradwell the right to practice law.† In a concurring opinion Justice Bradley looked beyond the Constitution to "the law of the Creator":

> Man is, or should be, woman's protector and defender. The natural and proper timidity and delicacy which belongs to the female sex evidently unfits it for many of the occupations of civil life. The constitution of the family organization, which is founded in the divine ordinance, as well as in the nature of things, indicates the domestic sphere as that which properly belongs to the domain and function of womanhood....
>
> It is true that many women are unmarried and not affected by any of the duties, complications and incapacities arising out of the married state, but these are exceptions to the general rule. The paramount destiny and mission of woman are to fulfil the noble and benign offices of wife and mother. This is the law of the Creator.

---

* "For if women have only a place, clearly the rest of the world must belong to someone else and, therefore, in default of God, to men." E. Janeway, *Man's World, Woman's Place: A Study in Social Mythology* 7 (1971).

† *Bradwell* was followed in *In re Lockwood*, 154 U.S. 116 (1894). It is now established that arbitrary denial of admission to the bar of a state violates the due process and equal protection guarantees of the fourteenth amendment. The *Bradwell* and *Lockwood* decisions are legal deadwood and should be museum pieces. But a century after the *Bradwell* decision, equal opportunity for women in the legal profession remains unfinished business.

Although the method of communication between the Creator and the jurist is never disclosed, "divine ordinance" has been a dominant theme in decisions justifying laws establishing sex-based classifications. Well past the middle of the Twentieth Century, laws delineating "a sharp line between the sexes" were sanctioned on the basis of assumptions unnecessary to prove, and impossible to disprove, for their lofty inspiration was an article of faith.

In *Minor v. Happersett*, 88 U.S. (21 Wall.) 162 (1874), the Court ruled that the right to vote was not among the "privileges and immunities of United States citizenship," hence states were not inhibited by the Constitution from committing "that important trust to men alone." But the Court emphasized that, beyond doubt, women are "persons" and may be "citizens" within the meaning of the fourteenth amendment. The significance of this clear statement has been discounted by some commentators, perhaps because the Court also pointed out that children qualify under both headings.

A landmark decision of the Court, responding to turn of the century conditions when women labored long into the night in sweatshop operations, *Muller v. Oregon*, 208 U.S. 412 (1908), is described by some commentators today as a "roadblock to the full equality of women." The issue in *Muller* was the constitutionality of an Oregon statute prohibiting the employment of women "in any mechanical establishment, or factory, or laundry" for more than ten hours per day. Muller, a laundry owner, was convicted of a violation of this statute. Three years earlier, in *Lochner v. New York*, 198 U.S. 45 (1905), the Court had declared unconstitutional a New York statute setting maximum hours of work at ten per day and sixty per week for all bakery employees, men as well as women. Not yet prepared to overrule *Lochner*, the Court distinguished it in an opinion reflecting the differences in the station occupied by men and women in the society of that day.

Interwoven in the *Muller* opinion are two themes: (1) recognition of the intolerable exploitation of women workers; (2) concern for the health of the sex believed to be weaker in physical structure but assigned the role of bearing the future generation ("The physical well-being of woman becomes an object of public interest and care in order to preserve the strength and vigor of the race."). Accepting as historic fact man's domination of woman, the Court stressed that women must "rest upon and look to [man] for protection" and, somewhat inconsistently, that she requires the aid of the law "to protect her from the greed as well as the passion of man."

Uncritical reliance upon *Muller* for the broad proposition that sex is a valid basis for legislative classification has been persistent and still occurs, although the issue in *Muller*—whether half a loaf would be allowed to state legislatures after the full loaf was denied in *Lochner*—long ago lost all vitality. Moreover, indicative of the changes in economic and social life in the decades since *Muller*, women workers—principally blue collar workers—have successfully challenged under Title VII laws restricting the hours women may work. As the work day shortened from twelve hours to eight, and the work week from six days to five, women found that these laws, however "protective" in origin, were "protecting" them from better-paying jobs and opportunities for promotion.

While *Muller* reflects constitutional interpretation in midpassage from *Lochner* to *Darby*, *Goesaert v. Cleary*, 335 U.S. 464 (1948), hardly exemplifies a first step toward enlightened change. It was retrogressive in its day and is intolerable a generation later. Unlike the "benign" classification upheld by the Court in *Muller*, the Michigan statute challenged in *Goesaert* [which allowed women to serve as waitresses in taverns but barred them from the more lucrative employment of bartender], like the classification challenged here, was difficult to construe as a measure intended to assist women "in the struggle for subsistence" or to safeguard women's competitive position....

The majority opinion in *Goesaert* reflects an antiquarian male attitude toward women—man as provider, man as protector, man as guardian of female morality. While the attitude is antiquarian, it is still indulged by judges who would automatically reject attribution of inferiority to racial or religious groups.

Twelve years later, the Court appeared to step away from *Goesaert*. In *United States v. Dege*, 364 U.S. 51 (1960), it refused to rely on "ancient doctrine" concerning the status of women. The Court declared, "we...do not allow ourselves to be obfuscated by medieval views regarding the legal status of women," and rejected precedent from an earlier age expressing a view of womanhood "offensive to the ethos of our society."

Goesaert's sanction of "a sharp line between the sexes," however, has not been reassessed by this Court. On the contrary, the Court cited *Goesaert* with seeming approval as recently as 1970. But enlightened jurists in federal and state courts have found *Goesaert* a burden and an embarrassment. They politely discard it as precedent, refusing "to be obfuscated by medieval views regarding the status of women."

This survey of pre-*Reed* precedent not squarely addressed by the Court in its *Reed* opinion appropriately ends with *Hoyt v. Florida*, 368 U.S. 57 (1961), in which the court again perceived a sex-based classification as "benign." In *Hoyt*, the Court sustained a Florida statute limiting jury service by women to those who registered with the court their desire to be placed on the jury list. Observing that "woman is still the center of home and family life," the Court concluded that the Florida legislature had not transgressed constitutional limitations by according her advantaged treatment: she had the right, but not the obligation to serve.

Special treatment of women as jurors was no advantage to defendant Hoyt whose crime was committed after an altercation in which she claimed her husband had insulted and humiliated her to the breaking point.* Nor is the classification "benign" for women generally. For example, in a 1970 decision a New York trial court rejected the challenge of a female plaintiff to a jury system with automatic exemption for women. As a result of this exemption, women constituted less than twenty percent of the available pool. In his published opinion, the judge relied on *Hoyt* to explain to the complainant that she was "in the wrong forum." Less chivalrous than this Court, but more accurately reflecting the impact of the stereotype, the judge stated that plaintiff's "lament" should be addressed to her sisters who prefer "cleaning and cooking, bridge and canasta, the beauty parlor and shopping, to becoming embroiled in plaintiff's problems...." *De Kosenko v. Brandt*, 313 N.Y.S.2d 827, 830 (Sup. Ct. 1970).

In 1972, this Court declined an invitation to review the constitutionality of a Louisiana statute limiting jury service by women to volunteers. The Court observed that "nothing in past adjudications [suggests] that [the male] petitioner has been denied equal protection by the alleged exclusion of women from grand jury service." *Alexander v. Louisiana*, 405 U.S. 625, 633. A short time later, the Court ruled that proof that blacks had been systematically excluded from state grand and petit juries that indicted and convicted a white defendant would entitle the white defendant to federal habeas corpus relief, even if he could not show he was harmed by the exclusion. *Peters v. Kiff*, 407 U.S. 493 (1972). The inference might well be drawn that full participation by women in community affairs is

---

* Empirical studies support the hypothesis that men jurors tend to favor men, while women jurors tend to favor women.

not yet recognized as a value worthy of "protection" in the interest of society.*

In 1971, two legal scholars—both of them male—examined the record of the judiciary in sex discrimination cases. They concluded that the performance of American judges in this area "can be succinctly described as ranging from poor to abominable. With some notable exceptions... [judges] have failed to bring to sex discrimination cases those virtues of detachment, reflection and critical analysis which have served them so well with respect to other sensitive social issues.... Judges have largely freed themselves from patterns of thought that can be stigmatized as 'racist.'... [But] 'sexism'—the making of unjustified (or at least unsupported) assumptions about individual capabilities, interests, goals and social roles solely on the basis of sex differences—is as easily discernible in contemporary judicial opinions as racism ever was." Johnston & Knapp, 46 N.Y.U.L. Rev. at 676 (1971).

While a new direction has been signalled in some of the state and lower federal courts, and in this Court's opinions in *Reed* and *Stanley v. Illinois*, 405 U.S. 645 (1972), the need for clear statement of the appropriate review standard is evident. Amicus urges that designation of sex as a suspect classification is overdue, provides the only wholly satisfactory standard for dealing with the claim in this case, and should be the starting point for assessing that claim.

III. The challenged classification is not justified by administrative convenience, the primary rationale relied on by the majority below.

A. The challenged classification does not result in substantial economies.
The majority below considered it

clear that the reason Congress established a conclusive presumption in favor of married servicemen was to avoid imposing on

---

* Compare *State v. Hall*, 187 So. 2d 861, 863 (Miss.), appeal dismissed, 385 U.S. 98 (1966) ("The legislature has the right to exclude women so they may continue their service as mothers, wives and homemakers and also to protect them...from the filth, obscenity and noxious atmosphere that so often pervades a courtroom during a jury trial."), with *Abbott v. Mines*, 411 F.2d 353, 355 (6th Cir. 1969) ("It is common knowledge that society no longer coddles women from the very real and sometimes brutal facts of life. Women, moreover, do not seek such oblivion.").

Despite *Hoyt*, state legislation concerning jury duty has progressed toward recognition that service is a responsibility shared equally by all citizens, male and female the uniformed services a substantial administrative burden of requiring actual proof from some 200,000 male officers and over 1,000,000 enlisted men that their wives were actually dependent upon them.

The majority further stated:

Congress apparently reached the conclusion that it would be more economical to require married female members claiming husbands to prove actual dependency than to extend the presumption of dependency to such members.

The assumption underlying the classification, and the defense of it offered below, is evident: nearly all women married to men in the military are financially dependent upon their husbands. Significantly, the statutes at issue define "dependent" as a person whose own income does not cover half of that person's expenses. It is not at all clear that nearly all women married to servicemen fall in this category.

In 1971, 43% of all women over the age of 16 were in the labor force, 18% of all women worked full-time the year round, and almost 60% of all married women living with their husbands were gainfully employed. The historical trend has been dramatically upward and further increases in labor force participation by women are expected. It is likely, then, that many married women earn enough to cover more than half of their own living expenses.* Such women would not qualify as "dependents" under the above criterion. Thus, it may well be that if servicemen were asked to prove the dependency of their wives, the resultant savings in benefits paid would be far greater than the cost of processing applications for benefits. Assuming vigorous enforcement, as is now the case with respect to servicewomen's applications, a high percentage of non-eligible servicemen would not bother to

alike. By 1970, the majority of states (including Florida) either treated women and men on the same basis, or relieved women only when family duties in the particular case warranted exemption.

* Note that under the statutory definition this need not mean that the wife earns more or as much as the husband. In the case at bar, for example, an income of only $2820 a year (Joseph Frontiero's) is enough to disqualify a spouse as a dependent. Many working women have substantially larger incomes. In 1970, for example, the median income for full-time women workers was $5,323.

apply, thereby reducing the application processing burden that so impressed the majority below.

But neither the armed forces nor the congressional committees involved ever have investigated whether the current arrangement does in fact effect any saving. Moreover, it is unlikely that Congress would require servicemen to prove dependency of their wives even if such a requirement would result in substantial economies. As the legislative history of these statutes reveals, the dominant purpose of Congress was to provide an incentive for married persons to choose a military career by offering benefits comparable to those available in civilian employment. The absence of any effort to determine whether the supposed economy of the present arrangement is real suggests that the principal reason for the distinction is not administrative convenience but the stereotypical notion that the husband, whatever his actual income, ought to be treated as principal family breadwinner.

While there is no evidence whatever supporting the economic prop for the challenged classification—that it costs less to grant benefits for wives than to require proof of dependency—it is undisputed that the relief sought by appellants, equalization of fringe benefits for married military personnel regardless of sex, would result in no increase in budget requirements of the Department of Defense.

B. Dissimilar treatment for men and women who are similarly situated cannot be justified by characterizing the benefits here at issue as a "privilege" or a "windfall." . . .

C. This Court and lower federal courts have rejected administrative convenience as a justification for discriminatory sex-based classifications.

In *Reed v. Reed*, the Court held unconstitutional a state statute providing that, as between persons equally entitled to administer an estate, "males must be preferred to females." The principal justification for the challenged provision was administrative convenience—the avoidance of a class of contests and, thereby, reduction of the probate court's workload. In rejecting this justification, Mr. Chief Justice Burger, writing for a unanimous Court, stated:

> Clearly the objective of reducing the workload on probate courts by eliminating one class of contests is not without some

legitimacy.... [But] to give a mandatory preference to members of either sex over members of the other, merely to accomplish the elimination of hearings on the merits, is to make the very kind of arbitrary legislative choice forbidden by the Equal Protection Clause of the Fourteenth Amendment.

As Judge Johnson stated in his dissent in the case at bar: "The basic message which comes from [the *Reed* case] is that administrative convenience is not a shibboleth, the mere recitation of which dictates constitutionality." In the case at bar, as in *Reed*, acceptance of the administrative convenience rationale would require approval of sex-role stereotyping as a legitimate basis for legislative distinction. As this Court has recognized, resort to group stereotype as a basis for legislative line-drawing is wholly at odds with the principle of equality of individuals before the law. In *Stanley v. Illinois*, decided two days before the decision by the court below but apparently not considered by that court, this Court declared unconstitutional legislation based on the administratively convenient assumption that unwed fathers are unsuitable and neglectful parents. In *Stanley*, as in the instant case, the barrier was not "insurmountable," for under the legislation at issue there an unwed father could affirmatively prove his qualification in an adoption or guardianship proceeding. But the Court held that he should not be subjected to a standard of proof more onerous than that applicable to other parents.

Most recently, the Court of Appeals for the District of Columbia rejected the argument that avoidance of administrative difficulties justified denial of medical benefits to children born to unmarried members of the armed forces. In striking down this classification (included in 10 U.S.C. Section 1072, one of the sections challenged in the case at bar),* the court stated:

While the Government may legitimately attempt to conserve its fisc, it may not accomplish that goal by drawing invidious classifications.

D. Congressional equalization of benefits paid to or for the "dependents" of male and female employees of the federal government demonstrates the

* The same distinction between children born to married parents and children born out of wedlock appears in 37 U.S.C. Section 401, the housing allowance provision challenged in the instant case.

administrative feasibility of equal treatment and congressional concern that sex-based discrimination be ended....

E. Federal prohibitions of discrimination on the basis of sex by private and state employers forbid practices of the kind authorized by the statutes at issue in the case at bar....

F. Summary and conclusion: The discrimination against women mandated by the challenged classification is neither (a) supported by a compelling state interest; (b) necessary to the accomplishment of legitimate legislative objectives; nor (c) reasonably related to a permissible legislative objective.

If, as amicus urges, the challenged sex-based classification is declared "suspect", this Court must consider whether a compelling state interest justifies the discriminatory practices embodied in the challenged provisions. The basic objective of the system of dependents' benefits is to attract and retain qualified personnel in the armed forces. There is no evidence that Congress believed that it was serving "a compelling state interest" by treating women differently from men and, as demonstrated in the discussion above, none is so served.

Convenience and simplicity, while grand virtues in the administration of public affairs, do not supersede the fundamental right of individuals to the equal protection of the law. Thus, such obviously convenient measures as restricting the ballot to "two old, established parties" (*Williams v. Rhodes*, 393 U.S. 23 (1968)), denying welfare payments to persons with less than a year's residency in the state (*Shapiro v. Thompson*, 394 U.S. 618 (1969)), and denying the right to vote in state elections to persons with less than a year's residency in the state (*Dunn v. Blumstein*, 405 U.S. 330 (1972)), did not survive measurement against the constitutional equal protection principle.

Dunn v. Blumstein involved governmental interests more substantial than administrative convenience. Yet the various reasons offered by the state in that case, even in combination, were found insufficient to overcome the heavy burden required by this Court.

In that case the state of Tennessee sought to justify its one-year residency requirement on two grounds: (1) to "insure purity of ballot box—protection against fraud through colonization and inability to identify persons offered to vote, and (2) [to] afford some surety that the voter has, in fact, become a member of the community and that as such, he [or she] has a common interest in all matters pertaining to its government and is, therefore, more likely to exercise his [or her] right more intelligently."

The Court implied that either or both of these reasons might constitute a legitimate government objective. And Mr. Chief Justice Burger in his dissent stated explicitly that the one year residency requirement was "reasonable." He objected to the application by the majority of the "compelling state interest" standard.

Thus while the reasons advanced by the state in *Dunn v. Blumstein* might be considered "rational," this Court concluded that, even in combination, they were not "compelling." In contrast to the relatively serious reasons asserted to save the Tennessee statute in *Dunn v. Blumstein*, the justification advanced here—administrative convenience—falls far short of a "compelling" interest when appraised in light of the interest of the class against which the statutes discriminate—an interest in treatment as full human personalities. As this Court said in *Williams v. Illinois*, 399 U.S. 235, 245 (1970), "the constitutional imperatives of the Equal Protection Clause must have priority over the comfortable convenience of the status quo."

Thus, if sex is a "suspect classification," the federal interest in limiting application processing or, alternatively, saving benefits that would be due to women if they were accorded the same fringe benefits as men, cannot justify rank discrimination against a person, solely because she is female.

If the Court concludes that sex is not a suspect classification, or determines not to reach that question, *amicus* urges application of an intermediate test. In part because of decisions of this Court, women continue to receive disadvantaged treatment by the law. In answer to the compelling claim of women for recognition by the law as full human personalities, this Court, at the very least, should apply a test similar to the one delineated by Chief Justice Burger in *Bullock v. Carter*, 405 U.S. 134 (1972). Regulations that disadvantaged women should be "closely scrutinized" with the burden on the proponent of the discriminatory action to establish that the sex-based classification is "necessary to accomplishment of legitimate [legislative] objectives."

Yet the discrimination embodied in 10 U.S.C. Sections 1072 and 1076 and 37 U.S.C. Sections 401 and 403 is so patently visible that the statute is readily assailable under the less stringent reasonable-relationship test. The exclusion of women from benefits to which similarly situated men are automatically entitled lacks the constitutionally required fair and substantial relation to a permissible legislative purpose and therefore must be held to violate the equal protection clause.

First, as shown above, it is not at all clear to what extent, if any, the challenged classification in the case at bar in fact conserves the federal fisc. Second, administrative convenience has been rejected by this Court as a justification for sex-based classifications even under the rational relationship test. Third, Congress and the Executive, in light of society's increasing awareness of the unfairness and waste of human resources engendered by sex-based discrimination, have prohibited state and municipal governments, nearly all private employers, and federal agencies other than the uniformed services from engaging in the discriminatory employment practice challenged in the case at bar. These comprehensive prohibitions clearly indicate that, in the view of Congress and the Executive, equal treatment of male and female employees for fringe benefit purposes is administratively feasible and, at this stage in our nation's history, a key element of equal employment opportunity policy.

The structure and mission of the armed forces are admittedly unique. But no suggestion has been made, nor does it appear, that, with regard to the benefits at issue here, equal treatment of men and women is more difficult to achieve in the armed forces than in private and other public employment. Rather, the discrimination embodied in 10 U.S.C. Sections 1072 and 1076 and 37 U.S.C. Sections 401 and 403 reflects the very different legislative and judicial perspective current in 1949 and 1956 when these provisions were enacted. At that time, equal employment opportunity for women was not a matter of legislative concern, and an unbroken line of precedent from this Court indicated that legislative lines drawn on the basis of sex, however "sharp," would be tolerated by the judiciary.

In view of the significant changes in the social and legal climate that have occurred since enactment of these provisions, it should be plain that the discriminatory practice countenanced by the challenged laws is no longer constitutionally tolerable. Equal pay must be an obligation in the military as it now is in all other areas of employment. Surely, there is no rational basis for exempting the military from the requirement that similarly situated male and female employees receive the same compensation. As Judge Johnson observed in his dissent below, it is "incongruous to say that the justification for denying the benefits [to women] is that it is cheaper not to give them.... If all that is required to uphold a congressional enactment is the conclusion that it is more economical to deny benefits than to extend them, then any statutory scheme can be established and no disqualified group can complain."

IV.

Upon determining that 10 U.S.C. Sections 1072 and 1076 and 37 U.S.C. Sections 401 and 403 as now limited violate the fifth amendment, the Court should, consistent with the dominant statutory purpose, remedy the defect by extending to female members of the armed forces the same benefits now available to similarly situated male members.

★ ★ ★

CONCLUSION

For the reasons stated above, the decision of the district court should be reversed, the provisions of 10 U.S.C. Sections 1072 and 1076 and 37 U.S.C. Sections 401 and 403 which deny female members of the armed forces benefits and allowances available to similarly situated male members should be declared unconstitutional and the benefits and allowances available to male members of the armed forces under these sections should be made available on the same terms to similarly situated female members.

CASPAR W. WEINBERGER, SECRETARY OF HEALTH, EDUCATION AND WELFARE, APPELLANT, V. STEPHEN CHARLES WIESENFELD, INDIVIDUALLY AND ON BEHALF OF ALL OTHER PERSONS SIMILARLY SITUATED, APPELLEE

APPEAL FROM THE UNITED STATES DISTRICT COURT FOR
THE MIDDLE DISTRICT OF ALABAMA
411 U.S. 677 (May 14, 1973)

Oral Argument

January 20, 1975

Warren E. Burger: Mrs. Ginsburg.
Ruth Bader Ginsburg: Mr. Chief Justice and may it please the Court.

Stephen Wiesenfeld's case concerns the entitlement of a female wage earner, a female wage earner's family to Social Insurance of the same quality as that accorded to the family of a male wage earner.

Four prime facts of the Wiesenfeld family's life situation bear special emphasis.

Paula Wiesenfeld, the deceased insured worker, was gainfully employed at all times during the seven years immediately preceding her death.

Throughout this period, maximum contributions were deducted from her salary and paid to Social Security.

During Paula's marriage to Stephen Wiesenfeld, both were employed.

Neither was attending school, and Paula was the family's principal income earner.

In 1972, Paula died giving birth to her son, Jason Paul, leaving the child's father, Stephen Wiesenfeld, with the sole responsibility for the care of Jason Paul.

For the eight months immediately following his wife's death and for all but a seven-month period thereafter, Stephen Wiesenfeld did not engage in substantial gainful employment.

Instead, he devoted himself to the care of the infant Jason Paul.

At issue is the constitutionality of the gender line drawn by 42 U.S.C. 402(g), the child in care provision of the Social Security Act.

Congress established this child in care insurance in 1939, as part of that year's conversion of Social Security from a system that insured only the worker to a system that provided a family basis of coverage.

The specific purpose of 402(g) was to protect families of deceased insured workers, by supplementing the child's benefit provided in 42 U.S.C. 402(d). Where the deceased insured worker is male, the family is afforded the full measure of protection, a child's benefit under 402(d), and a child in care benefit under 402(g).

Where the deceased worker is female, family protection is subject to a 50% discount.

A child in care benefit for survivors of a female insured worker is absolutely excluded even though, as here, the deceased mother was the family's principal breadwinner.

This absolutely exclusion, based on gender per se, operates to the disadvantage of female workers, their surviving spouses, and their children.

It denies the female worker social insurance family coverage of the same quality as the coverage available under the account of a male worker.

It denies the surviving spouse of the female worker the opportunity to care personally for his child, an opportunity afforded the surviving spouse of a male worker, and it denies the motherless child an opportunity for parental care afforded the fatherless child.

It is appellee's position that this three-fold discrimination violates the constitutional rights of Paula, Stephen, and Jason Paul Wiesenfeld to the equal protection of the laws, guaranteed to them with respect to federal legislation by the Fifth Amendment.

The care with which the judiciary should assess gender lines drawn by legislation is currently a matter of widespread uncertainty.

The District of Columbia Court of Appeals recently observed in *Waldie v. Schlesinger,* decided November 20, 1974, precedent is still evolving and existing decisions of this Court are variously interpreted by the lower courts.

Appellant had urged, in his brief, that it would be sufficient if any rationality can be conceived for the overt sex discrimination operating against the Wiesenfeld family.

But this Court acknowledged in *Reed v. Reed,* 404 U.S., that the legislative objective there in question, reducing probate court workloads, did not lack legitimacy.

Yet, in light of the differential based on gender per se, the Court required a more substantial relationship between legislative ends and means so that men and women similarly circumstanced would be treated alike.

Again, in the Court's eight-to-one judgment in *Frontiero v. Richardson*, 411 U.S., requiring the same fringe benefits for married men and women in the military, the Court evidenced a concern to analyze gender classifications with a view to the modern world and to be wary of gross, archaic, overbroad generalizations.

As in the case at bar, as in *Frontiero*, the underlying assumption was wives are typically dependent, husbands are not.

Hence, the statutory scheme in this case, as the scheme in *Frontiero*, favors one type of family unit over another, and in both cases, the basis for the distinction is that in the favored unit the husband's employment attracts the benefit in question.

Where the breadwinner is male, the family gets more, and where the breadwinner is female, the family gets less.

Kahn v. Shevin, 416 U.S., and *Schlesinger v. Ballard*, this Court's most recent expression, are viewed by some as reestablishing a slack or a cursory review standard, at least when the defender of the discrimination packages his argument with a protective or remedial label.

Kahn approved Florida's $15.00 real property tax saving for widows.

The decision reflects this Court's consistent deference to State policy in areas of local concern such as State tax systems, domestic relations, zoning, disposition of property within the state's borders.

By contrast, national workers insurance, and no issue of local concern, is in question here.

The differential in *Schlesinger v. Ballard*, this Court pointed out, did not reflect archaic, overbroad generalizations of the kind involved in *Frontiero* or in the instant case.

Indeed, there might have been a certain irony to a ruling in Lt. Ballard's favor.

To this day, women seeking careers in the uniform services are barred by federal statute and regulations from enlistment, training, and promotion opportunities open to men.

The Court's majority thought it a mismatch for federal law to mandate unequal treatment of women officers, denial to them of training and promotion opportunities open to men, a denial not challenged by Lt. Ballard, but to ignore that anterior discrimination for promotion and tenure purposes.

Perhaps most significantly, *Kahn* and *Ballard* are among the very few situations where a discriminatory advantage accorded some women is not readily perceived as a double-edged sword, a weapon that strikes directly against women who choose to be wives and mothers and at the same time to participate as full and equal individuals in a work-centered world.

But there could not be a clearer case than this one of the double-edged sword in operation—of differential treatment accorded similarly situated persons based grossly and solely on gender.

Paula Wiesenfeld, in fact the principal wage earner, is treated as though her use of work were of only secondary value to her family.

Stephen Wiesenfeld, in fact the nurturing parent, is treated as though he did not perform that function, and Jason Paul, a motherless infant with a father able and willing to provide care for him personally, is treated as an infant not entitled to the personal care of his sole surviving parent.

The line drawn is absolute, not merely a more onerous test for one sex than the other as in *Frontiero* and in *Stanley v. Illinois*, 405 U.S.

And the shutout is more extreme then it was in *Reed*, where a woman could qualify as administrator, if the man who opposed her were less closely related to the decedent.

This case, more than any other yet heard by this Court, illustrates the critical importance of careful judicial assessment of law-reinforced sex-role pigeonholing defended as a remedy.

For on any degree of scrutiny that is more than cursory, 402(g)'s conclusive presumption automatically and irrebuttably ranking husband principal breadwinner displays the pattern Justice Brennan identified in *Frontiero*: In practical effect, laws of this quality help to keep women, not on a pedestal, but in a cage.

They reinforce, not remedy, women's inferior position in the labor force.

Appellant has pointed out that women do not earn as much as men and urges that 402(g) responds to this condition by rectifying past and present economic discrimination against women.

This attempt to wrap a remedial rationale around a 1939 statute, originating in and reinforcing traditional sex-based assumptions, should attract strong suspicion.

In fact, Congress had in view male breadwinners, male heads of household, and the women and children dependent upon them.

Its attention to the families of insured male workers, their wives, and children is expressed in the scheme that heaps further disadvantage on the woman worker.

Far from rectifying economic discrimination against women, the scheme conspicuously discriminates against women workers by discounting the value to their family of their gainful employment, and it intrudes on private decision making in an area in which the law should maintain strict neutrality.

For when federal law provides a family benefit based on a husband's gainful employment, but absolutely bars that benefit based on a wife's gainful employment, the impact is to encourage the traditional division of labor between man and woman, to underscore twin assumptions: first, that labor for pay including attendant benefits is the prerogative of men; and second, that women, but not men, appropriately reduce their contributions in the working life to care for children.

On another day, the pernicious impact of gender lines like the one drawn by 402(g), was precisely and accurately discerned by appellant, in common with every government agency genuinely determined to break down artificial barriers and hindrances to women's economic advancement.

Appellant has instructed that employer's fringe benefit and pension schemes must not presume, as 402(g) does, that husband is head of household or principal wage earner.

It is surely irrational to condemn this sex line as discriminating against women when it appears in an employer's pension scheme, while asserting that it rectifies such discrimination when it appears in workers' social insurance.

[*Exchange with Justice Potter Stewart is omitted.*]

In sum, the prime generator of discrimination encountered by women in the economic sector is the pervasive attitude, now lacking functional justification, that pairs women with children, men with work.

This attitude is shored up and reinforced by laws of the 402(g) variety, laws that tell a woman her employment is less valuable to and supportive of the family than the employment of a male worker.

Surely, Paula Wiesenfeld would find unfathomable, this attempt to cast the compensatory cloak over the denial to her family of benefits available to the family of a male insured.

Nor does appellant's rationalization for discrimination even attempt to explain why Jason Paul, child of a fully insured deceased worker, can have the personal care of his sole surviving parent only if the deceased wage-earning parent was male.

Appellant has asserted that providing child and care benefits under a female worker's account would involve fiscal considerations.

The amount involved is considerably less than was indicated some moments ago.

He estimates the cost for this particular benefit to be 0.01% of taxable payroll in the appendix at 16, and other differentials are not now before this Court.

[*Exchanges with Justices Potter Stewart and Warren Burger about the cost for the benefit and the age of children being cared for are omitted.*]

…Comparing the cost analysis here with the *New Jersey Welfare Rights Organization* case, that case involved a wholly state-funded program for aid to families of the working poor.

This Court declared unconstitutional limitation of benefits under that program to families with wed parents.

Unlike *New Jersey Welfare Rights Organization*, the case at bar presents no issue of federal deference arguably due to state family law policy or any other local concern.

And surely, leeway for cost saving is no broader in federal workers' insurance than it is in a wholly state-financed and operated welfare program, a program funded by general state revenues rather than by contributions of insured workers and their employers.

Budgetary policy, like administrative convenience, simply cannot provide a fair and substantial basis for a scheme that establishes two classes of insured workers, both subject to the same contribution work rate: male workers, whose families receive full protection, and female workers, whose families receive diminished protection.

Finally, the appropriate remedy is correctly specified in the judgment below.

That judgment declares the gender line at issue unconstitutional because it discriminates in violation of the Fifth Amendment against gainfully employed women such as Paula Wiesenfeld as well as against men and children who have lost their wives and mothers.

The judgment enjoins enforcement of the statute insofar as it discriminates on the basis of sex.

Extension of child in care benefits under Paula Wiesenfeld's account is unquestionably the cause consistent with the dominant Congressional purpose to insure the family of deceased workers and the express Congressional concern to ameliorate the plight of the deceased worker's child by facilitating a close relationship with the sole surviving parent.

Unequal treatment of male and female workers surely is not a vital part of the Congressional plan.

Withdrawal of benefits from female parents who now receive them would conflict with the primary statutory objectives, to compensate the family unit for the loss of the insured individual and to facilitate parental care of the child.

Under the circumstances, extension of benefits to the surviving spouse of female insured workers—to the father who devotes himself to child rearing—is the only suitable remedy.

It accords with the express remedial preference of Congress in all recent measures eliminating gender-based differentials: for example, 5 U.S.C. 7152 cited at pages 39 to 40 of our brief, and with this Court's precedent in such cases as *U.S. Department of Agriculture v. Moreno*, 413 U.S., *New Jersey Welfare Rights Organization against Cahill*, 411 U.S., and *Frontiero v. Richardson*, 411 U.S.

I did want to comment very briefly on the point made with respect to women receiving Social Security benefits that exceed the amount of their contribution.

The reason for this, the prime reason of course, is that women live longer than men.

Most benefits are paid to retirement-age beneficiaries and women happen to be 58% of the population of persons over 65. That increases in time: they're about 54.5% of the 65-year olds, 58.5% of the 75-year olds, and about 64.5% of the 85-year olds.

But the critical point here is that payments to the elderly are based on the individual's life span not on his or her sex.

So, that if a man should live to a 100, he will continue to receive benefits and he won't be told, "Oh! Too bad, you should have died earlier, only women receive payments for that length of time."

In sum, appellee respectfully requests that the judgment below be affirmed, thereby establishing that under this nation's fundamental law, the woman worker's national social insurance is no less valuable to her family than is the social insurance of the working man.

Warren E. Burger: Thank you, Mrs. Ginsburg.

BRIEF FOR APPELLEE

Filed December 20, 1974

Excerpts from the brief follow, with most citations and footnotes omitted, as well as some punctuation (including brackets and internal quotation marks).

SUMMARY OF ARGUMENT

I.

The 42 U.S.C. §402(g) "child in care" Social Security benefit, furnished to the surviving spouse of a male insured individual, but not to the surviving spouse of a female insured individual, reflects the familiar stereotype that, throughout this Nation's history, has operated to devalue women's efforts in the economic sector. The female insured individual, who is treated equally for Social Security contribution purposes, is ranked as a secondary breadwinner for purposes of determining family benefits due under her account. Just as the female insured individual's status as a breadwinner is denigrated, so the parental status of her surviving spouse is discounted. For the sole reason that appellee is a father, not a mother, he is denied benefits that would permit him to attend personally to the care of his infant son, a child who has no other parent to provide that care.

The child, who supplies the *raison d'être* for the benefit in question, is the person ultimately disadvantaged by the 42 U.S.C. §402(g) gender line. A social insurance benefit, which is designed to facilitate close parent–child association, is not constitutionally allocated when it includes children with dead fathers, but excludes children with dead mothers.

II.

Exclusion of a deceased female worker's spouse from "child in care" benefits is not fairly and substantially related to the legislative purpose to provide for the families of deceased workers. Facilitating parental care for growing children, unquestionably an appropriate legislative purpose, may be advanced by a benefit tied to family need and the preference of the parent. However, gross gender classification may not be used as proxy for a need or parental preference criterion. Legislative provision for a "mother's benefit," but no father's benefit, cannot do service for functional classification when the effect is invidious discrimination against the families of working women.

III.

In enacting a "child in care" benefit, Congress used as its model and, for convenience, treated as universal, the one-earner family composed of breadwinning husband and child tending wife. Increasing female participation in the paid labor force has made it apparent that this rigidly stereotyped vision of man's work and woman's place lacks correspondence with reality for millions of American families.

IV.

Exclusion of the spouse of a working woman from social insurance benefits accorded the spouse of a working man does not operate to remedy the effects of past economic discrimination against women. On the contrary, the exclusion disadvantages working women, for their Social Security payments do not provide the same level of benefits for their families as do the payments of similarly positioned men. This tangible economic harm to working women and their families cannot be rationalized as part of a "benign" or "remedial" plan. Rather, the scheme "heaps on" an additional disadvantage, exacerbating, not alleviating, past discrimination encountered by women in the labor market....

ARGUMENT

"...To survive constitutional review, gender-based classifications, at a minimum, must be "reasonable, not arbitrary, and must rest upon some ground of difference having a fair and substantial relation to the object of the legislation, so that all persons similarly circumstanced shall be treated alike." *Reed v. Reed*, 404 U.S. 71, 76 (1971), quoting from *F. S. Royster Guano Co. v. Virginia*, 253 U.S. 412, 415 (1920). It is appellee's position that 42 U.S.C. §402(g) plainly fails to meet this standard. *A fortiori*, 42 U.S.C. §402(g) could not meet a heightened review standard, responding more precisely to the root cause of law-sanctioned gender lines that impact adversely upon women who seek to pursue economic or political activity on the same basis as men.

A. No legitimate governmental interest is fostered by denying to families of deceased female workers insured under Social Security benefits equal to those accorded families of deceased male workers.

...In short, the sharp line between the sexes drawn by 42 U.S.C. §402(g) plainly does not represent a fair, rational and functional approach to the allocation of family benefits. As in *Reed v. Reed* and *Frontiero v. Richardson*, the legislation here at issue impermissibly distinguishes between men and women without regard to individual or family need, ability, preference or life situation. The gender label employed, however convenient, cannot do service for functional classification when the effect is invidious discrimination against the families of women workers.

B. The gender line drawn by Congress rests on a gross, stereotypic view of the economic and parental roles of men and women.

In the case at bar, as in *Reed v. Reed* and *Frontiero v. Richardson*, upholding the gender-based criterion would require approval of gross sex-role stereotyping as a permissible basis for legislative distinction. In providing a "mother's benefit," but no father's benefit, Congress assumed a division of parental responsibility along gender lines: breadwinner was synonymous with father, child tenderer with mother. Increasing female participation in the paid labor force has placed in clear focus the invidious quality of this rigid sex-role delineation....

In contrast to the pattern assumed by Congress in 1939 [when this benefit was originally enacted], and not reconsidered by the national legislature in the context of Social Security since that time, women's dramatically increasing participation in the paid labor force is a prime fact of contemporary life. In 1940, women comprised less than 30% of gainfully-employed persons. By the start of the 1970's, they comprised nearly 43%. By 1974, close to 35 million women, including over 52% of all women between the ages of 18-64, were in the labor force. Close to 60% of gainfully-employed women were married and living with their husbands. Over 42% of women workers worked full-time the year round. Moreover, despite the discrimination against women workers still characteristic of the labor market, many married women earn more than their husbands....

Candid recognition that the rigid sex-role allocation reflected in 42 U.S.C. §402(g) does not correspond with reality for millions of families in the United States appears in a recent Social Security Administration Research Report:

> The concept that a man is responsible for the support of his wife and children led to the creation of a broad structure of social security family protection. At the same time, the steady growth of labor-force participation by women, particularly married women, has been reflected in a phenomenal growth in the number of women entitled to benefits on the basis of their own earnings records. Complaints that the...system discriminates against women have proliferated as a result of this growth.

...In sum, 42 U.S.C. §402(g)'s exclusion of coverage for a father who has in his care a child of the deceased insured female worker [rests] on the "arrogant assumption that merely because [the male breadwinner/female child tenderer] stereotypes are accurate for some individuals the [government] has a right to apply them to all individuals—and, indeed, to shape its official policy toward the end that [the stereotypes] shall continue to be accurate." Johnston & Knapp, Sex Discrimination by Law: A Study in Judicial Perspective, 46 N.Y.U.L. Rev. 675, 725-26 (1971)....

C. Exclusion of the spouse of a working woman from social insurance benefits accorded the spouse of a working man does not operate to remedy the effects of past economic discrimination against women.

In *Kahn v. Shevin*, 416 U.S. 351 (1974), this Court upheld a gender line regarded as operating solely to remedy past economic discrimination encountered by women. Rectifying the effects of past discrimination against women (or historically disadvantaged minorities) is a laudable legislative objective. In assessing a gender classification for consistency with equal protection, however, a court must assure itself that the classification in fact works to alleviate past discrimination, and does not perpetuate practices responsible for that discrimination. The case at bar presents a classic example of the double-edged discrimination characteristic of laws that chivalrous gentlemen, sitting in all-male chambers, misconceive as a favor to the ladies.

Significantly, when Congress genuinely determined to remedy overt discrimination against women in the economic sphere by focusing on "firmly entrenched practices" inhospitable to their claims to equal opportunity and equal remuneration in the job market, it rejected the gender stereotype that underlies 42 U.S.C. §402(g)....

Surely Paula Wiesenfeld would have found unfathomable the attempt to cast a compensatory cloak over the denial to her family of benefits available to the family of a male insured. Nor does appellant's rationale for discrimination begin to explain why the infant Jason Paul Wiesenfeld can have the personal care of a sole surviving parent only if that parent is female....

III. A.

...In *Frontiero v. Richardson*, this Court held that gender-based discrimination in the allocation of fringe benefits to members of the uniformed services violated the Constitution's guarantee of equal protection. A more extreme form of the same discriminatory pattern appears in the case at bar....

Frontiero concerned, as this case does, woman's status and associated benefits when she participates in economic activity outside the home. As a worker, she has been assigned an inferior place, often with the aid of laws purportedly intended for her protection. As Justice Brennan commented in *Frontiero*:

> There can be no doubt that our Nation has had a long and unfortunate history of sex discrimination. Traditionally, such discrimination was rationalized by an attitude of "romantic paternalism" which, in practical effect, put women not on a pedestal, but in a cage.

Spurred by a burgeoning feminist movement that has directed principal attention to employment-related inequities, legislatures and courts are responding with increased sensitivity to generators of a separate and unequal place for women in the labor force. As a perceptive male jurist observed:

One realizes with a shock what so many women now proclaim: Old accepted rules and customs often discriminate against women in ways that have long been taken for granted or have gone unnoticed. *Green v. Waterford Board of Education*, 473 F.2d 629, 634 (2d Cir. 1973)....

CONCLUSION

For the reasons stated above, the decision of the district court declaring unconstitutional and enjoining the enforcement of 42 U.S.C. §402(g) insofar as it discriminates on the basis of gender should be affirmed.

CURTIS CRAIG AND CAROLYN WHITENER, D/B/A "THE HONK AND HOLLER," APPELLANTS, V. HON. DAVID BOREN, GOVERNOR, STATE OF OKLAHOMA, ET AL., APPELLEES

429 U.S. 190 (December 20, 1976)

BRIEF *AMICUS CURIAE* FOR AMERICAN CIVIL LIBERTIES UNION

Filed February 26, 1976

Excerpts from the brief follow, with most citations and footnotes omitted, as well as some punctuation (including brackets and internal quotation marks).

SUMMARY OF ARGUMENT

I

37 Okla. Stat. §§241, 243 and 245, establishing a sex/age line to determine qualification for association with 3.2 beer, discriminates impermissibly on the basis of gender in violation of the fourteenth amendment's equal protection clause. This legislation places all 18–20 year old males in one pigeonhole, all 18–20 year old females in another, in conformity with familiar notions about "the way women (or men) are." Upholding the legislation, the court below relied upon overbroad generalizations concerning the drinking behavior, proclivities and preferences of the two sexes. Such overbroad generalization as a rationalization for line-drawing by gender cannot be tolerated under the Constitution.

The Oklahoma legislation in question is a curiosity, apparently the only law of its kind left in the nation. Similarly, the ruling below is an anomaly. It is inconsistent with this Court's decision in *Stanton v. Stanton*, 421 U.S. 7 (1975), and out of step with an array of authority in lower courts, federal and state, decisions that have made museum pieces of male/female age of majority differentials. . . .

On the surface, Oklahoma's 3.2 beer sex/age differential may appear to accord young women a liberty withheld from young men. Upon deeper inspection, the gender line drawn by Oklahoma is revealed as a manifestation of traditional attitudes about the expected behavior of males and females, part of the myriad signals and messages that daily underscore the notion of men as society's active members, women as men's quiescent companions.

II.

Beyond question, Oklahoma has broad authority to regulate effectively the sale and service of alcoholic beverages. But the twenty-first amendment does not insulate from review legislative resort to gross classification by gender. Just as drinking preferences and proclivities associated with a particular ethnic group or social class would be perceived as an unfair and insubstantial basis for a beverage sale or service prohibition directed to that group or class, so a gender-based classification should be recognized as an inappropriate, invidious means to the legislative end of rational regulation in the public interest.

III.

Even if the highly questionable statistical presentation on which the court below relied served to prove the proposition asserted by appellees (males "drive more, drink more, and commit more alcohol related offenses"), that proposition does not suffice to justify the sex/age classification here at issue. But in fact, the statistical presentation does not do the service claimed for it. . . .

In sum, the state officials utterly failed to demonstrate that the hypothesized legislative objective (protection of young men and the public from weaknesses male flesh is heir to) is fairly, substantially and sensibly served by a 3.2 beer sex/age line. The legislation in question is a bizarre and paradoxical remnant of the day when "anything goes" was the rule for line-drawing by gender. . . .

ARGUMENT

I. Oklahoma's sex/age classification to determine qualification for association with 3.2 beer pigeonholes impermissibly on the basis of gender in violation of the fourteenth amendment's equal protection principle.

A. This Court's precedent condemns legislative classification based on overbroad generalization about "the way women (or men) are."

Since *Reed v. Reed*, 404 U.S. 71 (1971), this Court has instructed consistently that gender-based legislative classification, premised on overbroad generalization concerning the behavior, proclivities and preferences of the two sexes, cannot be tolerated under the Constitution. The decision below rests exclusively upon such overbroad generalization. That decision, and the gender line it upholds, merit this Court's decisive disapprobation.

Recognizing that it is no longer in vogue to rely on the "demonstrated facts of life" to justify gender lines in the law, appellees offered statistics which, they asserted, tended to show that 18–20 year old males "drive more, drink more, and commit more alcohol related offenses." Even if the highly questionable statistical presentation served to prove the proposition asserted by appellees, that proposition does not suffice to justify the sex/age classification here at issue. . . .

For example, in *Reed*, the proposition that men have more business experience than women was not without empirical support. In *Frontiero* and in *Wiesenfeld*, the statistics tendered by the Government to document men's nondependency, and their labor-market orientation, were far more impressive than the concededly infirm data relied upon in the case at bar. In short, the essence of this Court's decisions condemning laws drawing "a sharp line between the sexes" escaped appellees and the court below: neither unsubstantiated stereotypes nor generalized factual data suffice to justify pigeonholing by gender; a legislature may not place all males in one pigeonhole, all females in another, based on assumed or documented notions about "the way women or men are.". . .

C. Gender-based discrimination in laws regulating the sale and consumption of alcohol is wholly without support in currently viable precedent.

This case involves more than an impermissible sex/age differential. It also involves the lore relating to women and liquor—a combination that has fascinated lawmen for generations. The legislation at issue is a manifestation, with a bizarre twist, of the erstwhile propensity of legislatures to prescribe the conditions under which women and alcohol may mix. In recent years, however, outside Oklahoma, such legislation has been relegated to history's scrap heap. As the Court of Appeals for the First Circuit said of once traditional judicial essays in this area, "the authority of those precedents . . . has waned with the metamorphosis of the attitudes which fed them. What was then gallantry now appears Victorian condescension or even misogyny, and this cultural evolution is now reflected in the Constitution." *Women's Liberation Union of Rhode Island v. Israel* (1st Cir. 1975). . . .

No legislative design has been advanced that would even remotely satisfy the constitutional requirement that, at the least, gender-based classification must be "reasonable, not arbitrary, and must rest upon some ground of difference having a fair and substantial relation to the object of the legislation . . ." *Reed v. Reed*, 404 U.S. at 76. For gender is no more rational or less arbitrary a criterion upon which to base liquor or traffic safety laws than is religion or national origin. If ethnic identification were the criterion, however buttressed by proof of drinking proclivities and preferences, the state officials would "concede error." Their willingness and the [lower] court's readiness to accept the gender line as unobjectionable warrant prompt correction by this Court. . . .

D. Laws such as 37 Okla. Stat. §§241, 243, 245 shore up artificial barriers to realization by men and women of their full human potential and retard society's progress toward equal opportunity, free from gender-based discrimination.

Oklahoma's sex/age 3.2 beer line may appear at first glance a sport, a ridiculous distinction. In comparison to other business vying for this Court's attention, 37 Okla. Stat. §§241, 243, 245 might be viewed as supplying comic relief. Yet if this Oklahoma legislative action is not checked, if the overbroad generalizations tendered in its support are allowed to stand as proof adequate to justify a gender-based criterion, then this Court will have turned back the clock to the day when "anything goes" was the approach to line drawing by gender. For any defender of a gender line, with a modicum of sophistication, could avoid express reliance on "old notions" and, instead, invoke statistics to "demonstrate the facts of life." But this Court's recent precedent should stand as a bulwark against "the imposition of special disabilities upon the members of a particular sex because of their sex." *Frontiero v. Richardson*, 411 U.S. at 686. . . .

. . . Laws such as 37 Okla. Stat. §§241, 243, 245 serve only to shore up artificial barriers to full realization by men and women of their human potential, and to retard progress toward equal opportunity, free from gender-based discrimination. Ultimately harmful to women by casting the weight of the state on the side of traditional notions concerning women's behavior and her relation to man, such laws have no place in a nation preparing to celebrate a 200-year commitment to equal justice under law....

CONCLUSION

For the reasons stated above, the decision of the District Court for the Western District of Oklahoma should be reversed and the gender line drawn in 37 Okla. Stat. §§241, 243 and 245 should be declared unconstitutional.

"The Way Women Are"
United States v. Virginia

By 1990, the Virginia Military Institute (VMI) in Lexington, Virginia, which was open only to men, had become the state's sole remaining single-sex public college or university. The United States government sued the state, claiming that to deny women admission to VMI violated the Fourteenth Amendment's guarantee of equal protection of the laws to all persons. In making that claim, the government relied on the U.S. Supreme Court gender discrimination cases that Justice Ginsburg had argued and won as a lawyer for the ACLU in the 1970s.

It was surely satisfying for the justice to write the Supreme Court's majority opinion in the case, ruling that VMI had to open its doors to women. As Ginsburg later explained, VMI was not about the value of single-sex schools; "instead, VMI was about a state that invested heavily in a college designed to produce business and civic leaders, that for generations succeeded admirably in the endeavor, and that strictly limited this unparalleled opportunity to men."[1]

Separate and Unequal

Virginia attempted to head off a ruling that VMI had to admit women by establishing a program at a private women's college that purported to parallel the VMI experience, called Virginia Women's Institute for Leadership, or VWIL. The resources that the state devoted to VWIL, however, and the standards and experiences offered to women students there, fell far short of what the state made available to men at VMI, as detailed in Justice Ginsburg's opinion.

Justice Ginsburg compared Virginia's effort with VWIL to Texas's attempt to avoid admitting African American students to the state's public law schools fifty years earlier, when Texas set up a separate school for African American law students that initially had no independent faculty, no library, and no accreditation. Even though the lower courts were satisfied that the school nonetheless offered black law students in Texas an opportunity to study law that was "substantially equivalent" to what was available to whites, the U.S. Supreme Court in 1946 unanimously ruled that the separate school was inadequate and ordered an end to the discriminatory admissions policy.

An "Exceedingly Persuasive" Justification

Legislation that makes distinctions among persons is acceptable under the equal protection clause of the Fourteenth Amendment to the U.S. Constitution if the law has a rational basis, unless a fundamental interest or a suspect classification like race or national origin is involved. In contrast, a "compelling governmental interest" is required to survive the strict scrutiny that courts give to laws that discriminate on the basis of race or national origin. Until Ginsburg's work with the ACLU in the 1970s, a rational basis was all that was required even for legislation that drew very stark lines between the sexes. By the 1990s, an intermediate standard was applied to laws that discriminated by sex, very often resulting in their being invalidated as unconstitutional.

Justice Ginsburg's opinion acknowledged that physical differences between the sexes had played a role in establishing a constitutional standard for legal gender discrimination that was different from the standard for legal racial or national origin discrimination. "'Inherent differences' between men and women, we have come to appreciate, remain cause for celebration, but not for denigration of the members of either sex or for artificial constraints on an individual's opportunity," she wrote.

The opinion announces the standard that applies in cases challenging laws that discriminate by gender as follows: "The reviewing court must determine whether the proffered justification is exceedingly persuasive. The burden of justification is demanding and it rests entirely on the State. The State must show at least that the challenged classification serves important governmental objectives and that the discriminatory means employed are substantially related to the achievement of those objectives. The justification must be genuine, not hypothesized or invented post hoc in response to litigation. And it must not rely on overbroad generalizations about the different talents, capacities, or preferences of males and females."

This characterization of the standard prompted Ginsburg's friend and fellow justice, Antonin Scalia, to write a dissent accusing Ginsburg and the majority of "smuggling politics into the law" through a "de facto abandonment of the intermediate scrutiny that has been our standard for sex-based classifications for some two decades" in favor of something much closer to strict scrutiny. He suggested that the better argument was to revert to requiring only a rational basis for legislation that discriminates by sex.

As she had done consistently since she began briefing and arguing gender discrimination cases in the U.S. Supreme Court in the 1970s, Ginsburg kept her focus on the way that gender stereotypes distort and obstruct human potential. "Generalizations about 'the way women are,'" she wrote, "estimates of what is appropriate for most women, no longer justify denying opportunity to women whose talent and capacity place them outside the average description."

UNITED STATES V. VIRGINIA ET AL.
CERTIORARI TO THE UNITED STATES COURT OF APPEALS
FOR THE FOURTH CIRCUIT
518 U.S. 515 (June 26, 1996)*
*Together with No. 94-2107, Virginia et al. v. United States, also on certiorari to the same court.

Opinion Announcement

William H. Rehnquist: The opinion of the Court in two cases, No. 94-1941, *United States against Virginia*, and No. 94-2107, *Virginia against United States*, will be announced by Justice Ginsburg.

Ruth Bader Ginsburg: This case concerns an incomparable military college, the Virginia Military Institute (VMI), the sole single-sex school among Virginia's public institutions of higher learning.

Since its founding in 1839, VMI has produced civilian and military leaders for the commonwealth and the nation.

The school's unique program and unparalleled record as a leadership training ground has led some women to seek admission.

The United States, on behalf of women capable of all the activities required of VMI cadets, instituted this lawsuit in 1990, maintaining that under the Equal Protection Clause of the Fourteenth Amendment to the United States Constitution, Virginia may not reserve exclusively to men the educational opportunities that VMI affords.

The case has had a long history in court.

In the first round, the district court ruled against the United States, reasoning that the all-male VMI served the state policy of affording a diverse array of educational programs.

The Fourth Circuit vacated that judgment, concluding that a diversity policy serving to favor one gender did not constitute equal protection. In the second round, the lower courts considered and found satisfactory the remedy Virginia proposed, a program for women called the Virginia Women's Institute for Leadership, or VWIL at a private women's college, Mary Baldwin College.

A VWIL degree, as the Fourth Circuit said, would not carry the historical benefits and prestige of a VMI degree, and the two programs differed markedly in methodology: VMI is rigorously adversative, VWIL would be cooperative.

But overall, the lower courts concluded, these schools were sufficiently comparable to meet the demand of equal protection.

We reverse that determination.

Our reasoning centers on the essence of the complaint of the United States and on facts that are undisputed.

Some women at least can meet the physical standards VMI imposes on men, are capable of all the activities required of VMI cadets, prefer VMI's methodology over VWIL, could be educated using VMI's methodology, and would want to attend VMI if they had the chance.

With recruitment, the district court recognized, VMI could achieve at least 10% female enrollment—a number, the district court said, sufficient to provide female cadets with a positive educational experience.

If most women would not choose VMI's adversative method, many men too would not want to be educated in VMI's environment.

The question before us, however, is not whether women or men should be forced to attend VMI. Rather the question is whether Virginia can constitutionally deny to women who have the will and capacity the training and attendant opportunity VMI uniquely affords—training and opportunity the VWIL program does not supply.

To answer that question, we must have a measuring rod—what lawyers call a standard of review.

In a nutshell, this is the standard our precedent establishes: Defenders of sex-based government action must demonstrate an exceedingly persuasive justification for that action to make that demonstration.

The defender of a gender line must show at least that the challenged classification served important governmental objectives and that any discriminatory means employed is substantially related to the achievement of those objectives.

The heightened review standard applicable to sex-based classification does not make sex a proscribed classification but it does mark as presumptively invalid, incompatible with equal protection, a law or official policy that denies to women, simply because they are women, equal opportunity to aspire, achieve, participate in, and contribute to society based upon what they can do.

Under this exacting standard, reliance on overbroad generalization, typically male or typically female tendencies, estimates about the way most women or most men are, will not suffice to deny opportunity to women whose talent and capacity place them outside the average description.

As this Court said in *Mississippi University for Women against Hogan* some 14 years ago, state actors may not close entrance gates based on fixed notions concerning the roles and abilities of males and females.

A remedial decree must [address] the constitutional violation in this case; the violation is the categorical exclusion of women from an extraordinary educational leadership development opportunity afforded men.

To cure that violation and to afford genuinely equal protection, women seeking and fit for a VMI quality education cannot be offered anything less.

We therefore reverse the Fourth Circuit's judgment and remand the case for proceedings consistent with this opinion.

OPINION

Most footnotes and citations have been omitted, as well as some punctuation (including brackets and internal quotation marks).

Justice Ginsburg delivered the opinion of the Court.

Virginia's public institutions of higher learning include an incomparable military college, Virginia Military Institute (VMI). The United States maintains that the Constitution's equal protection guarantee precludes Virginia from reserving exclusively to men the unique educational opportunities VMI affords. We agree.

I

Founded in 1839, VMI is today the sole single-sex school among Virginia's 15 public institutions of higher learning. VMI's distinctive mission is to produce "citizen-soldiers," men prepared for leadership in civilian life and in military service. VMI pursues this mission through pervasive training of a kind not available anywhere else in Virginia. Assigning prime place to character development, VMI uses an "adversative method" modeled on English public schools and once characteristic of military instruction. VMI constantly endeavors to instill physical and mental discipline in its cadets and impart to them a strong moral code. The school's graduates leave VMI with heightened comprehension of their capacity to deal with duress and stress, and a large sense of accomplishment for completing the hazardous course.

VMI has notably succeeded in its mission to produce leaders; among its alumni are military generals, Members of Congress, and business executives. The school's alumni overwhelmingly perceive that their VMI training helped them to realize their personal goals. VMI's endowment reflects the loyalty of its graduates; VMI has the largest per-student endowment of all public undergraduate institutions in the Nation.

Neither the goal of producing citizen-soldiers nor VMI's implementing methodology is inherently unsuitable to women. And the school's impressive record in producing leaders has made admission desirable to some women. Nevertheless, Virginia has elected to preserve exclusively for men the advantages and opportunities a VMI education affords.

II A

From its establishment in 1839 as one of the Nation's first state military colleges, VMI has remained financially supported by Virginia and "subject to the control of the [Virginia] General Assembly." First southern college to teach engineering and industrial chemistry, VMI once provided teachers for the Commonwealth's schools.* Civil War strife threatened the school's vitality, but a resourceful superintendent regained legislative support by highlighting "VMI's great potential, through its technical know-how," to advance Virginia's postwar recovery.

VMI today enrolls about 1,300 men as cadets.† Its academic offerings in the liberal arts, sciences, and engineering are also available at other public colleges and universities in Virginia. But VMI's mission is special. It is the

---

* During the Civil War, school teaching became a field dominated by women.

† Historically, most of Virginia's public colleges and universities were single sex; by the mid-1970's, however, all except VMI had become coeducational....

mission of the school "to produce educated and honorable men, prepared for the varied work of civil life, imbued with love of learning, confident in the functions and attitudes of leadership, possessing a high sense of public service, advocates of the American democracy and free enterprise system, and ready as citizen-soldiers to defend their country in time of national peril."

In contrast to the federal service academies, institutions maintained "to prepare cadets for career service in the armed forces," VMI's program "is directed at preparation for both military and civilian life"; "only about 15% of VMI cadets enter career military service."

VMI produces its "citizen-soldiers" through "an adversative, or doubting, model of education" which features "physical rigor, mental stress, absolute equality of treatment, absence of privacy, minute regulation of behavior, and indoctrination in desirable values." As one Commandant of Cadets described it, the adversative method "dissects the young student," and makes him aware of his "limits and capabilities," so that he knows "how far he can go with his anger, . . . how much he can take under stress, . . . exactly what he can do when he is physically exhausted."

VMI cadets live in spartan barracks where surveillance is constant and privacy nonexistent; they wear uniforms, eat together in the mess hall, and regularly participate in drills. Entering students are incessantly exposed to the rat line, "an extreme form of the adversative model," comparable in intensity to Marine Corps boot camp. Tormenting and punishing, the rat line bonds new cadets to their fellow sufferers and, when they have completed the 7-month experience, to their former tormentors.

VMI's "adversative model" is further characterized by a hierarchical "class system" of privileges and responsibilities, a "dyke system" for assigning a senior class mentor to each entering class "rat," and a stringently enforced "honor code," which prescribes that a cadet "does not lie, cheat, steal nor tolerate those who do."

VMI attracts some applicants because of its reputation as an extraordinarily challenging military school, and "because its alumni are exceptionally close to the school." "Women have no opportunity anywhere to gain the benefits of [the system of education at VMI]."

B

In 1990, prompted by a complaint filed with the Attorney General by a female high-school student seeking admission to VMI, the United States sued the Commonwealth of Virginia and VMI, alleging that VMI's exclusively male admission policy violated the Equal Protection Clause of the Fourteenth Amendment. Trial of the action consumed six days and involved an array of expert witnesses on each side.

In the two years preceding the lawsuit, the District Court noted, VMI had received inquiries from 347 women, but had responded to none of them. "Some women, at least," the court said, "would want to attend the school if they had the opportunity." The court further recognized that, with recruitment, VMI could "achieve at least 10% female enrollment"—"a sufficient 'critical mass' to provide the female cadets with a positive educational experience." And it was also established that "some women are capable of all of the individual activities required of VMI cadets." In addition, experts agreed that if VMI admitted women, "the VMI ROTC experience would become a better training program from the perspective of the armed forces, because it would provide training in dealing with a mixed-gender army."

The District Court ruled in favor of VMI, however, and rejected the equal protection challenge pressed by the United States. That court correctly recognized that *Mississippi Univ. for Women v. Hogan*, 458 U.S. 718 (1982), was the closest guide. There, this Court underscored that a party seeking to uphold government action based on sex must establish an "exceedingly persuasive justification" for the classification. To succeed, the defender of the challenged action must show "at least that the classification serves important governmental objectives and that the discriminatory means employed are substantially related to the achievement of those objectives."

The District Court reasoned that education in "a single-gender environment, be it male or female," yields substantial benefits. VMI's school for men brought diversity to an otherwise coeducational Virginia system, and that diversity was "enhanced by VMI's unique method of instruction." If single-gender education for males ranks as an important governmental objective, it becomes obvious, the District Court concluded, that the only means of achieving the objective "is to exclude women from the all-male institution—VMI."

"Women are [indeed] denied a unique educational opportunity that is available only at VMI," the District Court acknowledged. But "[VMI's] single-sex status would be lost, and some aspects of the [school's] distinctive method would be altered," if women were admitted: "Allowance for personal privacy would have to be made"; "physical education requirements would have to be altered, at least for the women"; the adversative environment could not

102

survive unmodified. Thus, "sufficient constitutional justification" had been shown, the District Court held, "for continuing [VMI's] single-sex policy."

The Court of Appeals for the Fourth Circuit disagreed and vacated the District Court's judgment. The appellate court held: "The Commonwealth of Virginia has not...advanced any state policy by which it can justify its determination, under an announced policy of diversity, to afford VMI's unique type of program to men and not to women."

The appeals court greeted with skepticism Virginia's assertion that it offers single-sex education at VMI as a facet of the Commonwealth's overarching and undisputed policy to advance "autonomy and diversity." The court underscored Virginia's nondiscrimination commitment: "It is extremely important that [colleges and universities] deal with faculty, staff, and students without regard to sex, race, or ethnic origin." "That statement," the Court of Appeals said, "is the only explicit one that we have found in the record in which the Commonwealth has expressed itself with respect to gender distinctions." Furthermore, the appeals court observed, in urging "diversity" to justify an all-male VMI, the Commonwealth had supplied "no explanation for the movement away from [single-sex education] in Virginia by public colleges and universities." In short, the court concluded, "a policy of diversity which aims to provide an array of educational opportunities, including single-gender institutions, must do more than favor one gender."

The parties agreed that "some women can meet the physical standards now imposed on men," and the court was satisfied that "neither the goal of producing citizen soldiers nor VMI's implementing methodology is inherently unsuitable to women." The Court of Appeals, however, accepted the District Court's finding that "at least these three aspects of VMI's program—physical training, the absence of privacy, and the adversative approach—would be materially affected by coeducation." Remanding the case, the appeals court assigned to Virginia, in the first instance, responsibility for selecting a remedial course. The court suggested these options for the Commonwealth: Admit women to VMI; establish parallel institutions or programs; or abandon state support, leaving VMI free to pursue its policies as a private institution. In May 1993, this Court denied certiorari.

C

In response to the Fourth Circuit's ruling, Virginia proposed a parallel program for women: Virginia Women's Institute for Leadership (VWIL).

The 4-year, state-sponsored undergraduate program would be located at Mary Baldwin College, a private liberal arts school for women, and would be open, initially, to about 25 to 30 students. Although VWIL would share VMI's mission—to produce "citizen-soldiers"—the VWIL program would differ, as does Mary Baldwin College, from VMI in academic offerings, methods of education, and financial resources.

The average combined SAT score of entrants at Mary Baldwin is about 100 points lower than the score for VMI freshmen. Mary Baldwin's faculty holds "significantly fewer Ph.D.'s than the faculty at VMI," and receives significantly lower salaries. While VMI offers degrees in liberal arts, the sciences, and engineering, Mary Baldwin, at the time of trial, offered only bachelor of arts degrees. A VWIL student seeking to earn an engineering degree could gain one, without public support, by attending Washington University in St. Louis, Missouri, for two years, paying the required private tuition.

Experts in educating women at the college level composed the Task Force charged with designing the VWIL program; Task Force members were drawn from Mary Baldwin's own faculty and staff. Training its attention on methods of instruction appropriate for "most women," the Task Force determined that a military model would be "wholly inappropriate" for VWIL.

VWIL students would participate in ROTC programs and a newly established, "largely ceremonial" Virginia Corps of Cadets, but the VWIL House would not have a military format, and VWIL would not require its students to eat meals together or to wear uniforms during the school day. In lieu of VMI's adversative method, the VWIL Task Force favored "a cooperative method which reinforces self-esteem." In addition to the standard bachelor of arts program offered at Mary Baldwin, VWIL students would take courses in leadership, complete an off-campus leadership externship, participate in community service projects, and assist in arranging a speaker series.

Virginia represented that it will provide equal financial support for instate VWIL students and VMI cadets, and the VMI Foundation agreed to supply a $5.4625 million endowment for the VWIL program. Mary Baldwin's own endowment is about $19 million; VMI's is $131 million. Mary Baldwin will add $35 million to its endowment based on future commitments; VMI will add $220 million. The VMI Alumni Association has developed a network of employers interested in hiring VMI graduates. The Association has agreed to open its network to VWIL graduates, but those graduates will not have the advantage afforded by a VMI degree.

D

Virginia returned to the District Court seeking approval of its proposed remedial plan, and the court decided the plan met the requirements of the Equal Protection Clause. The District Court again acknowledged evidentiary support for these determinations: "The VMI methodology could be used to educate women and, in fact, some women…may prefer the VMI methodology to the VWIL methodology." But the "controlling legal principles," the District Court decided, "do not require the Commonwealth to provide a mirror image VMI for women." The court anticipated that the two schools would "achieve substantially similar outcomes." It concluded: "If VMI marches to the beat of a drum, then Mary Baldwin marches to the melody of a fife and when the march is over, both will have arrived at the same destination."

A divided Court of Appeals affirmed the District Court's judgment. This time, the appellate court determined to give "greater scrutiny to the selection of means than to the [Commonwealth's] proffered objective." The official objective or purpose, the court said, should be reviewed deferentially. Respect for the "legislative will," the court reasoned, meant that the judiciary should take a "cautious approach," inquiring into the "legitimacy" of the governmental objective and refusing approval for any purpose revealed to be "pernicious."

"Providing the option of a single-gender college education may be considered a legitimate and important aspect of a public system of higher education," the appeals court observed; that objective, the court added, is "not pernicious." Moreover, the court continued, the adversative method vital to a VMI education "has never been tolerated in a sexually heterogeneous environment." The method itself "was not designed to exclude women," the court noted, but women could not be accommodated in the VMI program, the court believed, for female participation in VMI's adversative training "would destroy…any sense of decency that still permeates the relationship between the sexes."

Having determined, deferentially, the legitimacy of Virginia's purpose, the court considered the question of means. Exclusion of "men at Mary Baldwin College and women at VMI," the court said, was essential to Virginia's purpose, for without such exclusion, the Commonwealth could not "accomplish [its] objective of providing single-gender education."

The court recognized that, as it analyzed the case, means merged into end, and the merger risked "bypassing any equal protection scrutiny." The court therefore added another inquiry, a decisive test it called "substantive comparability." The key question, the court said, was whether men at VMI and women at VWIL would obtain "substantively comparable benefits at their institution or through other means offered by the State." Although the appeals court recognized that the VWIL degree "lacks the historical benefit and prestige" of a VMI degree, it nevertheless found the educational opportunities at the two schools "sufficiently comparable."

Senior Circuit Judge Phillips dissented. The court, in his judgment, had not held Virginia to the burden of showing an "exceedingly persuasive [justification]" for the Commonwealth's action. In Judge Phillips' view, the court had accepted "rationalizations compelled by the exigencies of this litigation," and had not confronted the Commonwealth's "actual overriding purpose." That purpose, Judge Phillips said, was clear from the historical record; it was "not to create a new type of educational opportunity for women,...nor to further diversify the Commonwealth's higher education system,...but [was] simply...to allow VMI to continue to exclude women in order to preserve its historic character and mission."

Judge Phillips suggested that the Commonwealth would satisfy the Constitution's equal protection requirement if it "simultaneously opened single-gender undergraduate institutions having substantially comparable curricular and extra-curricular programs, funding, physical plant, administration and support services, and faculty and library resources." But he thought it evident that the proposed VWIL program, in comparison to VMI, fell "far short...from providing substantially equal tangible and intangible educational benefits to men and women."

The Fourth Circuit denied rehearing en banc. Circuit Judge Motz, joined by Circuit Judges Hall, Murnaghan, and Michael, filed a dissenting opinion. Judge Motz agreed with Judge Phillips that Virginia had not shown an "exceedingly persuasive justification" for the disparate opportunities the Commonwealth supported. She asked: "How can a degree from a yet to be implemented supplemental program at Mary Baldwin be held 'substantively comparable' to a degree from a venerable Virginia military institution that was established more than 150 years ago?" "Women need not be guaranteed equal results," Judge Motz said, "but the Equal Protection Clause does require equal opportunity...[and] that opportunity is being denied here."

III

The cross-petitions in this suit present two ultimate issues. First, does Virginia's exclusion of women from the educational opportunities provided by VMI—extraordinary opportunities for military training and civilian leadership development—deny to women "capable of all of the individual activities required of VMI cadets" the equal protection of the laws guaranteed by the Fourteenth Amendment? Second, if VMI's "unique" situation—as Virginia's sole single-sex public institution of higher education—offends the Constitution's equal protection principle, what is the remedial requirement?

IV

We note, once again, the core instruction of this Court's pathmarking decisions in *J. E. B. v. Alabama ex rel. T. B.*, 511 U.S. 127, 136–137, and n. 6 (1994), and *Mississippi Univ. for Women*, 458 U.S., at 724: Parties who seek to defend gender-based government action must demonstrate an "exceedingly persuasive justification" for that action.

Today's skeptical scrutiny of official action denying rights or opportunities based on sex responds to volumes of history. As a plurality of this Court acknowledged a generation ago, "our Nation has had a long and unfortunate history of sex discrimination." *Frontiero v. Richardson*, 411 U.S. 677, 684 (1973). Through a century plus three decades and more of that history, women did not count among voters composing "We the People";* not until 1920 did women gain a constitutional right to the franchise. And for a half century thereafter, it remained the prevailing doctrine that government, both federal and state, could withhold from women opportunities accorded men so long as any "basis in reason" could be conceived for the discrimination. See, e.g., *Goesaert v. Cleary*, 335 U.S. 464, 467 (1948) (rejecting challenge of female tavern owner and her daughter to Michigan law denying bartender licenses to females—except for wives and daughters of male tavern owners; Court would not "give ear" to the contention that "an unchivalrous desire of male bartenders to...monopolize the calling" prompted the legislation).

In 1971, for the first time in our Nation's history, this Court ruled in favor of a woman who complained that her State had denied her the equal

---

* As Thomas Jefferson stated the view prevailing when the Constitution was new: "Were our State a pure democracy...there would yet be excluded from their deliberations...women, who, to prevent depravation of morals and ambiguity of issue, could not mix promiscuously in the public meetings of men."

protection of its laws. *Reed v. Reed*, 404 U.S. 71, 73 (holding unconstitutional Idaho Code prescription that, among "several persons claiming and equally entitled to administer [a decedent's estate], males must be preferred to females"). Since *Reed*, the Court has repeatedly recognized that neither federal nor state government acts compatibly with the equal protection principle when a law or official policy denies to women, simply because they are women, full citizenship stature—equal opportunity to aspire, achieve, participate in and contribute to society based on their individual talents and capacities. See, e. g., *Kirchberg v. Feenstra*, 450 U.S. 455, 462-463 (1981) (affirming invalidity of Louisiana law that made husband "head and master" of property jointly owned with his wife, giving him unilateral right to dispose of such property without his wife's consent); *Stanton v. Stanton*, 421 U.S. 7 (1975) (invalidating Utah requirement that parents support boys until age 21, girls only until age 18).

Without equating gender classifications, for all purposes, to classifications based on race or national origin, the Court, in post-*Reed* decisions, has carefully inspected official action that closes a door or denies opportunity to women (or to men). To summarize the Court's current directions for cases of official classification based on gender: Focusing on the differential treatment or denial of opportunity for which relief is sought, the reviewing court must determine whether the proffered justification is "exceedingly persuasive." The burden of justification is demanding and it rests entirely on the State. The State must show "at least that the [challenged] classification serves important governmental objectives and that the discriminatory means employed are substantially related to the achievement of those objectives." The justification must be genuine, not hypothesized or invented post hoc in response to litigation. And it must not rely on overbroad generalizations about the different talents, capacities, or preferences of males and females. See *Weinberger v. Wiesenfeld*, 420 U.S. 636, 643, 648 (1975); *Califano v. Goldfarb*, 430 U.S. 199, 223-224 (1977) (Stevens, J., concurring in judgment).

The heightened review standard our precedent establishes does not make sex a proscribed classification. Supposed "inherent differences" are no longer accepted as a ground for race or national origin classifications. See *Loving v. Virginia*, 388 U.S. 1 (1967). Physical differences between men and women, however, are enduring: "The two sexes are not fungible; a community made up exclusively of one [sex] is different from a community composed of both." *Ballard v. United States*, 329 U.S. 187, 193 (1946).

"Inherent differences" between men and women, we have come to appreciate, remain cause for celebration, but not for denigration of the members of either sex or for artificial constraints on an individual's opportunity. Sex classifications may be used to compensate women "for particular economic disabilities [they have] suffered," to "promote equal employment opportunity," to advance full development of the talent and capacities of our Nation's people.* But such classifications may not be used, as they once were, to create or perpetuate the legal, social, and economic inferiority of women.

Measuring the record in this case against the review standard just described, we conclude that Virginia has shown no "exceedingly persuasive justification" for excluding all women from the citizen-soldier training afforded by VMI. We therefore affirm the Fourth Circuit's initial judgment, which held that Virginia had violated the Fourteenth Amendment's Equal Protection Clause. Because the remedy proffered by Virginia—the Mary Baldwin VWIL program—does not cure the constitutional violation, i.e., it does not provide equal opportunity, we reverse the Fourth Circuit's final judgment in this case.

V

The Fourth Circuit initially held that Virginia had advanced no state policy by which it could justify, under equal protection principles, its determination "to afford VMI's unique type of program to men and not to women." Virginia challenges that "liability" ruling and asserts two justifications in defense of VMI's exclusion of women. First, the Commonwealth contends, "single-sex education provides important educational benefits," and the option of single-sex education contributes to "diversity in educational approaches." Second, the Commonwealth argues, "the unique VMI method of character development and leadership training," the school's adversative approach, would have to be modified were VMI to admit women. We consider these two justifications in turn.

---

* Several amici have urged that diversity in educational opportunities is an altogether appropriate governmental pursuit and that single-sex schools can contribute importantly to such diversity. Indeed, it is the mission of some single-sex schools "to dissipate, rather than perpetuate, traditional gender classifications." See Brief for Twenty-six Private Women's Colleges as Amici Curiae 5. We do not question the Commonwealth's prerogative evenhandedly to support diverse educational opportunities. We address specifically and only an educational opportunity recognized by the District Court and the Court of Appeals as "unique," an opportunity available only at Virginia's premier military institute, the Commonwealth's sole single-sex public university or college.

A

Single-sex education affords pedagogical benefits to at least some students, Virginia emphasizes, and that reality is uncontested in this litigation.* Similarly, it is not disputed that diversity among public educational institutions can serve the public good. But Virginia has not shown that VMI was established, or has been maintained, with a view to diversifying, by its categorical exclusion of women, educational opportunities within the Commonwealth. In cases of this genre, our precedent instructs that "benign" justifications proffered in defense of categorical exclusions will not be accepted automatically; a tenable justification must describe actual state purposes, not rationalizations for actions in fact differently grounded. See *Wiesenfeld*, 420 U.S., at 648, and n. 16 ("mere recitation of a benign [or] compensatory purpose" does not block "inquiry into the actual purposes" of government-maintained gender-based classifications).

Mississippi Univ. for Women is immediately in point. There the State asserted, in justification of its exclusion of men from a nursing school, that it was engaging in "educational affirmative action" by "compensating for discrimination against women." Undertaking a "searching analysis," the Court found no close resemblance between "the alleged objective" and "the actual purpose underlying the discriminatory classification." Pursuing a similar inquiry here, we reach the same conclusion.

Neither recent nor distant history bears out Virginia's alleged pursuit of diversity through single-sex educational options. In 1839, when the Commonwealth established VMI, a range of educational opportunities for men and women was scarcely contemplated. Higher education at the time was considered dangerous for women;† reflecting widely held views about

---

* On this point, the dissent sees fire where there is no flame. "Both men and women can benefit from a single-sex education," the District Court recognized, although "the beneficial effects" of such education, the court added, apparently "are stronger among women than among men." The United States does not challenge that recognition. Cf. C. Jencks & D. Riesman, *The Academic Revolution* 297–298 (1968): "The pluralistic argument for preserving all-male colleges is uncomfortably similar to the pluralistic argument for preserving all-white colleges.... The all-male college would be relatively easy to defend if it emerged from a world in which women were established as fully equal to men. But it does not. It is therefore likely to be a witting or unwitting device for preserving tacit assumptions of male superiority—assumptions for which women must eventually pay."

† Dr. Edward H. Clarke of Harvard Medical School, whose influential book, *Sex in Education*, went through 17 editions, was perhaps the most well-known speaker from the medical community opposing higher education for women. He maintained that the

women's proper place, the Nation's first universities and colleges—for example, Harvard in Massachusetts, William and Mary in Virginia—admitted only men. VMI was not at all novel in this respect: In admitting no women, VMI followed the lead of the Commonwealth's flagship school, the University of Virginia, founded in 1819.

"No struggle for the admission of women to a state university," a historian has recounted, "was longer drawn out, or developed more bitterness, than that at the University of Virginia." In 1879, the State Senate resolved to look into the possibility of higher education for women, recognizing that Virginia "has never, at any period of her history," provided for the higher education of her daughters, though she "has liberally provided for the higher education of her sons."*

Virginia eventually provided for several women's seminaries and colleges. Farmville Female Seminary became a public institution in 1884. Two women's schools, Mary Washington College and James Madison University, were founded in 1908; another, Radford University, was founded in 1910. By the mid-1970's, all four schools had become coeducational.

Debate concerning women's admission as undergraduates at the main university continued well past the century's midpoint. Familiar arguments were rehearsed. If women were admitted, it was feared, they "would encroach on the rights of men; there would be new problems of government, perhaps scandals; the old honor system would have to be changed; standards would be lowered to those of other coeducational schools; and the glorious reputation of the university, as a school for men, would be trailed in the dust."

Ultimately, in 1970, "the most prestigious institution of higher education in Virginia," the University of Virginia, introduced coeducation and, in 1972, began to admit women on an equal basis with men. A three-judge Federal District Court confirmed: "Virginia may not now deny to women, on the basis of sex, educational opportunities at the Charlottesville campus that are not afforded in other institutions operated by the State."

Virginia describes the current absence of public single-sex higher education for women as "an historical anomaly." But the historical record

physiological effects of hard study and academic competition with boys would interfere with the development of girls' reproductive organs....

* Virginia's Superintendent of Public Instruction dismissed the coeducational idea as "repugnant to the prejudices of the people" and proposed a female college similar in quality to Girton, Smith, or Vassar.

indicates action more deliberate than anomalous: First, protection of women against higher education; next, schools for women far from equal in resources and stature to schools for men; finally, conversion of the separate schools to coeducation. The state legislature, prior to the advent of this controversy, had repealed "all Virginia statutes requiring individual institutions to admit only men or women." And in 1990, an official commission, "legislatively established to chart the future goals of higher education in Virginia," reaffirmed the policy "of affording broad access" while maintaining "autonomy and diversity." Significantly, the commission reported:

> Because colleges and universities provide opportunities for students to develop values and learn from role models, it is extremely important that they deal with faculty, staff, and students without regard to sex, race, or ethnic origin.

This statement, the Court of Appeals observed, "is the only explicit one that we have found in the record in which the Commonwealth has expressed itself with respect to gender distinctions."

Our 1982 decision in *Mississippi Univ. for Women* prompted VMI to reexamine its male-only admission policy. Virginia relies on that reexamination as a legitimate basis for maintaining VMI's single-sex character. A Mission Study Committee, appointed by the VMI Board of Visitors, studied the problem from October 1983 until May 1986, and in that month counseled against "change of VMI status as a single-sex college." Whatever internal purpose the Mission Study Committee served—and however well meaning the framers of the report—we can hardly extract from that effort any commonwealth policy evenhandedly to advance diverse educational options. As the District Court observed, the Committee's analysis "primarily focused on anticipated difficulties in attracting females to VMI," and the report, overall, supplied "very little indication of how the conclusion was reached."

In sum, we find no persuasive evidence in this record that VMI's male-only admission policy "is in furtherance of a state policy of diversity." No such policy, the Fourth Circuit observed, can be discerned from the movement of all other public colleges and universities in Virginia away from single-sex education. That court also questioned "how one institution with autonomy, but with no authority over any other state institution, can give effect to a state policy of diversity among institutions." A purpose genuinely to advance an array of educational options, as the Court of Appeals recognized, is not served by VMI's historic and constant plan—a plan to "afford a unique educational benefit only to males." However "liberally" this plan serves the Commonwealth's sons, it makes no provision whatever for her daughters. That is not equal protection.

B

Virginia next argues that VMI's adversative method of training provides educational benefits that cannot be made available, unmodified, to women. Alterations to accommodate women would necessarily be "radical," so "drastic," Virginia asserts, as to transform, indeed "destroy," VMI's program. Neither sex would be favored by the transformation, Virginia maintains:

> Men would be deprived of the unique opportunity currently available to them; women would not gain that opportunity because their participation would "eliminate the very aspects of [the] program that distinguish [VMI] from...other institutions of higher education in Virginia."

The District Court forecast from expert witness testimony, and the Court of Appeals accepted, that coeducation would materially affect "at least these three aspects of VMI's program—physical training, the absence of privacy, and the adversative approach." And it is uncontested that women's admission would require accommodations, primarily in arranging housing assignments and physical training programs for female cadets. It is also undisputed, however, that "the VMI methodology could be used to educate women." The District Court even allowed that some women may prefer it to the methodology a women's college might pursue. "Some women, at least, would want to attend [VMI] if they had the opportunity," the District Court recognized, and "some women," the expert testimony established, "are capable of all of the individual activities required of VMI cadets." The parties, furthermore, agree that "some women can meet the physical standards [VMI] now imposes on men." In sum, as the Court of Appeals stated; "neither the goal of producing citizen soldiers," VMI's raison d'être, "nor VMI's implementing methodology is inherently unsuitable to women."

In support of its initial judgment for Virginia, a judgment rejecting all equal protection objections presented by the United States, the District Court made "findings" on "gender-based developmental differences." These "findings" restate the opinions of Virginia's expert witnesses, opinions about typically male or typically female "tendencies." For example, "males tend to need an atmosphere of adversativeness," while "females tend to thrive in a cooperative atmosphere." "I'm not saying that some women don't do well under [the] adversative model," VMI's expert on educational institutions testified, "undoubtedly there are some [women] who do"; but educational experiences must be designed "around the rule," this expert maintained, and not "around the exception."

The United States does not challenge any expert witness estimation on average capacities or preferences of men and women. Instead, the United States emphasizes that time and again since this Court's turning point decision in *Reed v. Reed*, 404 U.S. 71 (1971), we have cautioned reviewing courts to take a "hard look" at generalizations or "tendencies" of the kind pressed by Virginia, and relied upon by the District Court. State actors controlling gates to opportunity, we have instructed, may not exclude qualified individuals based on "fixed notions concerning the roles and abilities of males and females."

It may be assumed, for purposes of this decision, that most women would not choose VMI's adversative method. As Fourth Circuit Judge Motz observed, however, in her dissent from the Court of Appeals' denial of re-hearing en banc, it is also probable that "many men would not want to be educated in such an environment." (On that point, even our dissenting colleague might agree.) Education, to be sure, is not a "one size fits all" business. The issue, however, is not whether "women—or men—should be forced to attend VMI"; rather, the question is whether the Commonwealth can constitutionally deny to women who have the will and capacity, the training and attendant opportunities that VMI uniquely affords.

The notion that admission of women would downgrade VMI's stature, destroy the adversative system and, with it, even the school,* is a judgment hardly proved,† a prediction hardly different from other "self-fulfilling prophecies" once routinely used to deny rights or opportunities. When

---

* Forecasts of the same kind were made regarding admission of women to the federal military academies.

† See 766 F. Supp., at 1413 (describing testimony of expert witness David Riesman: "If VMI were to admit women, it would eventually find it necessary to drop the adversative

women first sought admission to the bar and access to legal education, concerns of the same order were expressed. For example, in 1876, the Court of Common Pleas of Hennepin County, Minnesota, explained why women were thought ineligible for the practice of law. Women train and educate the young, the court said, which

> "forbids that they shall bestow that time (early and late) and labor, so essential in attaining to the eminence to which the true lawyer should ever aspire. It cannot therefore be said that the opposition of courts to the admission of females to practice ... is to any extent the outgrowth of ... 'old fogyism.' ... It arises rather from a comprehension of the magnitude of the responsibilities connected with the successful practice of law, and a desire to grade up the profession." *In re Application of Martha Angle Dorsett to Be Admitted to Practice as Attorney and Counselor at Law* (Minn. C. P. Hennepin Cty., 1876).

A like fear, according to a 1925 report, accounted for Columbia Law School's resistance to women's admission, although "the faculty ... never maintained that women could not master legal learning.... No, its argument has been ... more practical. If women were admitted to the Columbia Law School, [the faculty] said, then the choicer, more manly and red-blooded graduates of our great universities would go to the Harvard Law School!"

Medical faculties similarly resisted men and women as partners in the study of medicine. More recently, women seeking careers in policing encountered resistance based on fears that their presence would "undermine male solidarity"; deprive male partners of adequate assistance; and lead to sexual misconduct. Field studies did not confirm these fears.

---

system altogether, and adopt a system that provides more nurturing and support for the students."). Such judgments have attended, and impeded, women's progress toward full citizenship stature throughout our Nation's history. Speaking in 1879 in support of higher education for females, for example, Virginia State Senator C. T. Smith of Nelson recounted that legislation proposed to protect the property rights of women had encountered resistance. A Senator opposing the measures objected that "there [was] no formal call for the [legislation]," and "depicted in burning eloquence the terrible consequences such laws would produce." The legislation passed, and a year or so later, its sponsor, C. T. Smith, reported that "not one of [the forecast "terrible consequences"] has or ever will happen, even unto the sounding of Gabriel's trumpet."

Women's successful entry into the federal military academies,* and their participation in the Nation's military forces, indicate that Virginia's fears for the future of VMI may not be solidly grounded.† The Commonwealth's justification for excluding all women from "citizen-soldier" training for which some are qualified, in any event, cannot rank as "exceedingly persuasive," as we have explained and applied that standard.

Virginia and VMI trained their argument on "means" rather than "end," and thus misperceived our precedent. Single-sex education at VMI serves an "important governmental objective," they maintained, and exclusion of women is not only "substantially related," it is essential to that objective. By this notably circular argument, the "straightforward" test Mississippi Univ. for Women described was bent and bowed.

The Commonwealth's misunderstanding and, in turn, the District Court's, is apparent from VMI's mission: to produce "citizen-soldiers," individuals

> "imbued with love of learning, confident in the functions and attitudes of leadership, possessing a high sense of public service, advocates of the American democracy and free enterprise system, and ready . . . to defend their country in time of national peril."

Surely that goal is great enough to accommodate women, who today count as citizens in our American democracy equal in stature to men. Just as surely, the Commonwealth's great goal is not substantially advanced by women's categorical exclusion, in total disregard of their individual merit, from the Commonwealth's premier "citizen-soldier" corps.‡ Virginia, in sum, "has fallen far short of establishing the exceedingly persuasive justification," *Mississippi Univ. for Women*, 458 U.S., at 731, that must be the solid base for any gender-defined classification.

---

* Women cadets have graduated at the top of their class at every federal military academy.

† Inclusion of women in settings where, traditionally, they were not wanted inevitably entails a period of adjustment. As one West Point cadet squad leader recounted: "The classes of '78 and '79 see the women as women, but the classes of '80 and '81 see them as classmates."

‡ VMI has successfully managed another notable change. The school admitted its first African-American cadets in 1968. See *The VMI Story* 347–349 (students no longer sing "Dixie," salute the Confederate flag or the tomb of General Robert E. Lee at ceremonies

VI

In the second phase of the litigation, Virginia presented its remedial plan—maintain VMI as a male-only college and create VWIL as a separate program for women. The plan met District Court approval. The Fourth Circuit, in turn, deferentially reviewed the Commonwealth's proposal and decided that the two single-sex programs directly served Virginia's reasserted purposes: single-gender education, and "achieving the results of an adversative method in a military environment." Inspecting the VMI and VWIL educational programs to determine whether they "afforded to both genders benefits comparable in substance, [if] not in form and detail," the Court of Appeals concluded that Virginia had arranged for men and women opportunities "sufficiently comparable" to survive equal protection evaluation. The United States challenges this "remedial" ruling as pervasively misguided.

A

A remedial decree, this Court has said, must closely fit the constitutional violation; it must be shaped to place persons unconstitutionally denied an opportunity or advantage in "the position they would have occupied in the absence of [discrimination]." The constitutional violation in this suit is the categorical exclusion of women from an extraordinary educational opportunity afforded men. A proper remedy for an unconstitutional exclusion, we have explained, aims to "eliminate [so far as possible] the discriminatory effects of the past" and to "bar like discrimination in the future."

Virginia chose not to eliminate, but to leave untouched, VMI's exclusionary policy. For women only, however, Virginia proposed a separate program, different in kind from VMI and unequal in tangible and intangible facilities. Having violated the Constitution's equal protection requirement, Virginia was obliged to show that its remedial proposal "directly addressed and related to" the violation, i.e., the equal protection denied to women ready, willing, and able to benefit from educational opportunities of the kind VMI offers. Virginia described VWIL as a "parallel program," and asserted that VWIL shares VMI's mission of producing "citizen-soldiers" and VMI's

and sports events). As the District Court noted, VMI established a program on "retention of black cadets" designed to offer academic and social-cultural support to "minority members of a dominantly white and tradition-oriented student body." The school maintains a "special recruitment program for blacks" which, the District Court found, "has had little, if any, effect on VMI's method of accomplishing its mission."

goals of providing "education, military training, mental and physical discipline, character...and leadership development." If the VWIL program could not "eliminate the discriminatory effects of the past," could it at least "bar like discrimination in the future"? A comparison of the programs said to be "parallel" informs our answer. In exposing the character of, and differences in, the VMI and VWIL programs, we recapitulate facts earlier presented.

VWIL affords women no opportunity to experience the rigorous military training for which VMI is famed. Instead, the VWIL program "deemphasizes" military education, and uses a "cooperative method" of education "which reinforces self-esteem."

VWIL students participate in ROTC and a "largely ceremonial" Virginia Corps of Cadets, but Virginia deliberately did not make VWIL a military institute. The VWIL House is not a military-style residence and VWIL students need not live together throughout the 4-year program, eat meals together, or wear uniforms during the school day. VWIL students thus do not experience the "barracks" life "crucial to the VMI experience," the spartan living arrangements designed to foster an "egalitarian ethic." "The most important aspects of the VMI educational experience occur in the barracks," the District Court found, yet Virginia deemed that core experience nonessential, indeed inappropriate, for training its female citizen-soldiers.

VWIL students receive their "leadership training" in seminars, externships, and speaker series, episodes and encounters lacking the "physical rigor, mental stress,... minute regulation of behavior, and indoctrination in desirable values" made hallmarks of VMI's citizen-soldier training.* Kept away from the pressures, hazards, and psychological bonding characteristic of VMI's adversative training, VWIL students will not know the "feeling of tremendous accomplishment" commonly experienced by VMI's successful cadets.

Virginia maintains that these methodological differences are "justified pedagogically," based on "important differences between men and women in learning and developmental needs," "psychological and sociological differences" Virginia describes as "real" and "not stereotypes." The Task Force charged with developing the leadership program for women, drawn from the staff and faculty at Mary Baldwin College, "determined that a military model and, especially VMI's adversative method, would be wholly inappropriate for

---

* Both programs include an honor system. Students at VMI are expelled forthwith for honor code violations; the system for VWIL students is less severe.

educating and training most women." The Commonwealth embraced the Task Force view, as did expert witnesses who testified for Virginia.

As earlier stated, generalizations about "the way women are," estimates of what is appropriate for most women, no longer justify denying opportunity to women whose talent and capacity place them outside the average description. Notably, Virginia never asserted that VMI's method of education suits most men. It is also revealing that Virginia accounted for its failure to make the VWIL experience "the entirely militaristic experience of VMI" on the ground that VWIL "is planned for women who do not necessarily expect to pursue military careers." By that reasoning, VMI's "entirely militaristic" program would be inappropriate for men in general or as a group, for "only about 15% of VMI cadets enter career military service."

In contrast to the generalizations about women on which Virginia rests, we note again these dispositive realities: VMI's "implementing methodology" is not "inherently unsuitable to women"; "some women...do well under [the] adversative model"; "some women, at least, would want to attend [VMI] if they had the opportunity"; "some women are capable of all of the individual activities required of VMI cadets" and "can meet the physical standards [VMI] now imposes on men." It is on behalf of these women that the United States has instituted this suit, and it is for them that a remedy must be crafted,* a remedy that will end their exclusion from a state-supplied educational opportunity for which they are fit, a decree that will "bar like discrimination in the future."

B

In myriad respects other than military training, VWIL does not qualify as VMI's equal. VWIL's student body, faculty, course offerings, and facilities hardly match VMI's. Nor can the VWIL graduate anticipate the benefits associated with VMI's 157-year history, the school's prestige, and its influential alumni network.

---

* Admitting women to VMI would undoubtedly require alterations necessary to afford members of each sex privacy from the other sex in living arrangements, and to adjust aspects of the physical training programs. Experience shows such adjustments are manageable. See U.S. Military Academy, A. Vitters, N. Kinzer, & J. Adams, Report of Admission of Women (Project Athena I–IV) (1977–1980) (4-year longitudinal study of the admission of women to West Point); Defense Advisory Committee on Women in the Services, Report on the Integration and Performance of Women at West Point 17-18 (1992).

Mary Baldwin College, whose degree VWIL students will gain, enrolls first-year women with an average combined SAT score about 100 points lower than the average score for VMI freshmen. The Mary Baldwin faculty holds "significantly fewer Ph.D.'s" and receives substantially lower salaries than the faculty at VMI.

Mary Baldwin does not offer a VWIL student the range of curricular choices available to a VMI cadet. VMI awards baccalaureate degrees in liberal arts, biology, chemistry, civil engineering, electrical and computer engineering, and mechanical engineering. VWIL students attend a school that "does not have a math and science focus"; they cannot take at Mary Baldwin any courses in engineering or the advanced math and physics courses VMI offers.

For physical training, Mary Baldwin has "two multipurpose fields" and "one gymnasium." VMI has "an NCAA competition level indoor track and field facility; a number of multi-purpose fields; baseball, soccer and lacrosse fields; an obstacle course; large boxing, wrestling and martial arts facilities; an 11-laps-to-the-mile indoor running course; an indoor pool; indoor and outdoor rifle ranges; and a football stadium that also contains a practice field and outdoor track."

Although Virginia has represented that it will provide equal financial support for in-state VWIL students and VMI cadets, and the VMI Foundation has agreed to endow VWIL with $5.4625 million, the difference between the two schools' financial reserves is pronounced. Mary Baldwin's endowment, currently about $19 million, will gain an additional $35 million based on future commitments; VMI's current endowment, $131 million—the largest public college per-student endowment in the Nation—will gain $220 million.

The VWIL student does not graduate with the advantage of a VMI degree. Her diploma does not unite her with the legions of VMI "graduates [who] have distinguished themselves" in military and civilian life. "[VMI] alumni are exceptionally close to the school," and that closeness accounts, in part, for VMI's success in attracting applicants. A VWIL graduate cannot assume that the "network of business owners, corporations, VMI graduates and non-graduate employers...interested in hiring VMI graduates" will be equally responsive to her search for employment.

Virginia, in sum, while maintaining VMI for men only, has failed to provide any "comparable single-gender women's institution." Instead, the Commonwealth has created a VWIL program fairly appraised as a "pale shadow" of VMI in terms of the range of curricular choices and faculty stature, funding, prestige, alumni support and influence.

Virginia's VWIL solution is reminiscent of the remedy Texas proposed 50 years ago, in response to a state trial court's 1946 ruling that, given the equal protection guarantee, African-Americans could not be denied a legal education at a state facility. See *Sweatt v. Painter*, 339 U.S. 629 (1950). Reluctant to admit African-Americans to its flagship University of Texas Law School, the State set up a separate school for Heman Sweatt and other black law students. As originally opened, the new school had no independent faculty or library, and it lacked accreditation. Nevertheless, the state trial and appellate courts were satisfied that the new school offered Sweatt opportunities for the study of law "substantially equivalent to those offered by the State to white students at the University of Texas."

Before this Court considered the case, the new school had gained "a faculty of five full-time professors; a student body of 23; a library of some 16,500 volumes serviced by a full-time staff; a practice court and legal aid association; and one alumnus who had become a member of the Texas Bar." This Court contrasted resources at the new school with those at the school from which Sweatt had been excluded. The University of Texas Law School had a full-time faculty of 16, a student body of 850, a library containing over 65,000 volumes, scholarship funds, a law review, and moot court facilities.

More important than the tangible features, the Court emphasized, are "those qualities which are incapable of objective measurement but which make for greatness" in a school, including "reputation of the faculty, experience of the administration, position and influence of the alumni, standing in the community, traditions and prestige." Facing the marked differences reported in the *Sweatt* opinion, the Court unanimously ruled that Texas had not shown "substantial equality in the [separate] educational opportunities" the State offered. Accordingly, the Court held, the Equal Protection Clause required Texas to admit African-Americans to the University of Texas Law School. In line with *Sweatt*, we rule here that Virginia has not shown substantial equality in the separate educational opportunities the Commonwealth supports at VWIL and VMI.

C

When Virginia tendered its VWIL plan, the Fourth Circuit did not inquire whether the proposed remedy, approved by the District Court, placed women denied the VMI advantage in "the position they would have occupied in the absence of [discrimination]." Instead, the Court of Appeals considered whether the Commonwealth could provide, with fidelity to the equal protection principle, separate and unequal educational programs for men and women.

The Fourth Circuit acknowledged that "the VWIL degree from Mary Baldwin College lacks the historical benefit and prestige of a degree from VMI." The Court of Appeals further observed that VMI is "an ongoing and successful institution with a long history," and there remains no "comparable single-gender women's institution." Nevertheless, the appeals court declared the substantially different and significantly unequal VWIL program satisfactory. The court reached that result by revising the applicable standard of review. The Fourth Circuit displaced the standard developed in our precedent and substituted a standard of its own invention.

We have earlier described the deferential review in which the Court of Appeals engaged, a brand of review inconsistent with the more exacting standard our precedent requires. Quoting in part from *Mississippi Univ. for Women*, the Court of Appeals candidly described its own analysis as one capable of checking a legislative purpose ranked as "pernicious," but generally according "deference to [the] legislative will." Recognizing that it had extracted from our decisions a test yielding "little or no scrutiny of the effect of a classification directed at [single-gender education]," the Court of Appeals devised another test, a "substantive comparability" inquiry, and proceeded to find that new test satisfied.

The Fourth Circuit plainly erred in exposing Virginia's VWIL plan to a deferential analysis, for "all gender-based classifications today" warrant "heightened scrutiny." Valuable as VWIL may prove for students who seek the program offered, Virginia's remedy affords no cure at all for the opportunities and advantages withheld from women who want a VMI education and can make the grade.* In sum, Virginia's remedy does not match the

---

* Virginia's prime concern, it appears, is that "placing men and women into the adversarial relationship inherent in the VMI program...would destroy, at least for that period of the adversative training, any sense of decency that still permeates the relationship between the sexes." It is an ancient and familiar fear. Compare *In re Lavinia Goodell*, 39 Wis. 232, 246 (1875) (denying female applicant's motion for admission to the bar of its court, Wisconsin Supreme Court explained: "Discussions are habitually necessary in courts of justice, which are unfit for female ears. The habitual presence of women at these would tend to relax the public sense of decency and propriety."), with Levine, Closing Comments, 6

constitutional violation; the Commonwealth has shown no "exceedingly persuasive justification" for withholding from women qualified for the experience premier training of the kind VMI affords.

VII

A generation ago, "the authorities controlling Virginia higher education," despite long established tradition, agreed "to innovate and favorably entertained the [then] relatively new idea that there must be no discrimination by sex in offering educational opportunity." Commencing in 1970, Virginia opened to women "educational opportunities at the Charlottesville campus that [were] not afforded in other [state-operated] institutions." A federal court approved the Commonwealth's innovation, emphasizing that the University of Virginia "offered courses of instruction ... not available elsewhere." The court further noted: "There exists at Charlottesville a 'prestige' factor [not paralleled in] other Virginia educational institutions."

VMI, too, offers an educational opportunity no other Virginia institution provides, and the school's "prestige"—associated with its success in developing "citizen-soldiers"—is unequaled. Virginia has closed this facility to its daughters and, instead, has devised for them a "parallel program," with a faculty less impressively credentialed and less well paid, more limited course offerings, fewer opportunities for military training and for scientific specialization. VMI, beyond question, "possesses to a far greater degree" than the VWIL program "those qualities which are incapable of objective measurement but which make for greatness in a ... school," including "position and influence of the alumni, standing in the community, traditions and prestige." Women seeking and fit for a VMI-quality education cannot be offered anything less, under the Commonwealth's obligation to afford them genuinely equal protection.

Law & Inequality 41 (1988); "Plato questioned whether women should be afforded equal opportunity to become guardians, those elite Rulers of Platonic society. Ironically, in that most undemocratic system of government, the Republic, women's native ability to serve as guardians was not seriously questioned. The concern was over the wrestling and exercise class in which all candidates for guardianship had to participate, for rigorous physical and mental training were prerequisites to attain the exalted status of guardian. And in accord with Greek custom, those exercise classes were conducted in the nude. Plato concluded that their virtue would clothe the women's nakedness and that Platonic society would not thereby be deprived of the talent of qualified citizens for reasons of mere gender."

A prime part of the history of our Constitution, historian Richard Morris recounted, is the story of the extension of constitutional rights and protections to people once ignored or excluded.* VMI's story continued as our comprehension of "We the People" expanded.

---

* R. Morris, *The Forging of the Union*, 1781–1789, setting out letter to a friend from Massachusetts patriot (later second President) John Adams, on the subject of qualifications for voting in his home State:

> "It is dangerous to open so fruitful a source of controversy and altercation as would be opened by attempting to alter the qualifications of voters; there will be no end of it. New claims will arise; women will demand a vote; lads from twelve to twenty-one will think their rights not enough attended to; and every man who has not a farthing, will demand an equal voice with any other, in all acts of state. It tends to confound and destroy all distinctions, and prostrate all ranks to one common level." Letter from John Adams to James Sullivan (May 26, 1776), in 9 Works of John Adams 378 (C. Adams ed. 1854).

❦ "The Magnitude and Permanence of the Loss": *M.L.B. v. S.L.J.*

M.L.B. (only initials were given to protect privacy) was a Mississippi mother of two children; S.L.J. was her ex-husband and the children's father. S.L.J. kept custody of the children following the agreement the parents made when they divorced. He remarried, and he and his new wife filed suit in the Mississippi chancery court to terminate M.L.B.'s parental rights and to have the stepmother's adoption of the children approved. The chancery court declared M.L.B. an unfit parent, without specifying any evidence or reasons for that decision. M.L.B. could not appeal the decision terminating her parental rights without prepaying court costs of more than $2,300, mostly for a transcript of the chancery court proceedings.

Different rules apply in criminal and noncriminal (civil) cases. Because a case to terminate parental rights is civil, not criminal, the law that requires the states to allow indigent criminal defendants to proceed in forma pauperis ("as a poor person") and to have access to an appeal, with court expenses waived, did not apply for M.L.B. The Supreme Court of Mississippi denied M.L.B.'s petition to appeal in forma pauperis, and she appealed that ruling to the U.S. Supreme Court.

In Justice Ginsburg's opinion for the majority, ruling in favor of M.L.B., Ginsburg reasoned that the preciousness of the bond between parent and child meant that a proceeding to terminate parental rights could not be treated like other civil actions. A proceeding to declare a parent unfit, she said, was "barely distinguishable from criminal condemnation in view of the magnitude and permanence of the loss at stake." For this reason, the state of Mississippi could not impose a barrier to M.L.B.'s appeal of the decision to terminate her parental rights by requiring prepayment of substantial court costs.

Justice Ginsburg has said of *M.L.B. v. S.L.J.*, "I think most women appreciate that the loss of one's child is more devastating than six months in jail, much more devastating. It was technically a civil case, but I was able to persuade a majority of the Court that depriving a parent of parental status is as devastating as a criminal conviction."[1]

M.L.B. V. S.L.J., INDIVIDUALLY AND AS NEXT FRIEND OF THE MINOR CHILDREN, S.L.J. AND M.L.J., ET UX.

CERTIORARI TO THE SUPREME COURT OF MISSISSIPPI

519 U.S. 102 (December 16, 1996)

Opinion Announcement

Ruth Bader Ginsburg: This case concerns a poor person's opportunity to challenge on appeal a court decree ending her status as a parent.

The petitioner, M.L.B., had two children, a boy born in 1985, a girl in 1987.

In 1994, on the application of M.L.B.'s former husband and his second wife, a Chancery Court in Mississippi decreed M.L.B. an unfit parent, terminated her parental rights, and approved adoption of the children by their stepmother.

The trial judge declared that the statutory requirements for parental status termination had been met, but he did not specify concretely the evidence, facts, or precise reasons for his decision.

M.L.B. sought to appeal and paid the $100 filing fee, but under Mississippi laws she could not perfect her appeal without paying at once an amount exceeding $2,300 for preparation of the record.

The largest part of that cost was for a transcript of the Chancery Court proceedings.

The Supreme Court of Mississippi denied M.L.B.'s request for permission to appeal without pre-payment of cost.

Mississippi courts granted such applications only for appeals from two categories of judgments: criminal convictions and involuntary civil commitment orders.

M.L.B. tenders this question: May a State, consistent with the Due Process and Equal Protection Clauses of the Fourteenth Amendment, render appellate review of parental termination decrees accessible only to parents who have the wherewithal to pay for a transcript plus other record preparation fees?

We reverse the judgment of the Mississippi Supreme Court and hold that Mississippi may not deny M.L.B. because of her poverty—her inability to pay for a transcript—access to appellate review to test the adequacy of the evidence on which she was judged unfit to remain a parent.

Our opinion surveys the court's prior decisions and points.

We take up, first, appeals from criminal convictions including convictions for petty offenses, penalized by fine but not incarceration.

In all cases typed criminal or quasi-criminal in nature, our prior decisions hold that a state may not bolt the door to a poor person's appeal by withholding the record necessary for appellate review.

On the other hand, we next point out, in most civil cases, our prior rulings established that the state need not permit poor persons to appeal free of charge.

Today's decision also reviews our case law recognizing that no ties are more precious than those binding parent and child, and that few decrees are so grave in their consequences as a court order permanently severing the parent-child bond.

Parental termination decrees, our prior decisions acknowledge, work a unique kind of deprivation. Unlike custody decrees, they totally destroy all legal recognition of a parent-child relationship.

We therefore distinguish M.L.B.'s case from the mine run of civil actions, including other domestic relations matters, and align it for appeal access purposes with criminal and petty offense cases.

The accusatory state action M.L.B. seeks to fend off, we explain, should not be obscured by the label "civil action," for parental unfitness judications are barely distinguishable from criminal condemnation in view of the magnitude and permanence of the loss at stake.

OPINION

Many citations and footnotes have been omitted, as well as some punctuation (including brackets and internal quotation marks).

Justice Ginsburg delivered the opinion of the Court.

By order of a Mississippi Chancery Court, petitioner M.L.B.'s parental rights to her two minor children were forever terminated. M.L.B. sought to appeal from the termination decree, but Mississippi required that she pay in advance record preparation fees estimated at $2,352.36. Because M.L.B. lacked funds to pay the fees, her appeal was dismissed.

Urging that the size of her pocketbook should not be dispositive when "an interest far more precious than any property right" is at stake, M.L.B. tenders this question, which we agreed to hear and decide: May a State, consistent with the Due Process and Equal Protection Clauses of the Fourteenth Amendment, condition appeals from trial court decrees terminating parental rights on the affected parent's ability to pay record preparation fees? We hold that, just as a State may not block an indigent petty offender's access to an appeal afforded others, so Mississippi may not deny M.L.B., because of her poverty, appellate review of the sufficiency of the evidence on which the trial court found her unfit to remain a parent.

I

Petitioner M.L.B. and respondent S.L.J. are, respectively, the biological mother and father of two children, a boy born in April 1985, and a girl born in February 1987. In June 1992, after a marriage that endured nearly eight years, M.L.B. and S.L.J. were divorced. The children remained in their father's custody, as M.L.B. and S.L.J. had agreed at the time of the divorce.

S.L.J. married respondent J.P.J. in September 1992. In November of the following year, S.L.J. and J.P.J. filed suit in Chancery Court in Mississippi, seeking to terminate the parental rights of M.L.B. and to gain court approval for adoption of the children by their stepmother, J.P.J. The complaint alleged that M.L.B. had not maintained reasonable visitation and was in arrears on child support payments. M.L.B. counterclaimed, seeking primary custody of both children and contending that S.L.J. had not permitted her reasonable visitation, despite a provision in the divorce decree that he do so.

After taking evidence on August 18, November 2, and December 12, 1994, the Chancellor, in a decree filed December 14, 1994, terminated all parental rights of the natural mother, approved the adoption, and ordered that J.P.J., the adopting parent, be shown as the mother of the children on their birth certificates. Twice reciting a segment of the governing Mississippi statute, Miss. Code Ann. § 93-15-103(3)(e) (1994), the Chancellor declared that there had been a "substantial erosion of the relationship between the natural mother, [M.L.B.], and the minor children," which had been caused "at least in part by [M.L.B.'s] serious neglect, abuse, prolonged and unreasonable absence or unreasonable failure to visit or communicate with her minor children."*

---

* Mississippi Code Ann. § 93-15-103(3) (1994) sets forth several grounds for termination of parental rights, including "when there is [a] substantial erosion of the relationship

The Chancellor stated, without elaboration, that the natural father and his second wife had met their burden of proof by "clear and convincing evidence." Nothing in the Chancellor's order describes the evidence, however, or otherwise reveals precisely why M.L.B. was decreed, forevermore, a stranger to her children.

In January 1995, M.L.B. filed a timely appeal and paid the $100 filing fee. The Clerk of the Chancery Court, several days later, estimated the costs for preparing and transmitting the record: $1,900 for the transcript (950 pages at $2 per page); $438 for other documents in the record (219 pages at $2 per page); $4.36 for binders; and $10 for mailing.

Mississippi grants civil litigants a right to appeal, but conditions that right on prepayment of costs. Relevant portions of a transcript must be ordered, and its preparation costs advanced by the appellant, if the appellant "intends to urge on appeal," as M.L.B. did, "that a finding or conclusion is unsupported by the evidence or is contrary to the evidence."

Unable to pay $2,352.36, M.L.B. sought leave to appeal in forma pauperis. The Supreme Court of Mississippi denied her application in August 1995. Under its precedent, the court said, "the right to proceed in forma pauperis in civil cases exists only at the trial level."*

M.L.B. had urged in Chancery Court and in the Supreme Court of Mississippi, and now urges in this Court, that

> "where the State's judicial processes are invoked to secure so severe an alteration of a litigant's fundamental rights—the termination of the parental relationship with one's natural child—basic notions of fairness [and] of equal protection under the law, . . . guaranteed by [the Mississippi and Federal Constitutions], require that a person

---

between the parent and child which was caused at least in part by the parent's serious neglect, abuse, prolonged and unreasonable absence, unreasonable failure to visit or communicate, or prolonged imprisonment."

M.L.B. notes that, "in repeating the catch-all language of [the statute], the Chancellor said that [she] was guilty of 'serious . . . abuse.'" "However," M.L.B. adds, "there was no allegation of abuse in the complaint in this case or at any other stage of the proceedings."

* In fact, Mississippi, by statute, provides for coverage of transcript fees and other costs for indigents in civil commitment appeals.

be afforded the right of appellate review though one is unable to pay the costs of such review in advance."*

II

Courts have confronted, in diverse settings, the "age-old problem" of "providing equal justice for poor and rich, weak and powerful alike." Concerning access to appeal in general, and transcripts needed to pursue appeals in particular, *Griffin v. Illinois*, 351 U.S. 12 (1956), is the foundation case.

Griffin involved an Illinois rule that effectively conditioned thoroughgoing appeals from criminal convictions on the defendant's procurement of a transcript of trial proceedings. Indigent defendants, other than those sentenced to death, were not excepted from the rule, so in most cases, defendants without means to pay for a transcript had no access to appellate review at all. Although the Federal Constitution guarantees no right to appellate review, once a State affords that right, *Griffin* held, the State may not "bolt the door to equal justice" (Frankfurter, J., concurring in judgment).

The plurality in *Griffin* recognized "the importance of appellate review to a correct adjudication of guilt or innocence." "To deny adequate review to the poor," the plurality observed, "means that many of them may lose their life, liberty or property because of unjust convictions which appellate courts would set aside." Judging the Illinois rule inconsonant with the Fourteenth Amendment, the *Griffin* plurality drew support from the Due Process and Equal Protection Clauses.

Justice Frankfurter, concurring in the judgment in *Griffin*, emphasized and explained the decision's equal protection underpinning: "Of course a State need not equalize economic conditions.... But when a State deems it wise and just that convictions be susceptible to review by an appellate court, it cannot by force of its exactions draw a line which precludes convicted indigent persons, forsooth erroneously convicted, from securing such a review...."

Summarizing the *Griffin* line of decisions regarding an indigent defendant's access to appellate review of a conviction, we said in *Rinaldi v. Yeager*, 384 U.S. 305, 310 (1966): "This Court has never held that the States are

* On the efficacy of appellate review in parental status termination cases, M.L.B. notes that of the eight reported appellate challenges to Mississippi trial court termination orders from 1980 through May 1996, three were reversed by the Mississippi Supreme Court for failure to meet the "clear and convincing" proof standard.

required to establish avenues of appellate review, but it is now fundamental that, once established, these avenues must be kept free of unreasoned distinctions that can only impede open and equal access to the courts."

Of prime relevance to the question presented by M.L.B.'s petition, *Griffin*'s principle has not been confined to cases in which imprisonment is at stake. The key case is *Mayer v. Chicago*, 404 U.S. 189 (1971). *Mayer* involved an indigent defendant convicted on nonfelony charges of violating two city ordinances. Fined $250 for each offense, the defendant petitioned for a transcript to support his appeal. He alleged prosecutorial misconduct and insufficient evidence to convict. The State provided free transcripts for indigent appellants in felony cases only. We declined to limit *Griffin* to cases in which the defendant faced incarceration. "The invidiousness of the discrimination that exists when criminal procedures are made available only to those who can pay," the Court said in *Mayer*, "is not erased by any differences in the sentences that may be imposed." Petty offenses could entail serious collateral consequences, the *Mayer* Court noted. The *Griffin* principle, *Mayer* underscored, "is a flat prohibition" against "making access to appellate processes from even [the State's] most inferior courts depend upon the [convicted] defendant's ability to pay." An impecunious party, the Court ruled, whether found guilty of a felony or conduct only "quasi criminal in nature" "cannot be denied a record of sufficient completeness to permit proper [appellate] consideration of his claims."*

In contrast to the "flat prohibition" of "bolted doors" that the *Griffin* line of cases securely established, the right to counsel at state expense, as delineated in our decisions, is less encompassing. A State must provide trial counsel for an indigent defendant charged with a felony, *Gideon v. Wainwright*, 372 U.S. 335, 339 (1963), but that right does not extend to nonfelony trials if no term of imprisonment is actually imposed. A State's obligation to provide appellate counsel to poor defendants faced with incarceration applies

---

* *Griffin* did not impose an inflexible requirement that a State provide a full trial transcript to an indigent defendant pursuing an appeal. In *Draper v. Washington*, 372 U.S. 487 (1963), we invalidated a state rule that tied an indigent defendant's ability to obtain a transcript at public expense to the trial judge's finding that the defendant's appeal was not frivolous. We emphasized, however, that the *Griffin* requirement is not rigid. "Alternative methods of reporting trial proceedings," we observed, "are permissible if they place before the appellate court an equivalent report of the events at trial from which the appellant's contentions arise." Moreover, we held, an indigent defendant is entitled only to those parts of the trial record that are "germane to consideration of the appeal."

to appeals of right. In *Ross v. Moffitt*, however, we held that neither the Due Process Clause nor the Equal Protection Clause requires a State to provide counsel at state expense to an indigent prisoner pursuing a discretionary appeal in the state system or petitioning for review in this Court.

III

We have also recognized a narrow category of civil cases in which the State must provide access to its judicial processes without regard to a party's ability to pay court fees. In *Boddie v. Connecticut*, 401 U.S. 371 (1971), we held that the State could not deny a divorce to a married couple based on their inability to pay approximately $60 in court costs. Crucial to our decision in *Boddie* was the fundamental interest at stake. "Given the basic position of the marriage relationship in this society's hierarchy of values and the concomitant state monopolization of the means for legally dissolving this relationship," we said, due process "prohibits a State from denying, solely because of inability to pay, access to its courts to individuals who seek judicial dissolution of their marriages."

Soon after *Boddie*, in *Lindsey v. Normet*, 405 U.S. 56 (1972), the Court confronted a double-bond requirement imposed by Oregon law only on tenants seeking to appeal adverse decisions in eviction actions. We referred first to precedent recognizing that, "if a full and fair trial on the merits is provided, the Due Process Clause of the Fourteenth Amendment does not require a State to provide appellate review." We next stated, however, that "when an appeal is afforded,... it cannot be granted to some litigants and capriciously or arbitrarily denied to others without violating the Equal Protection Clause." Oregon's double-bond requirement failed equal protection measurement, we concluded, because it raised a substantial barrier to appeal for a particular class of litigants—tenants facing eviction—a barrier "faced by no other civil litigant in Oregon." The Court pointed out in *Lindsey* that the classification there at issue disadvantaged nonindigent as well as indigent appellants; the *Lindsey* decision, therefore, does not guide our inquiry here.

The following year, in *United States v. Kras*, 409 U.S. 434 (1973), the Court clarified that a constitutional requirement to waive court fees in civil cases is the exception, not the general rule. *Kras* concerned fees, totaling $50, required to secure a discharge in bankruptcy. The Court recalled in *Kras* that "on many occasions we have recognized the fundamental importance...under our Constitution" of "the associational interests that surround the establishment and dissolution of the [marital] relationship."* But bankruptcy discharge entails no "fundamental interest," we said. Although "obtaining [a] desired new start in life [is] important," that interest, the Court explained, "does not rise to the same constitutional level" as the interest in establishing or dissolving a marriage. Nor is resort to court the sole path to securing debt forgiveness, we stressed; in contrast, termination of a marriage, we reiterated, requires access to the State's judicial machinery.

In *Ortwein v. Schwab*, 410 U.S. 656 (1973), the Court adhered to the line drawn in *Kras*. The appellants in *Ortwein* sought court review of agency determinations reducing their welfare benefits. Alleging poverty, they challenged, as applied to them, an Oregon statute requiring appellants in civil cases to pay a $25 fee. We summarily affirmed the Oregon Supreme Court's judgment rejecting appellants' challenge. As in *Kras*, the Court saw no "fundamental interest...gained or lost depending on the availability of the relief sought by [the complainants]." Absent a fundamental interest or classification attracting heightened scrutiny, we said, the applicable equal protection standard "is that of rational justification," a requirement we found satisfied by Oregon's need for revenue to offset the expenses of its court system. We expressly rejected the *Ortwein* appellants' argument that a fee waiver was required for all civil appeals simply because the State chose to permit in forma pauperis filings in special classes of civil appeals, including appeals from terminations of parental rights.

In sum, as *Ortwein* underscored, this Court has not extended *Griffin* to the broad array of civil cases. But tellingly, the Court has consistently set apart from the mine run of cases those involving state controls or intrusions on family relationships. In that domain, to guard against undue official intrusion, the Court has examined closely and contextually the importance of the governmental interest advanced in defense of the intrusion.

---

* As examples, the Court listed: *Eisenstadt v. Baird*, 405 U.S. 438, 453 (1972) (right to be free from government interference in deciding whether to bear or beget a child is "fundamental," and may not be burdened based upon marital status); *Loving v. Virginia*, 388 U.S. 1, 12 (1967) ("Marriage is [a] basic civil right," and cannot be denied based on a racial classification.); *Griswold v. Connecticut*, 381 U.S. 479, 485–486 (1965) (marital relationship "is an association that promotes a way of life,...a harmony in living,...a bilateral loyalty," and the use of contraception within marriage is protected against government intrusion); *Skinner v. Oklahoma ex rel. Williamson*, 316 U.S. 535, 541 (1942) (because the power to sterilize affects "a basic liberty,...strict scrutiny of the classification which a State makes in a sterilization law is essential."); *Meyer v. Nebraska*, 262 U.S. 390, 399 (1923) (recognizing liberty interest in raising children).

IV

Choices about marriage, family life, and the upbringing of children are among associational rights this Court has ranked as "of basic importance in our society," rights sheltered by the Fourteenth Amendment against the State's unwarranted usurpation, disregard, or disrespect. M.L.B.'s case, involving the State's authority to sever permanently a parent–child bond,* demands the close consideration the Court has long required when a family association so undeniably important is at stake. We approach M.L.B.'s petition mindful of the gravity of the sanction imposed on her and in light of two prior decisions most immediately in point: *Lassiter v. Department of Social Servs. of Durham Cty.*, 452 U.S. 18 (1981), and *Santosky v. Kramer*, 455 U.S. 745 (1982).

Lassiter concerned the appointment of counsel for indigent persons seeking to defend against the State's termination of their parental status. The Court held that appointed counsel was not routinely required to assure a fair adjudication; instead, a case-by-case determination of the need for counsel would suffice, an assessment to be made "in the first instance by the trial court, subject . . . to appellate review."

For probation-revocation hearings where loss of conditional liberty is at issue, the *Lassiter* Court observed, our precedent is not doctrinaire; due process is provided, we have held, when the decision whether counsel should be appointed is made on a case-by-case basis. In criminal prosecutions that do not lead to the defendant's incarceration, however, our precedent recognizes no right to appointed counsel. Parental termination cases, the *Lassiter* Court concluded, are most appropriately ranked with probation-revocation hearings: While the Court declined to recognize an automatic right to appointed counsel, it said that an appointment would be due when warranted by the character and difficulty of the case.†

Significant to the disposition of M.L.B.'s case, the *Lassiter* Court considered it "plain . . . that a parent's desire for and right to 'the companionship, care, custody, and management of his or her children' is an important

---

* Although the termination proceeding in this case was initiated by private parties as a prelude to an adoption petition, rather than by a state agency, the challenged state action remains essentially the same: M.L.B. resists the imposition of an official decree extinguishing, as no power other than the State can, her parent-child relationships.

† The Court noted, among other considerations, that petitions to terminate parental rights may charge criminal activity and that "parents so accused may need legal counsel to guide them in understanding the problems such petitions may create."

interest," one that "undeniably warrants deference and, absent a powerful countervailing interest, protection." The object of the proceeding is "not simply to infringe upon [the parent's] interest," the Court recognized, "but to end it"; thus, a decision against the parent "works a unique kind of deprivation." For that reason, "a parent's interest in the accuracy and justice of the decision . . . is . . . a commanding one."

Santosky held that a "clear and convincing" proof standard is constitutionally required in parental termination proceedings.* In so ruling, the Court again emphasized that a termination decree is "final and irrevocable." "Few forms of state action," the Court said, "are both so severe and so irreversible."† As in *Lassiter*, the Court characterized the parent's interest as "commanding," indeed, "far more precious than any property right."

Although both *Lassiter* and *Santosky* yielded divided opinions, the Court was unanimously of the view that "the interest of parents in their relationship with their children is sufficiently fundamental to come within the finite class of liberty interests protected by the Fourteenth Amendment" (Rehnquist, J., dissenting). It was also the Court's unanimous view that "few consequences of judicial action are so grave as the severance of natural family ties."

V

Guided by this Court's precedent on an indigent's access to judicial processes in criminal and civil cases, and on proceedings to terminate parental status, we turn to the classification question this case presents: Does the Fourteenth Amendment require Mississippi to accord M.L.B. access to an appeal—available but for her inability to advance required costs—before she is forever branded unfit for affiliation with her children? Respondents urge us to classify M.L.B.'s case with the generality of civil cases, in which indigent persons have no constitutional right to proceed in forma pauperis.

---

* Earlier, in *Addington v. Texas*, 441 U.S. 418 (1979), the Court concluded that the Fourteenth Amendment requires a "clear and convincing" standard of proof in civil commitment proceedings.

† In *Rivera v. Minnich*, 483 U.S. 574 (1987), the Court declined to extend *Santosky* to paternity proceedings. The Court distinguished the State's imposition of the legal obligations attending a biological relationship between parent and child from the State's termination of a fully existing parent–child relationship. In drawing this distinction, the Court found it enlightening that state legislatures had similarly separated the two proceedings: Most jurisdictions applied a "preponderance of the evidence" standard in paternity cases, while 38 jurisdictions, at the time *Santosky* was decided, required a higher standard of proof in proceedings to terminate parental rights.

M.L.B., on the other hand, maintains that the accusatory state action she is trying to fend off is barely distinguishable from criminal condemnation in view of the magnitude and permanence of the loss she faces. For the purpose at hand, M.L.B. asks us to treat her parental termination appeal as we have treated petty offense appeals; she urges us to adhere to the reasoning in *Mayer v. Chicago*, 404 U.S. 189 (1971), and rule that Mississippi may not withhold the transcript M.L.B. needs to gain review of the order ending her parental status. Guided by *Lassiter* and *Santosky*, and other decisions acknowledging the primacy of the parent-child relationship, we agree that the *Mayer* decision points to the disposition proper in this case.

We observe first that the Court's decisions concerning access to judicial processes, commencing with *Griffin* and running through *Mayer*, reflect both equal protection and due process concerns. As we said in *Bearden v. Georgia*, 461 U.S. 660, 665 (1983), in the Court's *Griffin*-line cases, "due process and equal protection principles converge." The equal protection concern relates to the legitimacy of fencing out would-be appellants based solely on their inability to pay core costs. The due process concern homes in on the essential fairness of the state-ordered proceedings anterior to adverse state action. A "precise rationale" has not been composed because cases of this order "cannot be resolved by resort to easy slogans or pigeonhole analysis." Nevertheless, "most decisions in this area," we have recognized, "rest on an equal protection framework," as M.L.B.'s plea heavily does, for, as we earlier observed, due process does not independently require that the State provide a right to appeal. We place this case within the framework established by our past decisions in this area. In line with those decisions, we inspect the character and intensity of the individual interest at stake, on the one hand, and the State's justification for its exaction, on the other.

We now focus on *Mayer* and the considerations linking that decision to M.L.B.'s case. *Mayer* applied *Griffin* to a petty offender, fined a total of $500, who sought to appeal from the trial court's judgment. An "impecunious medical student," the defendant in *Mayer* could not pay for a transcript. We held that the State must afford him a record complete enough to allow fair appellate consideration of his claims. The defendant in *Mayer* faced no term of confinement, but the conviction, we observed, could affect his professional prospects and, possibly, even bar him from the practice of medicine. The State's pocketbook interest in advance payment for a transcript, we concluded, was unimpressive when measured against the stakes for the defendant.

Similarly here, the stakes for petitioner M.L.B.—forced dissolution of her parental rights—are large, "more substantial than mere loss of money." In contrast to loss of custody, which does not sever the parent-child bond, parental status termination is "irretrievably destructive" of the most fundamental family relationship. And the risk of error, Mississippi's experience shows, is considerable.

Consistent with *Santosky*, Mississippi has, by statute, adopted a "clear and convincing proof" standard for parental status termination cases. Nevertheless, the Chancellor's termination order in this case simply recites statutory language; it describes no evidence, and otherwise details no reasons for finding M.L.B. "clearly and convincingly" unfit to be a parent. Only a transcript can reveal to judicial minds other than the Chancellor's the sufficiency, or insufficiency, of the evidence to support his stern judgment.

The countervailing government interest, as in *Mayer*, is financial. Mississippi urges, as the justification for its appeal cost prepayment requirement, the State's legitimate interest in offsetting the costs of its court system. But in the tightly circumscribed category of parental status termination cases, appeals are few, and not likely to impose an undue burden on the State. Mississippi's experience with criminal appeals is noteworthy in this regard. In 1995, the Mississippi Court of Appeals disposed of 298 first appeals from criminal convictions; of those appeals, only seven were appeals from misdemeanor convictions, notwithstanding our holding in *Mayer* requiring in forma pauperis transcript access in petty offense prosecutions.[*]

In States providing criminal appeals, as we earlier recounted, an indigent's access to appeal, through a transcript of relevant trial proceedings, is secure under our precedent. That equal access right holds for petty offenses as well as for felonies. But counsel at state expense, we have held, is a constitutional requirement, even in the first instance, only when the defendant faces time in confinement. When deprivation of parental status is at stake, however, counsel is sometimes part of the process that is due. It would be anomalous to recognize a right to a transcript needed to appeal a misdemeanor conviction—though trial counsel may be flatly denied—but hold, at the same time, that a transcript need not be prepared for M.L.B.—though

---

[*] Many States provide for in forma pauperis appeals, including transcripts, in civil cases generally. Several States deal discretely with in forma pauperis appeals, including transcripts, in parental status termination cases.

were her defense sufficiently complex, state-paid counsel, as *Lassiter* instructs, would be designated for her.

In aligning M.L.B.'s case and *Mayer*—parental status termination decrees and criminal convictions that carry no jail time—for appeal access purposes, we do not question the general rule, stated in *Ortwein*, that fee requirements ordinarily are examined only for rationality. The State's need for revenue to offset costs, in the mine run of cases, satisfies the rationality requirement; States are not forced by the Constitution to adjust all tolls to account for "disparity in material circumstances."

But our cases solidly establish two exceptions to that general rule. The basic right to participate in political processes as voters and candidates cannot be limited to those who can pay for a license.* Nor may access to judicial processes in cases criminal or "quasi criminal in nature" turn on ability to pay. In accord with the substance and sense of our decisions in *Lassiter* and *Santosky*, we place decrees forever terminating parental rights in the category of cases in which the State may not "bolt the door to equal justice."

VI

In numerous cases, respondents point out, the Court has held that government "need not provide funds so that people can exercise even fundamental rights." A decision for M.L.B., respondents contend, would dishonor our cases recognizing that the Constitution "generally confers no affirmative right to governmental aid, even where such aid may be necessary to secure life, liberty, or property interests of which the government itself may not deprive the individual."

---

* The pathmarking voting and ballot access decisions are *Harper v. Virginia Bd. of Elections*, 383 U.S. 663, 664, 666 (1966) (invalidating, as a denial of equal protection, an annual $1.50 poll tax imposed by Virginia on all residents over 21); *Bullock v. Carter*, 405 U.S. 134, 135, 145, 149 (1972) (invalidating Texas scheme under which candidates for local office had to pay fees as high as $8,900 to get on the ballot); *Lubin v. Panish*, 415 U.S. 709, 710, 718 (1974) (invalidating California statute requiring payment of a ballot-access fee fixed at a percentage of the salary for the office sought).

Notably, the Court in *Harper* recognized that "a State may exact fees from citizens for many different kinds of licenses." For example, the State "can demand from all an equal fee for a driver's license." But voting cannot hinge on ability to pay, the Court explained, for it is a "fundamental political right...preservative of all rights." *Bullock* rejected as justifications for excluding impecunious persons, the State's concern about unwieldy ballots and its interest in financing elections. *Lubin* reaffirmed that a State may not require from an indigent candidate "fees he cannot pay."

Complainants in the cases on which respondents rely sought state aid to subsidize their privately initiated action or to alleviate the consequences of differences in economic circumstances that existed apart from state action. M.L.B.'s complaint is of a different order. She is endeavoring to defend against the State's destruction of her family bonds, and to resist the brand associated with a parental unfitness adjudication. Like a defendant resisting criminal conviction, she seeks to be spared from the State's devastatingly adverse action. That is the very reason we have paired her case with *Mayer*, not with *Ortwein* or *Kras*.

Respondents also suggest that *Washington v. Davis*, 426 U.S. 229 (1976), is instructive because it rejects the notion "that a law, neutral on its face and serving ends otherwise within the power of government to pursue, is invalid under the Equal Protection Clause simply because it may affect a greater proportion of one race than of another." "This must be all the more true," respondents urge, "with respect to an allegedly disparate impact on a class [here, the poor] that, unlike race, is not suspect."

Washington v. Davis, however, does not have the sweeping effect respondents attribute to it. That case involved a verbal skill test administered to prospective Government employees. "A far greater proportion of blacks—four times as many—failed the test than did whites." But the successful test takers included members of both races, as did the unsuccessful examinees. Disproportionate impact, standing alone, the Court held, was insufficient to prove unconstitutional racial discrimination. Were it otherwise, a host of laws would be called into question, "a whole range of tax, welfare, public service, regulatory, and licensing statutes that may be more burdensome to the poor and to the average black than to the more affluent white."

To comprehend the difference between the case at hand and cases controlled by *Washington v. Davis*, one need look no further than this Court's opinion in *Williams v. Illinois*, 399 U.S. 235 (1970). *Williams* held unconstitutional an Illinois law under which an indigent offender could be continued in confinement beyond the maximum prison term specified by statute if his indigency prevented him from satisfying the monetary portion of the sentence. The Court described that law as "nondiscriminatory on its face," and recalled that the law found incompatible with the Constitution in *Griffin* had been so characterized ("A law nondiscriminatory on its face may be grossly discriminatory in its operation."). But the *Williams* Court went on to explain that "the Illinois statute in operative effect exposes only indigents to

139

the risk of imprisonment beyond the statutory maximum." Sanctions of the *Williams* genre, like the Mississippi prescription here at issue, are not merely disproportionate in impact. Rather, they are wholly contingent on one's ability to pay, and thus "visit different consequences on two categories of persons"; they apply to all indigents and do not reach anyone outside that class.

In sum, under respondents' reading of *Washington v. Davis*, our overruling of the *Griffin* line of cases would be two decades overdue. It suffices to point out that this Court has not so conceived the meaning and effect of our 1976 "disproportionate impact" precedent.*

Respondents and the dissenters urge that we will open floodgates if we do not rigidly restrict *Griffin* to cases typed "criminal" (Thomas, J., dissenting). But we have repeatedly noticed what sets parental status termination decrees apart from mine run civil actions, even from other domestic relations matters such as divorce, paternity, and child custody. To recapitulate, termination decrees "work a unique kind of deprivation." In contrast to matters modifiable at the parties' will or based on changed circumstances, termination adjudications involve the awesome authority of the State "to destroy permanently all legal recognition of the parental relationship." Our *Lassiter* and *Santosky* decisions, recognizing that parental termination decrees are among the most severe forms of state action, have not served as precedent in other areas. We are therefore satisfied that the label "civil" should not entice us to leave undisturbed the Mississippi courts' disposition of this case.

★ ★ ★

For the reasons stated, we hold that Mississippi may not withhold from M.L.B. "a 'record of sufficient completeness' to permit proper [appellate] consideration of [her] claims." Accordingly, we reverse the judgment of the Supreme Court of Mississippi and remand the case for further proceedings not inconsistent with this opinion.

It is so ordered.

---

* Six of the seven Justices in the majority in *Washington v. Davis*, 426 U.S. 229 (1976), had two Terms before *Davis* read our decisions in *Griffin* and related cases to hold that "the State cannot adopt procedures which leave an indigent defendant 'entirely cut off from any appeal at all,' by virtue of his indigency, or extend to such indigent defendants merely a 'meaningless ritual' while others in better economic circumstances have a 'meaningful appeal.'" *Ross v. Moffitt*, 417 U.S. 600, 612 (1974) (opinion of the Court by Rehnquist, J.).

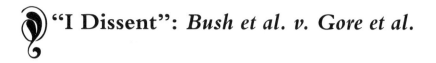

"I Dissent": *Bush et al. v. Gore et al.*

As many Americans well knew following the presidential election of 2016 if not sooner, the Electoral College, made up of representatives selected by state voting, decides who will be the U.S. president—not the popular vote of all voters in the nation as a whole. In the election of November 7, 2000, although Democratic presidential candidate Al Gore, an early advocate of measures to slow climate change, clearly won the popular vote, the vote of the Electoral College remained unclear for another month.

By the morning after the election, the Republican nominee, George W. Bush, had a total of 246 votes in the Electoral College, while the Democratic nominee, Al Gore, had a total of 250 electoral votes; 270 are needed to win the presidency. In three states—Wisconsin, Oregon, and Florida—the vote remained too close to call. Wisconsin and Oregon were added to Gore's column a few days after the election, but neither candidate could reach 270 electoral votes without Florida's 25, which remained up in the air.[1]

"The December Storm over the Supreme Court"

Gore conceded on election night, then withdrew his concession the next morning; the closeness of the vote in Florida triggered a mandatory machine recount. On November 26, Florida certified Bush as the winner by 537 votes. Gore contested these results, and when the Florida Supreme Court was again asked to intervene it ordered a recount of more than 70,000 ballots that had been rejected by machine counters as "undervotes."

Bush appealed to the U.S. Supreme Court, which granted a stay on December 9 to halt the recount while the Court was deliberating and on December 12 ruled that the recount order was unconstitutional, effectively awarding the presidency to Bush. For the first time since 1888, the winner of the popular vote (Gore, by about half a million votes) lost the vote in the Electoral College—a pattern that also, of course, characterized the 2016 presidential election (minus all the drama, suspense, and litigation).[2]

Bush v. Gore, the "December storm over the U.S. Supreme Court," as Justice Ginsburg called it, was a divisive and exhausting case, argued and decided in haste and literally in the spotlight; the justices were advised to draw their blinds against the bright lights from television networks' satellite trucks shining in the justices' windows as the media awaited the Court's decision.[3]

In the tension surrounding the decision, even relations between friends were strained. Conservative Justice Antonin Scalia—famously Justice Ginsburg's fellow vacationer, elephant rider, and opera lover—responded to a draft Ginsburg circulated, which contained a footnote suggesting that the Florida districts involved might have seen suppression of African American votes, by accusing her of "fouling our nest" and using "Al Sharpton tactics."[4]

"I Dissent"

In the end, the majority of the U.S. Supreme Court, ruling in favor of Bush, held that the recount would be unconstitutional under the equal protection clause of the Fourteenth Amendment to the U.S. Constitution. The majority opinion "per curiam" (by the Court as a whole rather than an individual author) reasoned that the recount procedures implemented in response to the state court's decision did not satisfy equal protection's minimum requirement for nonarbitrary treatment of voters. Standards for accepting or rejecting contested ballots varied not only from county to county but also from one recount team to another. It was obvious to the majority that the recount could not be conducted in compliance with the requirements of equal protection and due process without substantial additional work. The majority reasoned that there was not enough time for this work under a federal election statute, 3 U.S.C. § 5, that requires any controversy or contest designed to lead to a conclusive selection of electors to be completed by a "safe harbor" deadline of December 12 (the date of the court's ruling).

Justice Ginsburg and three other justices dissented from this ruling. In a break with precedent (although not for the first time), the conclusion to Justice Ginsburg's dissent famously omitted the word "respectfully": "I dissent," she stated baldly.

Justice Ginsburg argued that the Florida Supreme Court as the arbiter of state law should be allowed to determine how to select Florida's representatives to the Electoral College; that time had been shortened by the Court's granting a stay stopping the recount days earlier; and that the December 12 deadline was not crucially significant. What mattered was only "the sixth day of January," the date for which Congress had provided detailed rules for determining the validity of electoral votes. Finally, she called the majority's conclusion that a constitutionally adequate recount was impractical "a prophecy the Court's own judgment will not allow to be tested. Such an untested prophecy should not decide the Presidency of the United States."

"Never Beyond Repair"

Justice Stevens joined Justice Ginsburg's dissent and also wrote his own, more bitterly worded: The majority's ruling "can only lend credence to the most cynical appraisal of the work of judges throughout the land," he wrote. "Although we may never know with complete certainty the identity of the winner of this year's presidential election, the identity of the loser is perfectly clear. It is the nation's confidence in the judge as an impartial guardian of the rule of law."

Theodore Olson, who represented Bush before the Court, said of the case, "It was described as a circus, but that is an insult to the discipline of circuses."[5] Justice Ginsburg said shortly afterward, "Whatever final judgment awaits *Bush v. Gore* in the annals of history, I am certain that the good work and good faith of the U.S. federal judiciary as a whole will continue to sustain public confidence at a level never beyond repair."[6]

Once the storm had cleared, Justices Ginsburg and Scalia remained friends. Ginsburg prizes the Court culture that elevates the institution over the justices' individual egos.

BUSH ET AL. V. GORE ET AL.

531 U.S. 98 (December 12, 2000)

DISSENT

Most citations and all footnotes have been omitted for ease of reading, as well as some punctuation (including brackets and internal quotation marks).

Justice Ginsburg, with whom Justice Stevens joins, and with whom Justice Souter and Justice Breyer join as to Part I, dissenting.

I

The Chief Justice acknowledges that provisions of Florida's Election Code "may well admit of more than one interpretation." But instead of respecting the state high court's province to say what the State's Election Code means, the Chief Justice maintains that Florida's Supreme Court has veered so far from the ordinary practice of judicial review that what it did cannot properly be called judging. My colleagues have offered a reasonable construction of Florida's law. Their construction coincides with the view of one of Florida's seven Supreme Court justices. I might join the Chief Justice were it my commission to interpret Florida law. But disagreement with the Florida court's interpretation of its own State's law does not warrant the conclusion that the justices of that court have legislated. There is no cause here to believe that the members of Florida's high court have done less than "their mortal best to discharge their oath of office," and no cause to upset their reasoned interpretation of Florida law.

This Court more than occasionally affirms statutory, and even constitutional, interpretations with which it disagrees. For example, when reviewing challenges to administrative agencies' interpretations of laws they implement, we defer to the agencies unless their interpretation violates "the unambiguously expressed intent of Congress." We do so in the face of the declaration in Article I of the United States Constitution that "All legislative Powers herein granted shall be vested in a Congress of the United States." Surely the Constitution does not call upon us to pay more respect to a federal administrative agency's construction of federal law than to a state high court's interpretation of its own State's law. And not uncommonly, we let stand state-court interpretations of federal law with which we might disagree.

Notably, in the habeas context, the Court adheres to the view that "there is no intrinsic reason why the fact that a man is a federal judge should make him more competent, or conscientious, or learned with respect to [federal law] than his neighbor in the state courthouse."

No doubt there are cases in which the proper application of federal law may hinge on interpretations of state law. Unavoidably, this Court must sometimes examine state law in order to protect federal rights. But we have dealt with such cases ever mindful of the full measure of respect we owe to interpretations of state law by a State's highest court. In the Contract Clause case, *General Motors Corp. v. Romein*, 503 U.S. 181 (1992), for example, we said that although "ultimately we are bound to decide for ourselves whether a contract was made," the Court "accords respectful consideration and great weight to the views of the State's highest court." And in *Central Union Telephone Co. v. Edwardsville*, 269 U.S. 190 (1925), we upheld the Illinois Supreme Court's interpretation of a state waiver rule, even though that interpretation resulted in the forfeiture of federal constitutional rights. Refusing to supplant Illinois law with a federal definition of waiver, we explained that the state court's declaration "should bind us unless so unfair or unreasonable in its application to those asserting a federal right as to obstruct it."

In deferring to state courts on matters of state law, we appropriately recognize that this Court acts as an "outsider lacking the common exposure to local law which comes from sitting in the jurisdiction." That recognition has sometimes prompted us to resolve doubts about the meaning of state law by certifying issues to a State's highest court, even when federal rights are at stake. Notwithstanding our authority to decide issues of state law underlying federal claims, we have used the certification device to afford state high courts an opportunity to inform us on matters of their own State's law because such restraint "helps build a cooperative judicial federalism."

Just last Term, in *Fiore v. White*, 528 U.S. 23 (1999), we took advantage of Pennsylvania's certification procedure. In that case, a state prisoner brought a federal habeas action claiming that the State had failed to prove an essential element of his charged offense in violation of the Due Process Clause. Instead of resolving the state-law question on which the federal claim depended, we certified the question to the Pennsylvania Supreme Court for that court to "help determine the proper state-law predicate for our determination of the federal constitutional questions raised." The Chief Justice's willingness to reverse the Florida Supreme Court's interpretation of Florida law in this case is at least in tension with our reluctance in *Fiore* even to interpret Pennsylvania law before seeking instruction from the Pennsylvania Supreme Court. I would have thought the "cautious approach" we counsel when federal courts address matters of state law, and our commitment to "building cooperative judicial federalism," demanded greater restraint.

Rarely has this Court rejected outright an interpretation of state law by a state high court. *Fairfax's Devisee v. Hunter's Lessee*, 7 Cranch 603 (1813), *NAACP v. Alabama ex rel. Patterson*, 357 U.S. 449 (1958), and *Bouie v. City of Columbia*, 378 U.S. 347 (1964), cited by the Chief Justice, are three such rare instances. But those cases are embedded in historical contexts hardly comparable to the situation here. *Fairfax's Devisee*, which held that the Virginia Court of Appeals had misconstrued its own forfeiture laws to deprive a British subject of lands secured to him by federal treaties, occurred amidst vociferous States' rights attacks on the Marshall Court. The Virginia court refused to obey this Court's *Fairfax's Devisee* mandate to enter judgment for the British subject's successor in interest. That refusal led to the Court's pathmarking decision in *Martin v. Hunter's Lessee*, 1 Wheat. 304 (1816). *Patterson*, a case decided three months after *Cooper v. Aaron*, 358 U.S. 1 (1958), in the face of Southern resistance to the civil rights movement, held that the Alabama Supreme Court had irregularly applied its own procedural rules to deny review of a contempt order against the NAACP arising from its refusal to disclose membership lists. We said that "our jurisdiction is not defeated if the non-federal ground relied on by the state court is 'without any fair or substantial support.'" *Bouie*, stemming from a lunch counter "sit-in" at the height of the civil rights movement, held that the South Carolina Supreme Court's construction of its trespass laws—criminalizing conduct not covered by the text of an otherwise clear statute—was "unforeseeable" and thus violated due process when applied retroactively to the petitioners.

The Chief Justice's casual citation of these cases might lead one to believe they are part of a larger collection of cases in which we said that the Constitution impelled us to train a skeptical eye on a state court's portrayal of state law. But one would be hard pressed, I think, to find additional cases that fit the mold. As Justice Breyer convincingly explains (dissenting opinion), this case involves nothing close to the kind of recalcitrance by a state high court that warrants extraordinary action by this Court. The Florida

Supreme Court concluded that counting every legal vote was the overriding concern of the Florida Legislature when it enacted the State's Election Code. The court surely should not be bracketed with state high courts of the Jim Crow South.

The Chief Justice says that Article II, by providing that state legislatures shall direct the manner of appointing electors, authorizes federal superintendence over the relationship between state courts and state legislatures, and licenses a departure from the usual deference we give to state-court interpretations of state law. The Framers of our Constitution, however, understood that in a republican government, the judiciary would construe the legislature's enactments. In light of the constitutional guarantee to States of a "Republican Form of Government," U.S. Const., Art. IV, § 4, Article II can hardly be read to invite this Court to disrupt a State's republican regime. Yet the Chief Justice today would reach out to do just that. By holding that Article II requires our revision of a state court's construction of state laws in order to protect one organ of the State from another, the Chief Justice contradicts the basic principle that a State may organize itself as it sees fit. Article II does not call for the scrutiny undertaken by this Court.

The extraordinary setting of this case has obscured the ordinary principle that dictates its proper resolution: Federal courts defer to a state high court's interpretations of the State's own law. This principle reflects the core of federalism, on which all agree. "The Framers split the atom of sovereignty. It was the genius of their idea that our citizens would have two political capacities, one state and one federal, each protected from incursion by the other." The Chief Justice's solicitude for the Florida Legislature comes at the expense of the more fundamental solicitude we owe to the legislature's sovereign. Were the other Members of this Court as mindful as they generally are of our system of dual sovereignty, they would affirm the judgment of the Florida Supreme Court.

II

I agree with Justice Stevens that petitioners have not presented a substantial equal protection claim. Ideally, perfection would be the appropriate standard for judging the recount. But we live in an imperfect world, one in which thousands of votes have not been counted. I cannot agree that the recount adopted by the Florida court, flawed as it may be, would yield a result any less fair or precise than the certification that preceded that recount.

Even if there were an equal protection violation, I would agree with Justice Stevens, Justice Souter, and Justice Breyer that the Court's concern about the December 12 date is misplaced. Time is short in part because of the Court's entry of a stay on December 9, several hours after an able circuit judge in Leon County had begun to superintend the recount process. More fundamentally, the Court's reluctance to let the recount go forward—despite its suggestion that "the search for intent can be confined by specific rules designed to ensure uniform treatment"—ultimately turns on its own judgment about the practical realities of implementing a recount, not the judgment of those much closer to the process.

Equally important, as Justice Breyer explains (dissenting opinion), the December 12 date for bringing Florida's electoral votes into 3 U.S.C. § 5's safe harbor lacks the significance the Court assigns it. Were that date to pass, Florida would still be entitled to deliver electoral votes Congress must count unless both Houses find that the votes "had not been...regularly given." The statute identifies other significant dates. But none of these dates has ultimate significance in light of Congress' detailed provisions for determining, on "the sixth day of January," the validity of electoral votes.

The Court assumes that time will not permit "orderly judicial review of any disputed matters that might arise." But no one has doubted the good faith and diligence with which Florida election officials, attorneys for all sides of this controversy, and the courts of law have performed their duties. Notably, the Florida Supreme Court has produced two substantial opinions within 29 hours of oral argument. In sum, the Court's conclusion that a constitutionally adequate recount is impractical is a prophecy the Court's own judgment will not allow to be tested. Such an untested prophecy should not decide the Presidency of the United States.

I dissent.

⑨ "Today's Decision Is Alarming" ⑤ *Gonzales v. Carhart*

R uth Bader Ginsburg's approach to abortion rights has sometimes seemed a little complicated. When her name was floated for a U.S. Supreme Court position during President Bill Clinton's first term, Clinton initially dismissed the idea: "The women are against her," he responded—somewhat astonishingly, given all that Ginsburg had accomplished for women's rights in her work as a lawyer with the ACLU in the 1970s.[1] But Ginsburg had made some statements about *Roe v. Wade*, 410 U.S. 113 (1973), that threw her support for that decision in doubt, causing feminists to be unsure whether they could count on her to uphold it as a justice on the Court.

Roe: An Unstable Limb?

In a 1993 Madison lecture on constitutional law at New York University (NYU) School of Law, Ginsburg said, "Doctrinal limbs too swiftly shaped, experience teaches, may prove unstable. The most prominent example in recent decades is *Roe v. Wade*."

In *Roe v. Wade*, 410 U.S. 113 (1973), the Supreme Court decided that the due process clause of the U.S. Constitution's Fourteenth Amendment contains a "right to privacy." This right protects a pregnant woman's right to choose an abortion to an extent balanced against the government's interests in protecting women's health and prenatal life—interests that become stronger as a pregnancy proceeds. The *Roe* decision divided pregnancy into three consecutive trimesters, over the course of which increasing governmental regulation of the right to choose abortion was permitted.

Instead of just striking down the Texas criminal abortion law at issue in the case as excessive and draconian, Ginsburg explained, the *Roe* Court designed "a set of rules that displaced virtually every state law then in force," provoking a backlash that had already caused the Court to take a step back from the *Roe* scheme in *Planned Parenthood v. Casey*, 505 U.S. 833 (1992). "The *Roe* decision," Ginsburg said, "might have been less of a storm center had it both homed in more precisely on the women's equality dimension of the issue and, correspondingly, attempted nothing more bold at that time than the mode of decision-making the Court employed in the 1970s gender classification cases."[2]

Ginsburg went on to describe the case of *Struck v. Secretary of Defense*, which the Court had agreed to hear, 409 U.S. 947, but which then became moot when the policy at issue in the case was changed, 409 U.S. 1071 (1972). She thought the *Struck* case was a missed opportunity to place reproductive rights on a firmer foundation.

Privacy ... or Equal Protection?

In her work with the ACLU in the 1970s, Ginsburg had briefed the *Struck* case, which would have been heard in the same Supreme Court term as *Roe v. Wade*. U.S. Air Force Captain Susan Struck, a Catholic, sought relief from the Air Force policy that required a pregnant woman either to have an abortion or to quit the Air Force. The woman wanted both to keep her baby and to remain in the service. Ginsburg argued that since men in the Air Force were not barred from having children, the policy requiring a woman to choose between motherhood and service violated equal protection.

In keeping with the cases Ginsburg preferred, Struck's case presented circumstances that might evoke sympathy even from a justice not otherwise inclined to expand women's rights. The facts of the case also helpfully kept the focus on equality between men and women in reproductive choice rather than on abortion itself.[3] Ginsburg briefed the case, but it was dismissed as moot after the Air Force changed the policy. Instead, *Roe v. Wade* was decided that term. That decision based women's abortion rights on contraception case law that had created a zone of marital privacy constitutionally free from state interference, rather than on equal protection of the laws—an explicit guarantee of the U.S. Constitution—as Ginsburg thought wiser.

In her 1993 lecture at NYU, Ginsburg explained that the backdrop for the Court's rulings expanding women's rights in areas other than abortion in the 1970s and beyond was an expansion in women's employment and a change in culture set in motion by the civil rights movement. The Court, as Ginsburg characterized it, "opened a dialogue with the political branches of government ... [instructing] Congress and state legislatures: rethink ancient positions on these questions.... The ball, one might say, was tossed by the Justices back into the legislators' court, where the political forces of the day could operate."

In contrast, she said, "the *Roe* decision left virtually no state with laws fully conforming to the Court's delineation of abortion regulation still permissible. Around that extraordinary decision, a well-organized and vocal right-to-life movement rallied and succeeded, for a considerable time, in turning the legislative tide in the opposite direction.... *Roe* halted a political process that was moving in a reform direction and thereby, I believe, prolonged divisiveness and deferred stable settlement of the issue."[4]

Despite some women's wariness of Ginsburg in light of these remarks, in the Senate confirmation hearing following her 1993 nomination to the U.S. Supreme Court, Ginsburg succeeded in laying to rest any concerns from the senators about her support for *Roe v. Wade*. Questioned by Senator Joe Biden about an inconsistency between the boldness she had showed as a lawyer for the ACLU arguing for women's rights and her criticism of the Court for moving too far ahead of public opinion in *Roe v. Wade*, Ginsburg responded, "I saw my role in those days as an advocate."[5] She was confirmed by a vote of 96–3.

Polarized Politics and Ginsburg's Dissent

History seems to have proved Ginsburg correct in her assessment of the effect of *Roe v. Wade*. In the years that have followed, the debate over abortion has grown ever more polarized. *Roe v. Wade* helped equate feminism with abortion rights in the public mind and contributed to a backlash against the Equal Rights Amendment, which stalled in state legislatures after having made rapid progress in the early 1970s; Phyllis Schlafly, antifeminist activist, warned starting in 1974 that the "E.R.A. means abortion."[6] By the mid-1990s, even the original Jane Roe plaintiff in *Roe v. Wade*, Norma McCorvey, had been baptized as a born-again Christian by the director of Operation Rescue and had become an antiabortion activist.[7]

A decade later, the legislation at issue in *Gonzales v. Carhart*, the Partial-Birth Abortion Ban Act of 2003, reflected the ways that opposition to *Roe v. Wade* had helped to politically mobilize and organize conservatives and evangelical Christians, among others. With the Partial-Birth Abortion Ban Act, Congress enacted a national ban on the procedure known as "intact dilation and evacuation" (D&E), performed after the first trimester, without an exception for women's health.

Physicians who performed abortions and advocacy groups such as Planned Parenthood challenged the law as unconstitutional on its face, as written. The lower courts that had considered the ban found it was unconstitutional because medical authorities identified the banned procedure as the safest for some women in some circumstances.

Writing for the majority, Justice Anthony Kennedy reasoned that the ban did not, as a facial matter, present a substantial obstacle to women's access to abortion because the law, as the Court interpreted it, continued to permit abortions in which fetuses were not intact when extracted. The opinion stated that in *Planned Parenthood v. Casey*, the Court had recognized that "the government may use its voice and its regulatory authority to show profound respect for the life within the woman." The opinion also suggested that the law was intended to protect women from depression and guilt following an abortion, as "respect for human life finds an ultimate expression in the bond of love the mother has for her child." The opinion stated that the law could be challenged as applied, in a particular case in which the ban endangered a woman's health or life.

Ginsburg's passion on behalf of the decision-making autonomy, health, and safety of women struggling with real-life difficulties in what could be emergency situations is evident in her dissent from this ruling. She argued that the Court was ignoring precedent as well as the threat to women's health posed by permitting the Partial-Birth Abortion Ban Act to be challenged only as applied in a particular situation. She made the unusual choice of reading her dissent publicly, from the bench, at the time the decision was handed down.

ALBERTO R. GONZALES, ATTORNEY GENERAL, PETITIONER V. LEROY CARHART ET AL.

ON WRIT OF CERTIORARI TO THE UNITED STATES COURT OF APPEALS FOR THE EIGHTH CIRCUIT

ALBERTO R. GONZALES, ATTORNEY GENERAL, PETITIONER V. PLANNED PARENTHOOD FEDERATION OF AMERICA, INC., ET AL.

ON WRIT OF CERTIORARI TO THE UNITED STATES COURT OF APPEALS FOR THE NINTH CIRCUIT

550 U.S. 124 (April 18, 2007)

Dissent Announcement

Ruth Bader Ginsburg: Four members of this Court, Justices Stevens, Souter, Breyer, and I, strongly dissent from today's opinion.

Fifteen years ago in *Planned Parenthood of Southeastern Pennsylvania v. Casey*, the Court declared that liberty finds no refuge in the jurisprudence of doubt.

There was, the Court said, an "imperative" need to dispel doubt as to the meaning and reach of the Court's 7-to-2 judgment nearly two decades earlier in *Roe v. Wade*.

One of the clarifications *Casey* provided concerned the states' unconditional obligation to safeguard a woman's health. At all stages of pregnancy, the court reconfirmed, State regulation of abortion procedures must protect the health of the woman.

In reaffirming *Roe*, the *Casey* Court described the centrality of the decision whether to bear a child to a woman's dignity and autonomy, her destiny, her conception of her place in society.

Challenges to undo restriction on abortion procedures, the Court comprehended in *Casey*, do not seek to vindicate some vague or generalized notion of privacy. Rather, they home in on a woman's autonomy to decide for herself her life's course and thus to enjoy equal citizenship stature.

In keeping with this understanding of the right to reproductive choice, we have consistently required that laws regulating abortion, at any stage of pregnancy and in all cases, safeguard not only a woman's existence, her life, but her health as well.

Faithful to precedent unbroken from 1973 until today, the court held seven years ago in *Stenberg v. Carhart* that a state statute banning the very procedure at issue today—intact D&E—was unconstitutional in part because it lacked the health exception.

If substantial medical authority maintains that banning a particular abortion procedure could endanger women's health, we held, a health exception cannot be omitted by the legislators.

Despite that unambiguous ruling, Congress passed the Partial-Birth Abortion Ban Act without an exception for women's health, a ban that would operate nationwide.

After lengthy trials and thorough review of volumes of medical evidence, each of the District Courts to consider the statute found that it was unconstitutional for the same reason significant medical authority identified intact D&E as the safest procedure for some women.

In an alarming decision, the Court today reverses the judgments of other federal courts, decisions unanimously and uniformly made.

Today's decision refuses to take *Casey* and *Stenberg* seriously.

The Court's opinion tolerates, indeed applauds, federal intervention to ban nationwide a procedure found necessary and proper in certain cases by the American College of Obstetricians and Gynecologists.

For the first time since *Roe*, the Court blesses a prohibition with no exception protecting a woman's health.

The court asserts that its ruling furthers the government's interest in promoting fetus life.

But the Act scarcely furthers that interest, for it targets only a method of abortion. The woman may abort the fetus so long as her doctor uses another method, one her doctor judges less safe for her.

The Court further pretends that its decision protects women.

Women might come to regret that physician counseled choice of an intact D&E and suffer from severe depression and loss of esteem, the Court worries.

Notably, the solution the Court approves is not to require doctors to inform women adequately of the different procedures they might choose and the risks each entails.

Instead the Court shields the woman by denying her any choice in the matter, and this way of protecting women recalls ancient notions about women's place in society and under the Constitution—ideas that have long since been discredited.

If there is anything at all redemptive about today's opinion, it is that the Court is not willing to foreclose entirely a challenge to the constitutionality of the act.

But the as-applied challenges in discrete cases that the court would allow put women's health in danger and place doctors in an untenable position.

Even if courts were able slowly to carve out health exceptions for discrete and well defined instances through hard-fought, protracted, piece-meal litigation, women whose circumstances have not been anticipated by prior litigation could well remain unprotected.

In treating those women, physicians would risk criminal prosecution, conviction, and imprisonment if they exercise their best judgment as to the safest medical procedure for their patients.

The Court is thus gravely mistaken to conclude that narrow, as-applied challenges are the proper manner to protect the health of the woman.

As the Court wrote in *Casey*, overruling *Roe*'s central holding would not only reach an unjustifiable result under principles of stare decisis [the doctrine of following rules and principles set out in earlier judicial decisions unless contrary to justice], it would seriously weaken the Court's capacity to exercise the judicial power and to function as the Supreme Court of a nation dedicated to the rule of law.

Although today's opinion did not go so far as to discard *Roe* or *Casey*, the Court, differently composed than it was when we last considered a restrictive abortion regulation, is hardly faithful to *Casey*'s invocation of the rule of law and the principles of stare decisis.

In candor, the Partial-Birth Abortion Ban Act and the Court's defense of it cannot be understood as anything other than an effort to chip away at a right declared again and again by this Court and with increasing comprehension of its centrality to women's life.

A decision of the character the Court makes today should not have staying power.

DISSENT

Many citations and footnotes have been omitted, as well as some punctuation (including brackets and internal quotation marks).

Justice Ginsburg, with whom Justice Stevens, Justice Souter, and Justice Breyer join, dissenting.

In *Planned Parenthood of Southeastern Pa. v. Casey*, 505 U.S. 833, 844 (1992), the Court declared that "liberty finds no refuge in a jurisprudence of doubt." There was, the Court said, an "imperative" need to dispel doubt as to "the meaning and reach" of the Court's 7-to-2 judgment, rendered nearly two decades earlier in *Roe v. Wade*, 410 U.S. 113 (1973). Responsive to that need, the Court endeavored to provide secure guidance to "state and federal courts as well as legislatures throughout the Union," by defining "the rights of the woman and the legitimate authority of the State respecting the termination of pregnancies by abortion procedures."

Taking care to speak plainly, the *Casey* Court restated and reaffirmed *Roe*'s essential holding. First, the Court addressed the type of abortion regulation permissible prior to fetal viability. It recognized "the right of the woman to choose to have an abortion before viability and to obtain it without undue interference from the State." Second, the Court acknowledged "the State's power to restrict abortions after fetal viability, if the law contains exceptions for pregnancies which endanger the woman's life or health." Third, the Court confirmed that "the State has legitimate interests from the outset of the pregnancy in protecting the health of the woman and the life of the fetus that may become a child."

In reaffirming Roe, the *Casey* Court described the centrality of "the decision whether to bear...a child" to a woman's "dignity and autonomy," her "personhood" and "destiny," her "conception of...her place in society." Of signal importance here, the *Casey* Court stated with unmistakable clarity that state regulation of access to abortion procedures, even after viability, must protect "the health of the woman."

Seven years ago, in *Stenberg v. Carhart*, 530 U.S. 914 (2000), the Court invalidated a Nebraska statute criminalizing the performance of a medical procedure that, in the political arena, has been dubbed "partial-birth abortion."* With fidelity to the *Roe-Casey* line of precedent, the Court held the Nebraska statute unconstitutional in part because it lacked the requisite protection for the preservation of a woman's health.

Today's decision is alarming. It refuses to take *Casey* and *Stenberg* seriously. It tolerates, indeed applauds, federal intervention to ban nationwide a procedure found necessary and proper in certain cases by the American College of Obstetricians and Gynecologists (ACOG). It blurs the line, firmly drawn in *Casey*, between previability and postviability abortions. And, for the first time since *Roe*, the Court blesses a prohibition with no exception safeguarding a woman's health.

I dissent from the Court's disposition. Retreating from prior rulings that abortion restrictions cannot be imposed absent an exception safeguarding a woman's health, the Court upholds an Act that surely would not survive under the close scrutiny that previously attended state-decreed limitations on a woman's reproductive choices.

I
A

As *Casey* comprehended, at stake in cases challenging abortion restrictions is a woman's "control over her [own] destiny."† "There was a time, not so long ago," when women were "regarded as the center of home and family life, with attendant special responsibilities that precluded full and independent legal status under the Constitution." Those views, this Court made clear in *Casey*, "are no longer consistent with our understanding of the family, the individual, or the Constitution." Women, it is now acknowledged, have the talent, capacity, and right "to participate equally in the economic and social life of the Nation." Their ability to realize their full potential, the Court recognized, is intimately connected to "their ability to control their reproductive lives." Thus, legal challenges to undue restrictions on abortion

---

* The term "partial-birth abortion" is neither recognized in the medical literature nor used by physicians who perform second-trimester abortions. The medical community refers to the procedure as either dilation & extraction (D&X) or intact dilation and evacuation (intact D&E).

† *Planned Parenthood of Southeastern Pa. v. Casey*, 505 U.S. 833, 851–852 (1992), described more precisely than did *Roe v. Wade*, 410 U.S. 113 (1973), the impact of abortion restrictions on women's liberty. *Roe*'s focus was in considerable measure on "vindicating the right of the physician to administer medical treatment according to his professional judgment."

procedures do not seek to vindicate some generalized notion of privacy; rather, they center on a woman's autonomy to determine her life's course, and thus to enjoy equal citizenship stature.

In keeping with this comprehension of the right to reproductive choice, the Court has consistently required that laws regulating abortion, at any stage of pregnancy and in all cases, safeguard a woman's health. See, e.g., *Ayotte*, 546 U.S., at 327–328 ("Our precedents hold...that a State may not restrict access to abortions that are necessary, in appropriate medical judgment, for preservation of the life or health of the [woman]"; *Stenberg*, 530 U.S., at 930 ("Since the law requires a health exception in order to validate even a post-viability abortion regulation, it at a minimum requires the same in respect to previability regulation."). See also *Thornburgh v. American College of Obstetricians and Gynecologists*, 476 U.S. 747, 768–769 (1986) (invalidating a post-viability abortion regulation for "failure to require that [a pregnant woman's] health be the physician's paramount consideration").

We have thus ruled that a State must avoid subjecting women to health risks not only where the pregnancy itself creates danger, but also where state regulation forces women to resort to less safe methods of abortion. See *Planned Parenthood of Central Mo. v. Danforth*, 428 U.S. 52, 79 (1976) (holding unconstitutional a ban on a method of abortion that "forced a woman...to terminate her pregnancy by methods more dangerous to her health"). See also *Stenberg*, 530 U.S., at 931 ("[Our cases] make clear that a risk to...women's health is the same whether it happens to arise from regulating a particular method of abortion, or from barring abortion entirely."). Indeed, we have applied the rule that abortion regulation must safeguard a woman's health to the particular procedure at issue here—intact dilation and evacuation (D&E).*

---

* Dilation and evacuation (D&E) is the most frequently used abortion procedure during the second trimester of pregnancy; intact D&E is a variant of the D&E procedure. Second-trimester abortions (i.e., midpregnancy, previability abortions) are, however, relatively uncommon. Between 85 and 90 percent of all abortions performed in the United States take place during the first three months of pregnancy.

Adolescents and indigent women, research suggests, are more likely than other women to have difficulty obtaining an abortion during the first trimester of pregnancy. Minors may be unaware they are pregnant until relatively late in pregnancy, while poor women's financial constraints are an obstacle to timely receipt of services. Severe fetal anomalies and health problems confronting the pregnant woman are also causes of second-trimester abortions; many such conditions cannot be diagnosed or do not develop until the second trimester.

In *Stenberg*, we expressly held that a statute banning intact D&E was unconstitutional in part because it lacked a health exception. We noted that there existed a "division of medical opinion" about the relative safety of intact D&E, but we made clear that as long as "substantial medical authority supports the proposition that banning a particular abortion procedure could endanger women's health," a health exception is required. We explained:

> "The word 'necessary' in *Casey*'s phrase 'necessary, in appropriate medical judgment, for the preservation of the life or health of the [pregnant woman],' cannot refer to an absolute necessity or to absolute proof. Medical treatments and procedures are often considered appropriate (or inappropriate) in light of estimated comparative health risks (and health benefits) in particular cases. Neither can that phrase require unanimity of medical opinion. Doctors often differ in their estimation of comparative health risks and appropriate treatment. And *Casey*'s words 'appropriate medical judgment' must embody the judicial need to tolerate responsible differences of medical opinion...."

Thus, we reasoned, division in medical opinion "at most means uncertainty, a factor that signals the presence of risk, not its absence." "A statute that altogether forbids [intact D&E]...consequently must contain a health exception."

B

In 2003, a few years after our ruling in *Stenberg*, Congress passed the Partial-Birth Abortion Ban Act—without an exception for women's health.* The congressional findings on which the Partial-Birth Abortion Ban Act rests do not withstand inspection, as the lower courts have determined and this Court is obliged to concede.

---

* The Act's sponsors left no doubt that their intention was to nullify our ruling in *Stenberg*, 530 U.S. 914. See, e.g., 149 Cong. Rec. 5731 (2003) (statement of Sen. Santorum) ("Why are we here? We are here because the Supreme Court defended the indefensible.... We have responded to the Supreme Court."). See also 148 Cong. Rec. 14273 (2002) (statement of Rep. Linder) (rejecting proposition that Congress has "no right to legislate a ban on this horrible practice because the Supreme Court says [it] cannot").

Many of the Act's recitations are incorrect. For example, Congress determined that no medical schools provide instruction on intact D&E. But in fact, numerous leading medical schools teach the procedure. See…Brief for ACOG [American College of Obstetricians and Gynecologists] as Amicus Curiae 18 ("Among the schools that now teach the intact variant are Columbia, Cornell, Yale, New York University, Northwestern, University of Pittsburgh, University of Pennsylvania, University of Rochester, and University of Chicago.").

More important, Congress claimed there was a medical consensus that the banned procedure is never necessary. But the evidence "very clearly demonstrated the opposite."

Similarly, Congress found that "there is no credible medical evidence that partial-birth abortions are safe or are safer than other abortion procedures." But the congressional record includes letters from numerous individual physicians stating that pregnant women's health would be jeopardized under the Act, as well as statements from nine professional associations, including ACOG, the American Public Health Association, and the California Medical Association, attesting that intact D&E carries meaningful safety advantages over other methods. No comparable medical groups supported the ban. In fact, "all of the government's own witnesses disagreed with many of the specific congressional findings."

C

In contrast to Congress, the District Courts made findings after full trials at which all parties had the opportunity to present their best evidence. The courts had the benefit of "much more extensive medical and scientific evidence…concerning the safety and necessity of intact D&Es."

During the District Court trials, "numerous" "extraordinarily accomplished" and "very experienced" medical experts explained that, in certain circumstances and for certain women, intact D&E is safer than alternative procedures and necessary to protect women's health.

According to the expert testimony plaintiffs introduced, the safety advantages of intact D&E are marked for women with certain medical conditions, for example, uterine scarring, bleeding disorders, heart disease, or compromised immune systems. Further, plaintiffs' experts testified that intact D&E is significantly safer for women with certain pregnancy-related conditions, such as placenta previa and accreta, and for women carrying fetuses with certain abnormalities, such as severe hydrocephalus.

Intact D&E, plaintiffs' experts explained, provides safety benefits over D&E by dismemberment for several reasons: First, intact D&E minimizes the number of times a physician must insert instruments through the cervix and into the uterus, and thereby reduces the risk of trauma to, and perforation of, the cervix and uterus—the most serious complication associated with nonintact D&E. Second, removing the fetus intact, instead of dismembering it in utero, decreases the likelihood that fetal tissue will be retained in the uterus, a condition that can cause infection, hemorrhage, and infertility. Third, intact D&E diminishes the chances of exposing the patient's tissues to sharp bony fragments sometimes resulting from dismemberment of the fetus. Fourth, intact D&E takes less operating time than D&E by dismemberment, and thus may reduce bleeding, the risk of infection, and complications relating to anesthesia.

Based on thoroughgoing review of the trial evidence and the congressional record, each of the District Courts to consider the issue rejected Congress' findings as unreasonable and not supported by the evidence. The trial courts concluded, in contrast to Congress' findings, that "significant medical authority supports the proposition that in some circumstances, [intact D&E] is the safest procedure."*

The District Courts' findings merit this Court's respect. Today's opinion supplies no reason to reject those findings. Nevertheless, despite the District Courts' appraisal of the weight of the evidence, and in undisguised conflict with *Stenberg*, the Court asserts that the Partial-Birth Abortion Ban Act can survive "when...medical uncertainty persists." This assertion is bewildering. Not only does it defy the Court's longstanding precedent affirming the necessity of a health exception, with no carve-out for circumstances of medical uncertainty; it gives short shrift to the records before us, carefully canvassed by the District Courts. Those records indicate that "the majority of highly-qualified experts on the subject believe intact D&E to be the safest, most appropriate procedure under certain circumstances."

---

* Even the District Court for the Southern District of New York, which was more skeptical of the health benefits of intact D&E, recognized: "The Government's own experts disagreed with almost all of Congress's factual findings"; a "significant body of medical opinion" holds that intact D&E has safety advantages over nonintact D&E; "professional medical associations have also expressed their view that [intact D&E] may be the safest procedure for some women"; and "the evidence indicates that the same disagreement among experts found by the Supreme Court in *Stenberg* existed throughout the time that Congress was considering the legislation, despite Congress's findings to the contrary." *National Abortion Federation*, 330 F. Supp. 2d, at 480–482.

The Court acknowledges some of this evidence, but insists that, because some witnesses disagreed with the ACOG and other experts' assessment of risk, the Act can stand. In this insistence, the Court brushes under the rug the District Courts' well-supported findings that the physicians who testified that intact D&E is never necessary to preserve the health of a woman had slim authority for their opinions. They had no training for, or personal experience with, the intact D&E procedure, and many performed abortions only on rare occasions. Even indulging the assumption that the Government witnesses were equally qualified to evaluate the relative risks of abortion procedures, their testimony could not erase the "significant medical authority supporting the proposition that in some circumstances, [intact D&E] would be the safest procedure."*

II

A

The Court offers flimsy and transparent justifications for upholding a nationwide ban on intact D&E [without] any exception to safeguard a woman's health. Today's ruling, the Court declares, advances "a premise central to [*Casey*'s] conclusion"—i.e., the Government's "legitimate and substantial interest in preserving and promoting fetal life." But the Act scarcely furthers that interest: The law saves not a single fetus from destruction, for it targets only a method of performing abortion. And surely the statute was not designed to protect the lives or health of pregnant women. In short, the Court upholds a law that, while doing nothing to "preserve...fetal life," bars a woman from choosing intact D&E although her doctor "reasonably believes [that procedure] will best protect [her]."

As another reason for upholding the ban, the Court emphasizes that the Act does not proscribe the nonintact D&E procedure. But why not, one might ask. Nonintact D&E could equally be characterized as "brutal,"

---

* The majority contends that "if the intact D&E procedure is truly necessary in some circumstances, it appears likely an injection that kills the fetus is an alternative under the Act that allows the doctor to perform the procedure." But a "significant body of medical opinion believes that inducing fetal death by injection is almost always inappropriate to the preservation of the health of women undergoing abortion because it poses tangible risk and provides no benefit to the woman." The Court also identifies medical induction of labor as an alternative. That procedure, however, requires a hospital stay, rendering it inaccessible to patients who lack financial resources, and it too is considered less safe for many women, and impermissible for others.

involving as it does "tearing [a fetus] apart" and "ripping off" its limbs. "The notion that either of these two equally gruesome procedures...is more akin to infanticide than the other, or that the State furthers any legitimate interest by banning one but not the other, is simply irrational."

Delivery of an intact, albeit nonviable, fetus warrants special condemnation, the Court maintains, because a fetus that is not dismembered resembles an infant. But so, too, does a fetus delivered intact after it is terminated by injection a day or two before the surgical evacuation, or a fetus delivered through medical induction or cesarean. Yet, the availability of those procedures—along with D&E by dismemberment—the Court says, saves the ban on intact D&E from a declaration of unconstitutionality. Never mind that the procedures deemed acceptable might put a woman's health at greater risk.

Ultimately, the Court admits that "moral concerns" are at work, concerns that could yield prohibitions on any abortion. Notably, the concerns expressed are untethered to any ground genuinely serving the Government's interest in preserving life. By allowing such concerns to carry the day and case, overriding fundamental rights, the Court dishonors our precedent. See, e.g., *Casey*, 505 U.S., at 850 ("Some of us as individuals find abortion offensive to our most basic principles of morality, but that cannot control our decision. Our obligation is to define the liberty of all, not to mandate our own moral code."); *Lawrence v. Texas*, 539 U.S. 558, 571 (2003) (Though "for many persons [objections to homosexual conduct] are not trivial concerns but profound and deep convictions accepted as ethical and moral principles," the power of the State may not be used "to enforce these views on the whole society through operation of the criminal law." (citing *Casey*, 505 U.S., at 850)).

Revealing in this regard, the Court invokes an antiabortion shibboleth for which it concededly has no reliable evidence: Women who have abortions come to regret their choices, and consequently suffer from "severe depression and loss of esteem."* Because of women's fragile emotional state and because of the "bond of love the mother has for her child," the Court worries, doctors may withhold information about the nature of the intact

---

* The Court is surely correct that, for most women, abortion is a painfully difficult decision. But "neither the weight of the scientific evidence to date nor the observable reality of 33 years of legal abortion in the United States comports with the idea that having an abortion is any more dangerous to a woman's long-term mental health than delivering and parenting a child that she did not intend to have...."

D&E procedure.* The solution the Court approves, then, is not to require doctors to inform women, accurately and adequately, of the different procedures and their attendant risks. Instead, the Court deprives women of the right to make an autonomous choice, even at the expense of their safety.†

This way of thinking reflects ancient notions about women's place in the family and under the Constitution—ideas that have long since been discredited.

Though today's majority may regard women's feelings on the matter as "self-evident," this Court has repeatedly confirmed that "the destiny of the woman must be shaped... on her own conception of her spiritual imperatives and her place in society." *Casey*, 505 U.S., at 852.

B

In cases on a "woman's liberty to determine whether to [continue] her pregnancy," this Court has identified viability as a critical consideration. "There is no line [more workable] than viability," the Court explained in *Casey*, for viability is "the time at which there is a realistic possibility of maintaining and nourishing a life outside the womb, so that the independent existence of the second life can in reason and all fairness be the object of state protection that now overrides the rights of the woman.... In some broad sense it might be said that a woman who fails to act before viability has consented to the State's intervention on behalf of the developing child."

Today, the Court blurs that line, maintaining that "the Act [legitimately] applies both previability and postviability because... a fetus is a living organism while within the womb, whether or not it is viable outside the womb." Instead of drawing the line at viability, the Court refers to Congress' purpose to differentiate "abortion and infanticide" based not on whether a fetus can survive outside the womb, but on where a fetus is anatomically located when a particular medical procedure is performed.

---

* Notwithstanding the "bond of love" women often have with their children, not all pregnancies, this Court has recognized, are wanted, or even the product of consensual activity. See *Casey*, 505 U.S., at 891 ("On an average day in the United States, nearly 11,000 women are severely assaulted by their male partners. Many of these incidents involve sexual assault.").

† Eliminating or reducing women's reproductive choices is manifestly not a means of protecting them. When safe abortion procedures cease to be an option, many women seek other means to end unwanted or coerced pregnancies.

One wonders how long a line that saves no fetus from destruction will hold in face of the Court's "moral concerns." The Court's hostility to the right *Roe* and *Casey* secured is not concealed. Throughout, the opinion refers to obstetrician-gynecologists and surgeons who perform abortions not by the titles of their medical specialties, but by the pejorative label "abortion doctor." A fetus is described as an "unborn child," and as a "baby"; second-trimester, previability abortions are referred to as "late-term"; and the reasoned medical judgments of highly trained doctors are dismissed as "preferences" motivated by "mere convenience." Instead of the heightened scrutiny we have previously applied, the Court determines that a "rational" ground is enough to uphold the Act. And, most troubling, *Casey*'s principles, confirming the continuing vitality of "the essential holding of *Roe*," are merely "assumed" for the moment, rather than "retained" or "reaffirmed."

III
A

The Court further confuses our jurisprudence when it declares that "facial attacks" are not permissible in "these circumstances," i.e., where medical uncertainty exists. This holding is perplexing given that, in materially identical circumstances we held that a statute lacking a health exception was unconstitutional on its face. *Stenberg*, 530 U.S., at 930 (in facial challenge, law held unconstitutional because "significant body of medical opinion believes [the] procedure may bring with it greater safety for some patients").

Without attempting to distinguish *Stenberg* and earlier decisions, the majority asserts that the Act survives review because respondents have not shown that the ban on intact D&E would be unconstitutional "in a large fraction of relevant cases." But *Casey* makes clear that, in determining whether any restriction poses an undue burden on a "large fraction" of women, the relevant class is not "all women," nor "all pregnant women," nor even all women "seeking abortions." Rather, a provision restricting access to abortion, "must be judged by reference to those [women] for whom it is an actual rather than an irrelevant restriction." Thus the absence of a health exception burdens all women for whom it is relevant—women who, in the judgment of their doctors, require an intact D&E because other procedures would place their health at risk.* It makes no sense to conclude that this facial challenge fails because respondents have not shown that a health exception is necessary for a large fraction of second-trimester abortions, including those for which a health exception is unnecessary: The very purpose of a health exception is to protect women in exceptional cases.

B

If there is anything at all redemptive to be said of today's opinion, it is that the Court is not willing to foreclose entirely a constitutional challenge to the Act. "The Act is open," the Court states, "to a proper as-applied challenge in a discrete case." But the Court offers no clue on what a "proper" lawsuit might look like. Nor does the Court explain why the injunctions ordered by the District Courts should not remain in place, trimmed only to exclude instances in which another procedure would safeguard a woman's health at least equally well. Surely the Court cannot mean that no suit may be brought until a woman's health is immediately jeopardized by the ban on intact D&E. A woman "suffering from medical complications" needs access to the medical procedure at once and cannot wait for the judicial process to unfold.

The Court appears, then, to contemplate another lawsuit by the initiators of the instant actions. In such a second round, the Court suggests, the challengers could succeed upon demonstrating that "in discrete and well-defined instances a particular condition has or is likely to occur in which the procedure prohibited by the Act must be used." One may anticipate that such a preenforcement challenge will be mounted swiftly, to ward off serious, sometimes irremediable harm, to women whose health would be endangered by the intact D&E prohibition.

The Court envisions that in an as-applied challenge, "the nature of the medical risk can be better quantified and balanced." But it should not escape notice that the record already includes hundreds and hundreds of pages of testimony identifying "discrete and well-defined instances" in which recourse to an intact D&E would better protect the health of women with particular conditions. Record evidence also documents that medical exigencies, unpredictable in advance, may indicate to a well-trained doctor that

---

* There is, in short, no fraction because the numerator and denominator are the same: The health exception reaches only those cases where a woman's health is at risk. Perhaps for this reason, in mandating safeguards for women's health, we have never before invoked the "large fraction" test.

intact D&E is the safest procedure. In light of this evidence, our unanimous decision just one year ago in *Ayotte* counsels against reversal. See 546 U.S., at 331 (remanding for reconsideration of the remedy for the absence of a health exception, suggesting that an injunction prohibiting unconstitutional applications might suffice).

The Court's allowance only of an "as-applied challenge in a discrete case" jeopardizes women's health and places doctors in an untenable position. Even if courts were able to carve out exceptions through piecemeal litigation for "discrete and well-defined instances," women whose circumstances have not been anticipated by prior litigation could well be left unprotected. In treating those women, physicians would risk criminal prosecution, conviction, and imprisonment if they exercise their best judgment as to the safest medical procedure for their patients. The Court is thus gravely mistaken to conclude that narrow as-applied challenges are "the proper manner to protect the health of the woman."

IV

As the Court wrote in *Casey*, "overruling *Roe*'s central holding would not only reach an unjustifiable result under principles of stare decisis, but would seriously weaken the Court's capacity to exercise the judicial power and to function as the Supreme Court of a Nation dedicated to the rule of law." "The very concept of the rule of law underlying our own Constitution requires such continuity over time that a respect for precedent is, by definition, indispensable."

Though today's opinion does not go so far as to discard *Roe* or *Casey*, the Court, differently composed than it was when we last considered a restrictive abortion regulation, is hardly faithful to our earlier invocations of "the rule of law" and the "principles of stare decisis." Congress imposed a ban despite our clear prior holdings that the State cannot proscribe an abortion procedure when its use is necessary to protect a woman's health. Although Congress' findings could not withstand the crucible of trial, the Court defers to the legislative override of our Constitution-based rulings. A decision so at odds with our jurisprudence should not have staying power.

In sum, the notion that the Partial-Birth Abortion Ban Act furthers any legitimate governmental interest is, quite simply, irrational. The Court's defense of the statute provides no saving explanation. In candor, the Act, and the Court's defense of it, cannot be understood as anything other than an effort to chip away at a right declared again and again by this Court—and with increasing comprehension of its centrality to women's lives. When "a statute burdens constitutional rights and all that can be said on its behalf is that it is the vehicle that legislators have chosen for expressing their hostility to those rights, the burden is undue." *Stenberg*, 530 U.S., at 952 (Ginsburg, J., concurring).

★ ★ ★

For the reasons stated, I dissent from the Court's disposition and would affirm the judgments before us for review.

⟩ "The Ball Lies in Congress's Court" ⟨ Ledbetter v. Goodyear Tire and Rubber Company

Lilly Ledbetter worked as a manager at a Goodyear Tire and Rubber plant in Alabama for nineteen years. Just before she was due to retire, she received an anonymous note containing salary information that showed she was being paid about $1,500 a month less than the lowest-paid man in the department with the same job.

Title VII's 180-Day Deadline

Under Title VII of the Civil Rights Act of 1964, it is an unlawful employment practice to discriminate against any individual with respect to compensation because of the person's sex. Crucially, however, as a first step toward getting a court to hear an employee's claims of wage discrimination and possibly award back pay, in Alabama an employee has to file a charge of employment discrimination with the Equal Employment Opportunity Commission (EEOC) within 180 days after the alleged unlawful employment practice occurred (in some states, this time limit is 300 days).

After Ledbetter retired, she filed a complaint of employment discrimination with the EEOC. The EEOC considered each pay period of uncorrected discrimination a new act of discrimination. Since Ledbetter had filed her complaint within the EEOC time limit of six months from her last paycheck, the EEOC ruled that she could sue Goodyear.

At the trial of Ledbetter's case, a picture emerged of widespread past discrimination against women at the plant where Ledbetter worked. Goodyear's position that Ledbetter was paid less because her performance was poor was undermined by evidence that the company had given her an award as a top performer. Ledbetter claimed that her performance was evaluated discriminatorily in the past during her earlier career at Goodyear because she was a woman and that as a result her more recent paychecks were smaller than they should have been.

Ledbetter was awarded back pay and punitive damages totaling $3.3 million. Goodyear appealed. The U.S. Court of Appeals for the Eleventh

Circuit reversed the trial court's award, holding that most of Ledbetter's claims could not be addressed at all because too much time had passed since the pay-setting decisions were made; the court also held that Ledbetter did not prove intentional discrimination in her last pay-setting period, six months before she filed her charge with the EEOC.

Wage Complaints and Timeliness

Ledbetter appealed this decision, and the U.S. Supreme Court agreed to hear her appeal to settle the question of how to determine whether claims of wage discrimination are timely under Title VII. U.S. Courts of Appeal for regions other than the Eleventh Circuit had agreed with the EEOC that if an employee's recent paychecks (within the previous six months) were undersized because of the cumulative effect of intentional wage discrimination that took place in the more distant past, the employee could still take the employer to court to try to get back pay and other relief. This interpretation of Title VII made it possible for employees to try to rectify wage discrimination even if, like Ledbetter, they were not certain that their paychecks had never measured up to those of others doing the same job until long after the employer made wage decisions that were intentionally discriminatory.[1]

At the U.S. Supreme Court, the majority rejected Ledbetter's claim that the paychecks were unlawful because they would have been larger if she had been evaluated in a nondiscriminatory way before the EEOC charging period. Writing the opinion for the majority, Justice Samuel Alito noted that Ledbetter did not claim that Goodyear decisionmakers acted with discriminatory intent when they issued her paychecks during the EEOC charging period or when they denied her a raise just before she retired; the cumulative effect of discriminatory evaluations before the six-month time limitation, he wrote, could not be considered. Alito suggested that the rule Justice Ginsburg argued for in her dissent would allow employees to wait for years after an adverse employment decision to sue their employers, even if the employee knew at the time of the decision that the employer was acting with discriminatory intent.

Justice Ginsburg responded that the majority ignored Ledbetter's uncertainty that she was being paid much less than men in the same job until just before she retired. Alito's concern about employees waiting a long time to sue employers for wage claims also ignored the familiar common law doctrines of estoppel and laches, which judges routinely use to prevent plaintiffs from suing defendants too long after an alleged wrong occurred. Ginsburg pointed out that the majority's narrow, crabbed interpretation of the time limitations in Title VII, a statute that Congress intended to be broadly remedial, invalidated the approach taken in pay cases by the EEOC itself and by a majority of the regional U.S. Courts of Appeal.

Ginsburg's vigorous dissent was the second that she took the unusual step of reading from the bench that term.[2] The dissent ended with an invitation to Congress to undo the damage the majority had done to wage discrimination law. Evidently, Justice Alito suppressed any impulse to roll his eyes as Justice Ginsburg spoke—although he gave in to that impulse several years later, in 2013, when Justice Ginsburg again vigorously dissented from the majority rulings in a pair of employment discrimination cases.[3]

With the ball in its court—where Justice Ginsburg put it—Congress then passed the Lilly Ledbetter Fair Pay Act of 2009, which superseded the majority's ruling and reinstituted the policy Justice Ginsburg's dissent advocated. It was the first bill President Barack Obama signed into law after he took office in 2009.

LILLY M. LEDBETTER, PETITIONER V. THE GOODYEAR TIRE & RUBBER COMPANY, INC.

ON WRIT OF CERTIORARI TO THE UNITED STATES COURT OF APPEALS FOR THE ELEVENTH CIRCUIT

550 U.S. 618 (May 29, 2007)

Dissent Announcement

Ruth Bader Ginsburg: As Justice Alito announced, four members of this Court, Justices Stevens, Souter, Breyer, and I, dissent from today's decision.

In our view, the Court does not comprehend or is indifferent to the insidious way in which women can be victims of pay discriminations.

Today's decision counsels, sue early on when it is uncertain whether discrimination accounts for the pay disparity you are beginning to experience.

Indeed, initially you may not know that men are receiving more for substantially similar work.

Of course, you are likely to lose such a less-than-fully baked case.

If you sue only when the pay disparity becomes steady and large enough to enable you to mount a winnable case, you will be cut off at the Court's threshold for suing too late. That situation cannot be what Congress intended when in Title VII it outlawed discrimination on the basis of race, color, religion, sex, or national origin in our nation's workplaces.

Lilly Ledbetter, the plaintiff in this case, was engaged as an Area Manager at a Goodyear Tire and Rubber plant in Alabama in 1979.

Her starting salary was in line with the salaries of men performing similar work, but over time her pay slipped in comparison to the pay of male employees with equal or less seniority.

By the end of 1997, Ledbetter was the only woman left working as an Area Manager, and the pay discrepancy between Ledbetter and her 15 male counterparts was stark.

Ledbetter's pay was 15% to 40% less than every other Area Manager.

Ledbetter complained to the Equal Employment Opportunity Commission in March 1998. She charged that in violation of Title VII, Goodyear paid her a discriminatorily low salary because of her sex.

The charge was eventually brought to court and tried to a jury.

The jury found it more likely than not that Goodyear paid Ledbetter an unequal salary because of her sex.

The court today nullifies that verdict, holding that Ledbetter's claim is time barred.

Title VII provides that a charge of discrimination shall be filed within 180 days after the alleged unlawful employment practice occurred.

Ledbetter charged and proved at trial that the paychecks she received within the 180 day filing period were substantially lower than the paychecks received by men doing the same work.

Further, she introduced substantial evidence showing that discrimination accounted for the pay differential—indeed that discrimination against women as supervisors was pervasive at Goodyear's plant.

That evidence was unavailing, the Court holds, because it was incumbent on Ledbetter to file charges of discrimination year by year, each time Goodyear failed to increase her salary commensurate with the salaries of her male peers.

Any annual pay decision not contested properly within 180 days, the Court affirmed, becomes grandfathered beyond the province of Title VII ever to repair.

Title VII was meant to govern real world employment practices, and that world is what the court ignores today.

Pay disparities often occur as they did in Ledbetter's case in small increments. Only over time is there strong cause to suspect that discrimination is at work.

Comparative pay information is not routinely communicated to employees; instead it is often hidden from the employees' view.

Small initial discrepancies, even if the employee knows they exist, may not be seen as grounds for a federal case.

An employee like Ledbetter trying to succeed in a male dominated workplace in a job filled only by men before she was hired, understandably may be anxious to avoid making waves.

Pay discrimination that recurs and swells in impact is significantly different from discrete adverse actions properly communicated and easy to identify as discriminatory.

Events in that category include firing, denial of a promotion, or refusal to hire.

In contrast to those unambiguous actions, until a pay disparity becomes apparent and sizeable, an employee is unlikely to comprehend her plight and therefore to complain about it.

Ledbetter's initial readiness to give her employer the benefit of the doubt does not preclude her from later seeking redress for the continuing payment to her of a salary depressed because of her sex.

Yet, as the Court reads Title VII, each and every pay decision Ledbetter did not promptly challenge wiped the slate clean.

Never mind the cumulative effect of a series of decisions that, together, set her pay well below that of every male Area Manager.

Knowingly carrying past pay discrimination forward must be treated as lawful.

Ledbetter may not be compensated under Title VII for the lower pay she was in fact receiving when she complained to the EEOC.

Notably, the same denial of relief would occur had Ledbetter encountered pay discrimination based on race, religion, age, national origin, or disability.

This is not the first time this Court has ordered a cramped interpretation of Title VII, incompatible with the statute's broad remedial purpose.

In 1991, Congress passed a Civil Rights Act that effectively overruled several of this Court's similarly restrictive decisions, including one on which the court relies today.

Today, the ball again lies in Congress's court. As in 1991, the legislature has cause to note and to correct this court's parsimonious reading of Title VII.

DISSENT

Footnotes and most citations have been omitted, as well as some punctuation (including brackets and internal quotation marks).

Justice Ginsburg, with whom Justice Stevens, Justice Souter, and Justice Breyer join, dissenting.

Lilly Ledbetter was a supervisor at Goodyear Tire and Rubber's plant in Gadsden, Alabama, from 1979 until her retirement in 1998. For most of those years, she worked as an area manager, a position largely occupied by men. Initially, Ledbetter's salary was in line with the salaries of men performing substantially similar work. Over time, however, her pay slipped in comparison to the pay of male area managers with equal or less seniority. By the end of 1997, Ledbetter was the only woman working as an area manager and the pay discrepancy between Ledbetter and her 15 male counterparts was stark: Ledbetter was paid $3,727 per month; the lowest paid male area manager received $4,286 per month, the highest paid, $5,236.

Ledbetter launched charges of discrimination before the Equal Employment Opportunity Commission (EEOC) in March 1998. Her formal administrative complaint specified that, in violation of Title VII, Goodyear paid her a discriminatorily low salary because of her sex. That charge was eventually tried to a jury, which found it "more likely than not that [Goodyear] paid [Ledbetter] an unequal salary because of her sex." In accord with the jury's liability determination, the District Court entered judgment for Ledbetter for backpay and damages, plus counsel fees and costs.

The Court of Appeals for the Eleventh Circuit reversed. Relying on Goodyear's system of annual merit-based raises, the court held that Ledbetter's claim, in relevant part, was time barred. Title VII provides that a charge of discrimination "shall be filed within [180] days after the alleged unlawful employment practice occurred." Ledbetter charged, and proved at trial, that within the 180-day period, her pay was substantially less than the pay of men doing the same work. Further, she introduced evidence sufficient to establish that discrimination against female managers at the Gadsden plant, not performance inadequacies on her part, accounted for the pay differential. That evidence was unavailing, the Eleventh Circuit held, and the Court today agrees, because it was incumbent on Ledbetter to file charges year-by-year, each time Goodyear failed to increase her salary commensurate with the salaries of male peers. Any annual pay decision not contested immediately (within 180 days), the Court affirms, becomes grandfathered, a fait accompli beyond the province of Title VII ever to repair.

The Court's insistence on immediate contest overlooks common characteristics of pay discrimination. Pay disparities often occur, as they did in Ledbetter's case, in small increments; cause to suspect that discrimination is at work develops only over time. Comparative pay information, moreover, is often hidden from the employee's view. Employers may keep under wraps the pay differentials maintained among supervisors, no less the reasons for those differentials. Small initial discrepancies may not be seen as meet for a federal case, particularly when the employee, trying to succeed in a nontraditional environment, is averse to making waves.

Pay disparities are thus significantly different from adverse actions "such as termination, failure to promote,...or refusal to hire," all involving fully communicated discrete acts, "easy to identify" as discriminatory. It is only when the disparity becomes apparent and sizable, e.g., through future raises calculated as a percentage of current salaries, that an employee in Ledbetter's situation is likely to comprehend her plight and, therefore, to complain. Her initial readiness to give her employer the benefit of the doubt should not preclude her from later challenging the then current and continuing payment of a wage depressed on account of her sex.

On questions of time under Title VII, we have identified as the critical inquiries: "What constitutes an 'unlawful employment practice' and when has that practice 'occurred'?" Our precedent suggests, and lower courts have overwhelmingly held, that the unlawful practice is the current payment of salaries infected by gender-based (or race-based) discrimination—a practice that occurs whenever a paycheck delivers less to a woman than to a similarly situated man.

I

Title VII proscribes as an "unlawful employment practice" discrimination "against any individual with respect to his compensation...because of such individual's race, color, religion, sex, or national origin." An individual seeking to challenge an employment practice under this proscription must file a charge with the EEOC within 180 days "after the alleged unlawful employment practice occurred."

Ledbetter's petition presents a question important to the sound application of Title VII: What activity qualifies as an unlawful employment practice in cases of discrimination with respect to compensation. One answer identifies the pay-setting decision, and that decision alone, as the unlawful practice. Under this view, each particular salary-setting decision is discrete from prior and subsequent decisions, and must be challenged within 180 days on pain of forfeiture. Another response counts both the pay-setting decision and the actual payment of a discriminatory wage as unlawful practices. Under this approach, each payment of a wage or salary infected by sex-based discrimination constitutes an unlawful employment practice; prior decisions, outside the 180-day charge-filing period, are not themselves actionable, but they are relevant in determining the lawfulness of conduct within the period. The Court adopts the first view, but the second is more faithful to precedent, more in tune with the realities of the workplace, and more respectful of Title VII's remedial purpose.

A

In *Bazemore* [*Bazemore v. Friday*, 478 U.S. 385 (1986)], we unanimously held that an employer, the North Carolina Agricultural Extension Service, committed an unlawful employment practice each time it paid black employees less than similarly situated white employees. Before 1965, the Extension Service was divided into two branches: a white branch and a "Negro branch." Employees in the "Negro branch" were paid less than their white counterparts. In response to the Civil Rights Act of 1964, which included Title VII, the State merged the two branches into a single organization, made adjustments to reduce the salary disparity, and began giving annual raises based on nondiscriminatory factors. Nonetheless, "some pre-existing salary disparities continued to linger on." We rejected the Court of Appeals' conclusion that the plaintiffs could not prevail because the lingering disparities were simply a continuing effect of a decision lawfully made prior to the effective date of Title VII. Rather, we reasoned, "each week's paycheck that delivers less to a black than to a similarly situated white is a wrong actionable under Title VII." Paychecks perpetuating past discrimination, we thus recognized, are actionable not simply because they are "related" to a decision made outside the charge-filing period, but because they discriminate anew each time they issue.

Subsequently, in *Morgan* [*National Railroad Passenger Corporation v. Morgan*, 536 U.S. 101 (2002)], we set apart, for purposes of Title VII's timely filing requirement, unlawful employment actions of two kinds: "discrete acts" that are "easy to identify" as discriminatory, and acts that recur and are cumulative in impact. "A discrete act such as termination, failure to promote, denial of transfer, or refusal to hire," we explained, " 'occurs' on the day that it 'happens.' A party, therefore, must file a charge within...180...days of the date of the act or lose the ability to recover for it." [See *Morgan*] at 113 ("Discrete discriminatory acts are not actionable if time barred, even when they are related to acts alleged in timely filed charges. Each discrete discriminatory act starts a new clock for filing charges alleging that act.").

"Different in kind from discrete acts," we made clear, are "claims... based on the cumulative effect of individual acts." The *Morgan* decision placed hostile work environment claims in that category. "Their very nature involves repeated conduct." "The unlawful employment practice" in hostile work environment claims, "cannot be said to occur on any particular day. It occurs over a series of days or perhaps years and, in direct contrast to discrete acts, a single act of harassment may not be actionable on its own." The persistence of the discriminatory conduct both indicates that management should have known of its existence and produces a cognizable harm. Because the very nature of the hostile work environment claim involves repeated conduct, "it does not matter, for purposes of the statute, that some of the component acts of the hostile work environment fall outside the statutory time period. Provided that an act contributing to the claim occurs within the filing period, the entire time period of the hostile environment may be considered by a court for the purposes of determining liability." Consequently, although the unlawful conduct began in the past, "a charge may be filed at a later date and still encompass the whole."

Pay disparities, of the kind Ledbetter experienced, have a closer kinship to hostile work environment claims than to charges of a single episode of discrimination. Ledbetter's claim, resembling Morgan's, rested not on one particular paycheck, but on "the cumulative effect of individual acts." She charged insidious discrimination building up slowly but steadily. Initially in line with the salaries of men performing substantially the same work, Ledbetter's salary fell 15 to 40 percent behind her male counterparts only after successive evaluations and percentage-based pay adjustments. Over time, she alleged and proved, the repetition of pay decisions undervaluing her work gave rise to the current discrimination of which she complained. Though component acts fell outside the charge-filing period, with each new paycheck, Goodyear contributed incrementally to the accumulating harm.

B

The realities of the workplace reveal why the discrimination with respect to compensation that Ledbetter suffered does not fit within the category of singular discrete acts "easy to identify." A worker knows immediately if she is denied a promotion or transfer, if she is fired or refused employment. And promotions, transfers, hirings, and firings are generally public events, known to co-workers. When an employer makes a decision of such open and definitive character, an employee can immediately seek out an explanation and evaluate it for pretext. Compensation disparities, in contrast, are often hidden from sight. It is not unusual, decisions in point illustrate, for management to decline to publish employee pay levels, or for employees to keep private their own salaries. Tellingly, as the record in this case bears out, Goodyear kept salaries confidential; employees had only limited access to information regarding their colleagues' earnings.

The problem of concealed pay discrimination is particularly acute where the disparity arises not because the female employee is flatly denied a raise but because male counterparts are given larger raises. Having received a pay increase, the female employee is unlikely to discern at once that she has experienced an adverse employment decision. She may have little reason even to suspect discrimination until a pattern develops incrementally and she ultimately becomes aware of the disparity. Even if an employee suspects that the reason for a comparatively low raise is not performance but sex (or another protected ground), the amount involved may seem too small, or the employer's intent too ambiguous, to make the issue immediately actionable—or winnable.

Further separating pay claims from the discrete employment actions identified in *Morgan*, an employer gains from sex-based pay disparities in a way it does not from a discriminatory denial of promotion, hiring, or transfer. When a male employee is selected over a female for a higher level position, someone still gets the promotion and is paid a higher salary; the employer is not enriched. But when a woman is paid less than a similarly situated man, the employer reduces its costs each time the pay differential is implemented. Furthermore, decisions on promotions, like decisions installing seniority systems, often implicate the interests of third-party employees in a way that pay differentials do not. Disparate pay, by contrast, can be remedied at any time solely at the expense of the employer who acts in a discriminatory fashion.

C

In light of the significant differences between pay disparities and discrete employment decisions of the type identified in *Morgan*, the cases on which the Court relies hold no sway (discussing *United Air Lines, Inc. v. Evans*, 431 U.S. 553 (1977), *Delaware State College v. Ricks*, 449 U.S. 250 (1980), and *Lorance v. AT&T Technologies, Inc.*, 490 U.S. 900 (1989)). *Evans* and *Ricks* both involved a single, immediately identifiable act of discrimination: in *Evans*, a constructive discharge; in *Ricks*, a denial of tenure. In each case, the employee filed charges well after the discrete discriminatory act occurred: When United Airlines forced Evans to resign because of its policy barring married female flight attendants, she filed no charge; only four years later, when Evans was rehired, did she allege that the airline's former no-marriage rule was unlawful and therefore should not operate to deny her seniority credit for her prior service. Similarly, when Delaware State College denied Ricks tenure, he did not object until his terminal contract came to an end, one year later. No repetitive, cumulative discriminatory employment practice was at issue in either case.

Lorance is also inapposite, for, in this Court's view, it too involved a one-time discrete act: the adoption of a new seniority system that "had its genesis in sex discrimination." The Court's extensive reliance on *Lorance,* moreover, is perplexing for that decision is no longer effective: In the 1991 Civil Rights Act, Congress superseded *Lorance*'s holding. Repudiating our judgment that a facially neutral seniority system adopted with discriminatory intent must be challenged immediately, Congress provided: "For purposes of this section, an unlawful employment practice occurs... when the seniority system is adopted, when an individual becomes subject to the seniority system, or when a person aggrieved is injured by the application of the seniority system or provision of the system." Congress thus agreed with the dissenters in *Lorance* that "the harsh reality of [that] decision," was "glaringly at odds with the purposes of Title VII" (1991 Civil Rights Act was designed "to respond to recent decisions of the Supreme Court by expanding the scope of relevant civil rights statutes in order to provide adequate protection to victims of discrimination").

True, §112 of the 1991 Civil Rights Act directly addressed only seniority systems. But Congress made clear (1) its view that this Court had unduly contracted the scope of protection afforded by Title VII and other civil rights statutes, and (2) its aim to generalize the ruling in *Bazemore*. As the Senate Report accompanying the proposed Civil Rights Act of 1990, the precursor to the 1991 Act, explained: "Where, as was alleged in *Lorance*, an employer adopts a rule or decision with an unlawful discriminatory motive, each application of that rule or decision is a new violation of the law. In *Bazemore...*, for example,... the Supreme Court properly held that each application of the racially motivated salary structure, i.e., each new paycheck, constituted a distinct violation of Title VII. Section 7(a)(2) generalizes the result correctly reached in *Bazemore*."

Until today, in the more than 15 years since Congress amended Title VII, the Court had not once relied upon *Lorance*. It is mistaken to do so now.

Just as Congress' "goals in enacting Title VII...never included conferring absolute immunity on discriminatorily adopted seniority systems that survive their first [180] days," Congress never intended to immunize forever discriminatory pay differentials unchallenged within 180 days of their adoption. This assessment gains weight when one comprehends that even a relatively minor pay disparity will expand exponentially over an employee's working life if raises are set as a percentage of prior pay.

A clue to congressional intent can be found in Title VII's backpay provision. The statute expressly provides that backpay may be awarded for a period of up to two years before the discrimination charge is filed. This prescription indicates that Congress contemplated challenges to pay discrimination commencing before, but continuing into, the 180-day filing period. As we recognized in *Morgan*, "the fact that Congress expressly limited the amount of recoverable damages elsewhere to a particular time period [i.e., two years] indicates that the [180-day] timely filing provision was not meant to serve as a specific limitation...[on] the conduct that may be considered."

D

In tune with the realities of wage discrimination, the Courts of Appeals have overwhelmingly judged as a present violation the payment of wages infected by discrimination: Each paycheck less than the amount payable had the employer adhered to a nondiscriminatory compensation regime, courts have held, constitutes a cognizable harm.

Similarly in line with the real-world characteristics of pay discrimination, the EEOC—the federal agency responsible for enforcing Title VII—has interpreted the Act to permit employees to challenge disparate pay each time it is received. The EEOC's Compliance Manual provides that "repeated occurrences of the same discriminatory employment action, such as discriminatory paychecks, can be challenged as long as one discriminatory act occurred within the charge filing period."

The EEOC has given effect to its interpretation in a series of administrative decisions. And in this very case, the EEOC urged the Eleventh Circuit to recognize that Ledbetter's failure to challenge any particular pay-setting decision when that decision was made "does not deprive her of the right to seek relief for discriminatory paychecks she received in 1997 and 1998."

II

The Court asserts that treating pay discrimination as a discrete act, limited to each particular pay-setting decision, is necessary to "protect employers from the burden of defending claims arising from employment decisions that are long past." But the discrimination of which Ledbetter complained is not long past. As she alleged, and as the jury found, Goodyear continued to treat Ledbetter differently because of sex each pay period, with mounting harm. Allowing employees to challenge discrimination "that extends over long periods of time," into the charge-filing period, we have previously explained, "does not leave employers defenseless" against unreasonable or prejudicial delay. Doctrines such as "waiver, estoppel, and equitable tolling" "allow us to honor Title VII's remedial purpose without negating the particular purpose of the filing requirement, to give prompt notice to the employer."

In a last-ditch argument, the Court asserts that this dissent would allow a plaintiff to sue on a single decision made 20 years ago "even if the employee had full knowledge of all the circumstances relating to the . . . decision at the time it was made." It suffices to point out that the defenses just noted would make such a suit foolhardy. No sensible judge would tolerate such inexcusable neglect.

Ledbetter, the Court observes, dropped an alternative remedy she could have pursued: Had she persisted in pressing her claim under the Equal Pay Act of 1963 (EPA), 29 U.S.C. §206(d), she would not have encountered a time bar. Notably, the EPA provides no relief when the pay discrimination charged is based on race, religion, national origin, age, or disability. Thus, in truncating the Title VII rule this Court announced in *Bazemore*, the Court does not disarm female workers from achieving redress for unequal pay, but it does impede racial and other minorities from gaining similar relief.

Furthermore, the difference between the EPA's prohibition against paying unequal wages and Title VII's ban on discrimination with regard to compensation is not as large as the Court's opinion might suggest. The key distinction is that Title VII requires a showing of intent. In practical effect, "if the trier of fact is in equipoise about whether the wage differential is motivated by gender discrimination," Title VII compels a verdict for the employer, while the EPA compels a verdict for the plaintiff. In this case, Ledbetter carried the burden of persuading the jury that the pay disparity she suffered was attributable to intentional sex discrimination.

III

To show how far the Court has strayed from interpretation of Title VII with fidelity to the Act's core purpose, I return to the evidence Ledbetter presented at trial. Ledbetter proved to the jury the following: She was a member of a protected class; she performed work substantially equal to work of the dominant class (men); she was compensated less for that work; and the disparity was attributable to gender-based discrimination.

Specifically, Ledbetter's evidence demonstrated that her current pay was discriminatorily low due to a long series of decisions reflecting Goodyear's pervasive discrimination against women managers in general and Ledbetter in particular. Ledbetter's former supervisor, for example, admitted to the jury that Ledbetter's pay, during a particular one-year period, fell below Goodyear's minimum threshold for her position. Although Goodyear claimed the pay disparity was due to poor performance, the supervisor acknowledged that Ledbetter received a "Top Performance Award" in 1996. The jury also heard testimony that another supervisor—who evaluated Ledbetter in 1997 and whose evaluation led to her most recent raise denial—was openly biased against women. And two women who had previously worked as managers at the plant told the jury they had been subject to pervasive discrimination and were paid less than their male counterparts. One was paid less than the men she supervised. Ledbetter herself testified about the discriminatory animus conveyed to her by plant officials. Toward the end of her career, for instance, the plant manager told Ledbetter that the "plant did not need women, that [women] didn't help it, [and] caused problems." After weighing all the evidence, the jury found for Ledbetter, concluding that the pay disparity was due to intentional discrimination.

Yet, under the Court's decision, the discrimination Ledbetter proved is not redressable under Title VII. Each and every pay decision she did not immediately challenge wiped the slate clean. Consideration may not be given to the cumulative effect of a series of decisions that, together, set her pay well below that of every male area manager. Knowingly carrying past pay discrimination forward must be treated as lawful conduct. Ledbetter may not be compensated for the lower pay she was in fact receiving when she complained to the EEOC. Nor, were she still employed by Goodyear, could she gain, on the proof she presented at trial, injunctive relief requiring, prospectively, her receipt of the same compensation men receive for substantially similar work. The Court's approbation of these consequences is totally at odds with the robust protection against workplace discrimination Congress intended Title VII to secure.

This is not the first time the Court has ordered a cramped interpretation of Title VII, incompatible with the statute's broad remedial purpose [citing Lindemann and Grossman's hornbook *Employment Discrimination Law*: "A spate of Court decisions in the late 1980s drew congressional fire and resulted in demands for legislative change," culminating in the 1991 Civil Rights Act]. Once again, the ball is in Congress' court. As in 1991, the Legislature may act to correct this Court's parsimonious reading of Title VII.

For the reasons stated, I would hold that Ledbetter's claim is not time barred and would reverse the Eleventh Circuit's judgment.

"Throwing Away Your Umbrella in a Rainstorm": *Shelby County v. Holder*

The Fifteenth Amendment to the U.S. Constitution, ratified in 1870, five years after the end of the Civil War, guaranteed that "the right of citizens of the United States to vote shall not be denied or abridged by the United States or by any State on account of race, color, or previous condition of servitude." In the century that followed, however, this promise was routinely broken by state and local governments that used poll taxes, literacy tests, and other methods to ensure that African Americans had no access to the voting booth.

The Voting Rights Act of 1965

In response to the civil rights movement of the 1950s and 1960s, Congress, using its power granted in the Constitution to enforce the Fifteenth Amendment by appropriate legislation, passed the Voting Rights Act of 1965. This law included, in Section 5, a "preclearance remedy" that required certain state and county governments with a history of suppressing the African American vote to clear with the U.S. Department of Justice (DOJ) any new state or local legislation concerning elections or voting before implementing the changes.

In 2006, Congress reauthorized the Voting Rights Act, with overwhelming support in both Houses of Congress, from members of both political parties. President George W. Bush signed the reauthorization into law. This reauthorization included Section 5, with its preclearance remedy.

"Things Have Changed Dramatically"

Shelby County, Alabama, which was covered by Section 5 as a jurisdiction with a history of suppressing the African American vote, sued the U.S. attorney general, asking the lower court to declare that Section 5 was unconstitutional on its face and to enjoin its enforcement. The two lower courts found that the evidence Congress considered in 2006 that the preclearance remedy was still needed was sufficient to uphold the reauthorization of Section 5.

The U.S. Supreme Court reversed, ruling that Section 5 was unconstitutional. Writing for the majority, Chief Justice John Roberts reasoned that the coverage formula underlying the Section 5 preclearance requirement—used to determine which states and counties had to request review from the DOJ before changing election and voting provisions—had not actually been updated by Congress since the Voting Rights Act was originally written. "Nearly 50 years later," he wrote, "things have changed dramatically," citing parity in voter turnout and registration rates, "unprecedented levels" of minorities holding office, and the rarity of "blatantly discriminatory evasions of federal decrees."

"A Steadfast Commitment"

Justice Ginsburg's dissent pointed out that these dramatic changes were due to the full-potency Voting Rights Act with Section 5's preclearance remedy in active operation as Congress intended. She asked why the Court would want to dispense with a tool that was doing its intended job: "Throwing out preclearance when it has worked and is continuing to work to stop discriminatory changes is like throwing away your umbrella in a rainstorm because you are not getting wet."

She completed her dissent with a famous quote from Reverend Martin Luther King Jr. Ginsburg stressed the conditional nature of progress: "The arc of the moral universe is long...but it bends toward justice if there is a steadfast commitment to see the task through to completion."

Aftermath of *Shelby County v. Holder*

The results of this decision, in a country with a fraught history of racial conflict and aggression, ought to have been predictable. Voter-identification requirements, racial gerrymandering, closings of registration locations and polling places, voter roll purges, and other practices that make it more difficult for poor people, elderly people, and people of color to vote have proliferated since the decision.[1] Moreover, in two opinions authored by Justice Samuel Alito, the Court has since gone even farther than the majority in *Shelby County v. Holder* did, ruling that "the presumption of legislative good faith" in making state and local election laws was "not changed by a finding of past discrimination."[2]

SHELBY COUNTY, ALABAMA V. HOLDER, ATTORNEY GENERAL, ET AL.
CERTIORARI TO THE UNITED STATES COURT OF APPEALS
FOR THE DISTRICT OF COLUMBIA CIRCUIT
570 U.S. 529 (June 25, 2013)

Dissent Announcement

Ruth Bader Ginsburg: The majority and the dissenters agree on two points.

First, race-based voting discrimination still exists; no one doubts that.

Second, the Voting Rights Act addresses an extraordinary problem, a near century of disregard for the dictates of the Fifteenth Amendment, and Congress has taken extraordinary measures to meet the problem.

Beyond those two points the Court divides sharply.

Congress failed to redo the coverage formula, the Court holds. The Court holds that that renders inoperative the preclearance remedy of Section 5.

Section 5 cannot operate without the formula.

Section 5 is the provision far more effective than any other in securing minority voting rights and stopping backsliding.

Justices Breyer, Sotomayor, Kagan, and I are of the view that Congress's decision to renew the Act and keep the coverage formula was an altogether rational means to serve the end of achieving what was once the subject of a dream, the equal citizenship stature of all in our polity, a voice to every voter in our democracy undiluted by race.

Most fundamentally, we see the issue as a "who decides" question.

In this regard we note that the very First Amendment to our Constitution exhibits a certain suspicion of Congress.

It instructs, Congress shall make no law abridging the freedom of speech or of the press.

The Civil War Amendments are of a distinctly different thrust, as the Fifteenth Amendment instructs that the right to vote shall not be denied or abridged on account of race, and it vests in Congress as do the Thirteenth and Fourteenth Amendments, power to enforce the guaranteed right by appropriate legislation.

As the standard-setting decision, *South Carolina v. Katzenbach*, puts it, as against the reserved powers of states, Congress may use any rational means to effectuate the constitutional prohibition of race discrimination in voting.

Congress sought to do just that in 1965, when it initially passed the Voting Rights Act, and in each reauthorization, including the most recent one.

Indeed, the 2006 reauthorization was the product of the most earnest consideration.

Over a span of more than 20 months, the House and Senate Judiciary Committees held 21 hearings, heard from scores of witnesses, received numerous investigative reports and other documentation showing that serious and widespread intentional discrimination persists in covered jurisdictions.

In all, the legislative records filled more than 15,000 pages. Representative Sensenbrenner, then the Chair of the House Judiciary Committee, described the record supporting the authorization as one of the most extensive considerations of any piece of legislation that the United States Congress had dealt with in the 27 and a half years he had served in the House.

The reauthorization passed the House by a vote of 390-to-33.

The vote in the Senate was 98-to-0.

President Bush signed the reauthorization a week after he received it, noting the need for further work in the fight against injustice and calling the extension an example of our continued commitment to a united America where every person is treated with dignity and respect.

Why was Congress intent on renewing Section 5 particularly?

As the Chief Justice explained, Section 5 requires covered jurisdictions to obtain preclearance before making changes in voting laws that might introduce new methods of voting discrimination.

Congress found, first of all, that Section 5 had been enormously successful in increasing minority registration and access to the ballot.

But it also learned how essential Section 5 was to prevent a return to old ways.

In 1995, for example, the State of Mississippi was stopped by Section 5 from bringing back its Jim Crow era to its voter registration system.

And in 2006, Texas was stopped from curtailing early voting in a predominantly Latino district in defiance of this Court's order to reinstate the district after Texas tried to eliminate it.

Congress confronted similar examples of discrimination in covered jurisdictions by the score.

Of signal importance, Congress found that as registration and voting by minority citizens impressively increased, other barriers sprang up to replace the tests and devices that once impeded access to the ballot.

The second-generation barriers included racial gerrymandering, switching from district by district voting to at-large voting, discriminatory annexations—methods more subtle than the visible methods used in 1965 but serving effectively to diminish a minority community's ability to exercise clout in the electoral process.

Congress retained Section 5 to put down the second-generation barriers before they got off the ground.

But the coverage formula is no good, the Court insists, for it is based on decades-old data and eradicated practices, so Congress must start from scratch.

But suppose the record shows, as engaging with it would reveal, that the formula continues to identify the jurisdictions of gravest concern, jurisdictions with the worst current records of voting discrimination.

If Congress could determine from the reams of evidence it gathered that these jurisdictions still belonged under the preclearance regime, why did it need to alter the formula?

Bear in mind that Shelby County has mounted a facial challenge to the reauthorization.

By what right does the Court address the county's claim?

On other days, the Court has explained that facial challenges are the most difficult to mount successfully.

The challenger will not be heard to complain on the ground that the statute in question might be applied unconstitutionally to others in situations not before the Court.

Congress continued preclearance over Alabama, including Shelby County, only after considering barriers remaining there to minority voting clout.

There were many, they were shocking, and they were recent; they are spelled out in the dissenting opinion.

What has become of the Court's usual restraint, its readiness to turn away facial attacks unless there is no set of circumstances under which an Act would be valid?

The Court points to the success of Section 5 in eliminating the tests and devices extant in 1965 and in increasing citizens' registration and ballot access.

Does that provide cause to believe Section 5 remedy is no longer needed?

The notion that it does is hardly new.

The same assumption that the problem can be solved when particular methods of voting discrimination are identified and eliminated was indulged and proved wrong repeatedly prior to the enactment of the Voting Rights Act.

That is why the 2006 renewal targeted no particular practices but instead aimed to reach in all their variety and persistence measures that effectively impaired minority voting rights.

And it is why Congress found in the second-generation barriers demonstrative evidence that a remedy as strong as preclearance remains vital and should not be removed from the federal arsenal.

It was the judgment of Congress that 40 years has not been sufficient amount of time to eliminate the vestiges of discrimination. That judgment of the body empowered to enforce the Civil War Amendments by appropriate legislation should go under this Court's unstinting approbation.

The great man who led the march from Selma to Montgomery and their call for the passage of the Voting Rights Act foresaw progress, even in Alabama.

"The arc of the moral universe is long," he said, "but it bends toward justice if there is a steadfast commitment to see the task through to completion."

That commitment has been disserved by today's decision.

DISSENT

Many citations and footnotes have been omitted, as well as some punctuation (including brackets and internal quotation marks).

Justice Ginsburg, with whom Justice Breyer, Justice Sotomayor, and Justice Kagan join, dissenting.

In the Court's view, the very success of §5 of the Voting Rights Act demands its dormancy. Congress was of another mind. Recognizing that large progress has been made, Congress determined, based on a voluminous record, that the scourge of discrimination was not yet extirpated. The question this case presents is who decides whether, as currently operative, §5 remains justifiable,* this Court, or a Congress charged with the obligation to enforce the post-Civil War Amendments by appropriate legislation. With overwhelming support in both Houses, Congress concluded that, for two prime reasons, §5 should continue in force, unabated. First, continuance would facilitate completion of the impressive gains thus far made; and second, continuance would guard against backsliding. Those assessments were well within Congress' province to make and should elicit this Court's unstinting approbation.

I

"Voting discrimination still exists; no one doubts that." But the Court today terminates the remedy that proved to be best suited to block that discrimination. The Voting Rights Act of 1965 (VRA) has worked to combat voting discrimination where other remedies had been tried and failed. Particularly effective is the VRA's requirement of federal preclearance for all changes to voting laws in the regions of the country with the most aggravated records of rank discrimination against minority voting rights.

A century after the Fourteenth and Fifteenth Amendments guaranteed citizens the right to vote free of discrimination on the basis of race, the "blight of racial discrimination in voting" continued to "infect the electoral process in parts of our country." *South Carolina v. Katzenbach*, 383 U.S. 301, 308 (1966). Early attempts to cope with this vile infection resembled battling the Hydra. Whenever one form of voting discrimination was identified and prohibited, others sprang up in its place. This Court repeatedly encountered the remarkable "variety and persistence" of laws disenfranchising minority citizens. To take just one example, the Court, in 1927, held unconstitutional a Texas law barring black voters from participating in primary elections, *Nixon v. Herndon*, 273 U.S. 536; in 1944, the Court struck down a "reenacted" and slightly altered version of the same law; and in 1953, the Court once again confronted an attempt by Texas to "circumvent" the Fifteenth Amendment by adopting yet another variant of the all-white primary, *Terry v. Adams*, 345 U.S. 461.

During this era, the Court recognized that discrimination against minority voters was a quintessentially political problem requiring a political

---

* The Court purports to declare unconstitutional only the coverage formula set out in §4(b). But without that formula, §5 is immobilized.

solution. As Justice Holmes explained: If "the great mass of the white population intends to keep the blacks from voting," "relief from [that] great political wrong, if done, as alleged, by the people of a State and the State itself, must be given by them or by the legislative and political department of the government of the United States." *Giles v. Harris*, 189 U.S. 475 (1903).

Congress learned from experience that laws targeting particular electoral practices or enabling case-by-case litigation were inadequate to the task. In the Civil Rights Acts of 1957, 1960, and 1964, Congress authorized and then expanded the power of "the Attorney General to seek injunctions against public and private interference with the right to vote on racial grounds." But circumstances reduced the ameliorative potential of these legislative Acts: "Voting suits are unusually onerous to prepare, sometimes requiring as many as 6,000 man-hours spent combing through registration records in preparation for trial. Litigation has been exceedingly slow, in part because of the ample opportunities for delay afforded voting officials and others involved in the proceedings. Even when favorable decisions have finally been obtained, some of the States affected have merely switched to discriminatory devices not covered by the federal decrees or have enacted difficult new tests designed to prolong the existing disparity between white and Negro registration. Alternatively, certain local officials have defied and evaded court orders or have simply closed their registration offices to freeze the voting rolls."

Patently, a new approach was needed.

Answering that need, the Voting Rights Act became one of the most consequential, efficacious, and amply justified exercises of federal legislative power in our Nation's history. Requiring federal preclearance of changes in voting laws in the covered jurisdictions—those States and localities where opposition to the Constitution's commands were most virulent—the VRA provided a fit solution for minority voters as well as for States. Under the preclearance regime established by §5 of the VRA, covered jurisdictions must submit proposed changes in voting laws or procedures to the Department of Justice (DOJ), which has 60 days to respond to the changes. A change will be approved unless DOJ finds it has "the purpose [or]...the effect of denying or abridging the right to vote on account of race or color." In the alternative, the covered jurisdiction may seek approval by a three-judge District Court in the District of Columbia.

After a century's failure to fulfill the promise of the Fourteenth and Fifteenth Amendments, passage of the VRA finally led to signal improvement on this front. "The Justice Department estimated that in the five years after [the VRA's] passage, almost as many blacks registered [to vote] in Alabama, Mississippi, Georgia, Louisiana, North Carolina, and South Carolina as in the entire century before 1965." And in assessing the overall effects of the VRA in 2006, Congress found that "significant progress has been made in eliminating first generation barriers experienced by minority voters, including increased numbers of registered minority voters, minority voter turnout, and minority representation in Congress, State legislatures, and local elected offices. This progress is the direct result of the Voting Rights Act of 1965." Fannie Lou Hamer, Rosa Parks, and Coretta Scott King Voting Rights Act Reauthorization and Amendments Act of 2006 (hereinafter 2006 Reauthorization), §2(b)(1). On that matter of cause and effects there can be no genuine doubt.

Although the VRA wrought dramatic changes in the realization of minority voting rights, the Act, to date, surely has not eliminated all vestiges of discrimination against the exercise of the franchise by minority citizens. Jurisdictions covered by the preclearance requirement continued to submit, in large numbers, proposed changes to voting laws that the Attorney General declined to approve, auguring that barriers to minority voting would quickly resurface were the preclearance remedy eliminated. Congress also found that as "registration and voting of minority citizens increased, other measures may be resorted to which would dilute increasing minority voting strength." Efforts to reduce the impact of minority votes, in contrast to direct attempts to block access to the ballot, are aptly described as "second-generation barriers" to minority voting.

Second-generation barriers come in various forms. One of the blockages is racial gerrymandering, the redrawing of legislative districts in an "effort to segregate the races for purposes of voting." Another is adoption of a system of at-large voting in lieu of district-by-district voting in a city with a sizable black minority. By switching to at-large voting, the overall majority could control the election of each city council member, effectively eliminating the potency of the minority's votes. A similar effect could be achieved if the city engaged in discriminatory annexation by incorporating majority white areas into city limits, thereby decreasing the effect of VRA-occasioned increases in black voting. Whatever the device employed, this Court has long recognized that vote dilution, when adopted with a discriminatory purpose, cuts down the right to vote as certainly as denial of access to the ballot.

In response to evidence of these substituted barriers, Congress reauthorized the VRA for five years in 1970, for seven years in 1975, and for 25 years in 1982. Each time, this Court upheld the reauthorization as a valid exercise of congressional power. As the 1982 reauthorization approached its 2007 expiration date, Congress again considered whether the VRA's preclearance mechanism remained an appropriate response to the problem of voting discrimination in covered jurisdictions.

Congress did not take this task lightly. Quite the opposite. The 109th Congress that took responsibility for the renewal started early and conscientiously. In October 2005, the House began extensive hearings, which continued into November and resumed in March 2006. In April 2006, the Senate followed suit, with hearings of its own. In May 2006, the bills that became the VRA's reauthorization were introduced in both Houses. The House held further hearings of considerable length, as did the Senate, which continued to hold hearings into June and July. In mid-July, the House considered and rejected four amendments, then passed the reauthorization by a vote of 390 yeas to 33 nays. The bill was read and debated in the Senate, where it passed by a vote of 98 to 0. President Bush signed it a week later, on July 27, 2006, recognizing the need for "further work . . . in the fight against injustice," and calling the reauthorization "an example of our continued commitment to a united America where every person is valued and treated with dignity and respect."

In the long course of the legislative process, Congress "amassed a sizable record." The House and Senate Judiciary Committees held 21 hearings, heard from scores of witnesses, received a number of investigative reports and other written documentation of continuing discrimination in covered jurisdictions. In all, the legislative record Congress compiled filled more than 15,000 pages. The compilation presents countless "examples of flagrant racial discrimination" since the last reauthorization; Congress also brought to light systematic evidence that "intentional racial discrimination in voting remains so serious and widespread in covered jurisdictions that section 5 preclearance is still needed."

After considering the full legislative record, Congress made the following findings: The VRA has directly caused significant progress in eliminating first-generation barriers to ballot access, leading to a marked increase in minority voter registration and turnout and the number of minority elected officials. But despite this progress, "second generation barriers constructed to prevent minority voters from fully participating in the electoral process" continued to exist, as well as racially polarized voting in the covered jurisdictions, which increased the political vulnerability of racial and language minorities in those jurisdictions. Extensive "evidence of continued discrimination," Congress concluded, "clearly showed the continued need for Federal oversight" in covered jurisdictions. The overall record demonstrated to the federal lawmakers that, "without the continuation of the Voting Rights Act of 1965 protections, racial and language minority citizens will be deprived of the opportunity to exercise their right to vote, or will have their votes diluted, undermining the significant gains made by minorities in the last 40 years."

Based on these findings, Congress reauthorized preclearance for another 25 years, while also undertaking to reconsider the extension after 15 years to ensure that the provision was still necessary and effective. The question before the Court is whether Congress had the authority under the Constitution to act as it did.

II

In answering this question, the Court does not write on a clean slate. It is well established that Congress' judgment regarding exercise of its power to enforce the Fourteenth and Fifteenth Amendments warrants substantial deference. The VRA addresses the combination of race discrimination and the right to vote, which is "preservative of all rights." When confronting the most constitutionally invidious form of discrimination, and the most fundamental right in our democratic system, Congress' power to act is at its height.

The basis for this deference is firmly rooted in both constitutional text and precedent. The Fifteenth Amendment, which targets precisely and only racial discrimination in voting rights, states that, in this domain, "Congress shall have power to enforce this article by appropriate legislation."* In choosing this language, the Amendment's framers invoked Chief Justice Marshall's formulation of the scope of Congress' powers under the Necessary and Proper Clause:

---

* The Constitution uses the words "right to vote" in five separate places: the Fourteenth, Fifteenth, Nineteenth, Twenty-Fourth, and Twenty-Sixth Amendments. Each of these Amendments contains the same broad empowerment of Congress to enact "appropriate legislation" to enforce the protected right. The implication is unmistakable: Under our constitutional structure, Congress holds the lead rein in making the right to vote equally real for all U.S. citizens. These Amendments are in line with the special role assigned to Congress in protecting the integrity of the democratic process in federal elections.

"Let the end be legitimate, let it be within the scope of the constitution, and all means which are appropriate, which are plainly adapted to that end, which are not prohibited, but consist with the letter and spirit of the constitution, are constitutional." *McCulloch v. Maryland*, 4 Wheat. 316, 421 (1819).

It cannot tenably be maintained that the VRA, an Act of Congress adopted to shield the right to vote from racial discrimination, is inconsistent with the letter or spirit of the Fifteenth Amendment, or any provision of the Constitution read in light of the Civil War Amendments. Nowhere in today's opinion, or in Northwest Austin, is there clear recognition of the transformative effect the Fifteenth Amendment aimed to achieve. Notably, "the Founders' first successful amendment told Congress that it could 'make no law' over a certain domain"; in contrast, the Civil War Amendments used "language [that] authorized transformative new federal statutes to uproot all vestiges of unfreedom and inequality" and provided "sweeping enforcement powers... to enact 'appropriate' legislation targeting state abuses."

The stated purpose of the Civil War Amendments was to arm Congress with the power and authority to protect all persons within the Nation from violations of their rights by the States. In exercising that power, then, Congress may use "all means which are appropriate, which are plainly adapted" to the constitutional ends declared by these Amendments. So when Congress acts to enforce the right to vote free from racial discrimination, we ask not whether Congress has chosen the means most wise, but whether Congress has rationally selected means appropriate to a legitimate end. "It is not for us to review the congressional resolution of [the need for its chosen remedy]. It is enough that we be able to perceive a basis upon which the Congress might resolve the conflict as it did."

Unil today, in considering the constitutionality of the VRA, the Court has accorded Congress the full measure of respect its judgments in this domain should garner. *South Carolina v. Katzenbach* supplies the standard of review: "As against the reserved powers of the States, Congress may use any rational means to effectuate the constitutional prohibition of racial discrimination in voting." Faced with subsequent reauthorizations of the VRA, the Court has reaffirmed this standard. Today's Court does not purport to alter settled precedent establishing that the dispositive question is whether Congress has employed "rational means."

For three reasons, legislation reauthorizing an existing statute is especially likely to satisfy the minimal requirements of the rational-basis test. First, when reauthorization is at issue, Congress has already assembled a legislative record justifying the initial legislation. Congress is entitled to consider that preexisting record as well as the record before it at the time of the vote on reauthorization. This is especially true where, as here, the Court has repeatedly affirmed the statute's constitutionality and Congress has adhered to the very model the Court has upheld.

Second, the very fact that reauthorization is necessary arises because Congress has built a temporal limitation into the Act. It has pledged to review, after a span of years (first 15, then 25) and in light of contemporary evidence, the continued need for the VRA.

Third, a reviewing court should expect the record supporting reauthorization to be less stark than the record originally made. Demand for a record of violations equivalent to the one earlier made would expose Congress to a catch-22. If the statute was working, there would be less evidence of discrimination, so opponents might argue that Congress should not be allowed to renew the statute. In contrast, if the statute was not working, there would be plenty of evidence of discrimination, but scant reason to renew a failed regulatory regime.

This is not to suggest that congressional power in this area is limitless. It is this Court's responsibility to ensure that Congress has used appropriate means. The question meet for judicial review is whether the chosen means are "adapted to carry out the objects the amendments have in view." The Court's role, then, is not to substitute its judgment for that of Congress, but to determine whether the legislative record sufficed to show that "Congress could rationally have determined that [its chosen] provisions were appropriate methods."

In summary, the Constitution vests broad power in Congress to protect the right to vote, and in particular to combat racial discrimination in voting. This Court has repeatedly reaffirmed Congress' prerogative to use any rational means in exercise of its power in this area. And both precedent and logic dictate that the rational-means test should be easier to satisfy, and the burden on the statute's challenger should be higher, when what is at issue is the reauthorization of a remedy that the Court has previously affirmed, and that Congress found, from contemporary evidence, to be working to advance the legislature's legitimate objective.

III

The 2006 reauthorization of the Voting Rights Act fully satisfies the standard stated in McCulloch, 4 Wheat., at 421: Congress may choose any means "appropriate" and "plainly adapted to" a legitimate constitutional end. As we shall see, it is implausible to suggest otherwise.

A

I begin with the evidence on which Congress based its decision to continue the preclearance remedy. The surest way to evaluate whether that remedy remains in order is to see if preclearance is still effectively preventing discriminatory changes to voting laws. On that score, the record before Congress was huge. In fact, Congress found there were more DOJ [Department of Justice] objections between 1982 and 2004 (626) than there were between 1965 and the 1982 reauthorization (490).

All told, between 1982 and 2006, DOJ objections blocked over 700 voting changes based on a determination that the changes were discriminatory. Congress found that the majority of DOJ objections included findings of discriminatory intent and that the changes blocked by preclearance were "calculated decisions to keep minority voters from fully participating in the political process." On top of that, over the same time period the DOJ and private plaintiffs succeeded in more than 100 actions to enforce the §5 preclearance requirements.

In addition to blocking proposed voting changes through preclearance, DOJ may request more information from a jurisdiction proposing a change. In turn, the jurisdiction may modify or withdraw the proposed change. The number of such modifications or withdrawals provides an indication of how many discriminatory proposals are deterred without need for formal objection. Congress received evidence that more than 800 proposed changes were altered or withdrawn since the last reauthorization in 1982.* Congress also received empirical studies finding that DOJ's requests for more information

---

* This number includes only changes actually proposed. Congress also received evidence that many covered jurisdictions engaged in an "informal consultation process" with DOJ before formally submitting a proposal, so that the deterrent effect of preclearance was far broader than the formal submissions alone suggest. All agree that an unsupported assertion about "deterrence" would not be sufficient to justify keeping a remedy in place in perpetuity. But it was certainly reasonable for Congress to consider the testimony of witnesses who had worked with officials in covered jurisdictions and observed a real-world deterrent effect.

had a significant effect on the degree to which covered jurisdictions "complied with their obligation" to protect minority voting rights.

Congress also received evidence that litigation under §2 of the VRA was an inadequate substitute for preclearance in the covered jurisdictions. Litigation occurs only after the fact, when the illegal voting scheme has already been put in place and individuals have been elected pursuant to it, thereby gaining the advantages of incumbency. An illegal scheme might be in place for several election cycles before a §2 plaintiff can gather sufficient evidence to challenge it. And litigation places a heavy financial burden on minority voters. Congress also received evidence that preclearance lessened the litigation burden on covered jurisdictions themselves, because the preclearance process is far less costly than defending against a §2 claim, and clearance by DOJ substantially reduces the likelihood that a §2 claim will be mounted.

The number of discriminatory changes blocked or deterred by the preclearance requirement suggests that the state of voting rights in the covered jurisdictions would have been significantly different absent this remedy. Surveying the type of changes stopped by the preclearance procedure conveys a sense of the extent to which §5 continues to protect minority voting rights. Set out below are characteristic examples of changes blocked in the years leading up to the 2006 reauthorization:

- In 1995, Mississippi sought to reenact a dual voter registration system, "which was initially enacted in 1892 to disenfranchise Black voters," and for that reason, was struck down by a federal court in 1987.
- Following the 2000 census, the City of Albany, Georgia, proposed a redistricting plan that DOJ found to be "designed with the purpose to limit and retrogress the increased black voting strength...in the city as a whole."
- In 2001, the mayor and all-white five-member Board of Aldermen of Kilmichael, Mississippi, abruptly canceled the town's election after "an unprecedented number" of African-American candidates announced they were running for office. DOJ required an election, and the town elected its first black mayor and three black aldermen.
- In 2006, this Court found that Texas' attempt to redraw a congressional district to reduce the strength of Latino voters bore "the mark of intentional discrimination that could give rise to an equal protection violation," and ordered the district redrawn in compliance with the VRA. In response, Texas sought to undermine this Court's order by curtailing

early voting in the district, but was blocked by an action to enforce the §5 preclearance requirement.

- In 2003, after African-Americans won a majority of the seats on the school board for the first time in history, Charleston County, South Carolina, proposed an at-large voting mechanism for the board. The proposal, made without consulting any of the African-American members of the school board, was found to be an "exact replica" of an earlier voting scheme that, a federal court had determined, violated the VRA. DOJ invoked §5 to block the proposal.

- In 1993, the City of Millen, Georgia, proposed to delay the election in a majority-black district by two years, leaving that district without representation on the city council while the neighboring majority white district would have three representatives. DOJ blocked the proposal. The county then sought to move a polling place from a predominantly black neighborhood in the city to an inaccessible location in a predominantly white neighborhood outside city limits.

- In 2004, Waller County, Texas, threatened to prosecute two black students after they announced their intention to run for office. The county then attempted to reduce the availability of early voting in that election at polling places near a historically black university.

- In 1990, Dallas County, Alabama, whose county seat is the City of Selma, sought to purge its voter rolls of many black voters. DOJ rejected the purge as discriminatory, noting that it would have disqualified many citizens from voting "simply because they failed to pick up or return a voter update form, when there was no valid requirement that they do so."

These examples, and scores more like them, fill the pages of the legislative record. The evidence was indeed sufficient to support Congress' conclusion that "racial discrimination in voting in covered jurisdictions [remained] serious and pervasive."*

---

* For an illustration postdating the 2006 reauthorization, see *South Carolina v. United States*, 898 F. Supp. 2d 30 (DC 2012), which involved a South Carolina voter-identification law enacted in 2011. Concerned that the law would burden minority voters, DOJ brought a §5 enforcement action to block the law's implementation. In the course of the litigation, South Carolina officials agreed to binding interpretations that made it "far easier than some might have expected or feared" for South Carolina citizens to vote. A three-judge panel precleared the law after adopting both interpretations as an express "condition of preclearance." Two of the judges commented that the case demonstrated

Congress further received evidence indicating that formal requests of the kind set out above represented only the tip of the iceberg. There was what one commentator described as an "avalanche of case studies of voting rights violations in the covered jurisdictions," ranging from "outright intimidation and violence against minority voters" to "more subtle forms of voting rights deprivations." This evidence gave Congress ever more reason to conclude that the time had not yet come for relaxed vigilance against the scourge of race discrimination in voting.

True, conditions in the South have impressively improved since passage of the Voting Rights Act. Congress noted this improvement and found that the VRA was the driving force behind it. But Congress also found that voting discrimination had evolved into subtler second-generation barriers, and that eliminating preclearance would risk loss of the gains that had been made. Concerns of this order, the Court previously found, gave Congress adequate cause to reauthorize the VRA. Facing such evidence, then, the Court expressly rejected the argument that disparities in voter turnout and number of elected officials were the only metrics capable of justifying reauthorization of the VRA.

B

I turn next to the evidence on which Congress based its decision to reauthorize the coverage formula in §4(b). Because Congress did not alter the coverage formula, the same jurisdictions previously subject to preclearance continue to be covered by this remedy. The evidence just described, of preclearance's continuing efficacy in blocking constitutional violations in the covered jurisdictions, itself grounded Congress' conclusion that the remedy should be retained for those jurisdictions. There is no question, moreover, that the covered jurisdictions have a unique history of problems with racial discrimination in voting. Consideration of this long history, still in living memory, was altogether appropriate. The Court criticizes Congress for failing to recognize that "history did not end in 1965." But the Court ignores that "what's past is prologue." W. Shakespeare, *The Tempest*, act 2, sc. 1. And "those who cannot remember the past are condemned to repeat it." G. Santayana, *The Life of Reason* 284 (1905). Congress was especially mindful

"the continuing utility of Section 5 of the Voting Rights Act in deterring problematic, and hence encouraging non-discriminatory, changes in state and local voting laws."

of the need to reinforce the gains already made and to prevent backsliding. Of particular importance, even after 40 years and thousands of discriminatory changes blocked by preclearance, conditions in the covered jurisdictions demonstrated that the formula was still justified by "current needs."

Congress learned of these conditions through a report, known as the Katz study, that looked at §2 suits between 1982 and 2004. To Examine the Impact and Effectiveness of the Voting Rights Act: Hearing before the Subcommittee on the Constitution of the House Committee on the Judiciary, 109th Cong., 1st Sess. (2005). Because the private right of action authorized by §2 of the VRA applies nationwide, a comparison of §2 lawsuits in covered and noncovered jurisdictions provides an appropriate yardstick for measuring differences between covered and noncovered jurisdictions. If differences in the risk of voting discrimination between covered and noncovered jurisdictions had disappeared, one would expect that the rate of successful §2 lawsuits would be roughly the same in both areas.* The study's findings, however, indicated that racial discrimination in voting remains "concentrated in the jurisdictions singled out for preclearance."

Although covered jurisdictions account for less than 25 percent of the country's population, the Katz study revealed that they accounted for 56 percent of successful §2 litigation since 1982. Controlling for population, there were nearly four times as many successful §2 cases in covered jurisdictions as there were in noncovered jurisdictions. The Katz study further found that §2 lawsuits are more likely to succeed when they are filed in covered jurisdictions than in noncovered jurisdictions. From these findings—ignored by the Court—Congress reasonably concluded that the coverage formula continues to identify the jurisdictions of greatest concern.

The evidence before Congress, furthermore, indicated that voting in the covered jurisdictions was more racially polarized than elsewhere in the country. While racially polarized voting alone does not signal a constitutional violation, it is a factor that increases the vulnerability of racial minorities to discriminatory changes in voting law. The reason is twofold. First, racial polarization means that racial minorities are at risk of being systematically outvoted and having their interests underrepresented in legislatures.

---

* Because preclearance occurs only in covered jurisdictions and can be expected to stop the most obviously objectionable measures, one would expect a lower rate of successful §2 lawsuits in those jurisdictions if the risk of voting discrimination there were the same as elsewhere in the country.

Second, "when political preferences fall along racial lines, the natural inclinations of incumbents and ruling parties to entrench themselves have predictable racial effects. Under circumstances of severe racial polarization, efforts to gain political advantage translate into race-specific disadvantages."

In other words, a governing political coalition has an incentive to prevent changes in the existing balance of voting power. When voting is racially polarized, efforts by the ruling party to pursue that incentive "will inevitably discriminate against a racial group." Just as buildings in California have a greater need to be earthquake-proofed, places where there is greater racial polarization in voting have a greater need for prophylactic measures to prevent purposeful race discrimination. This point was understood by Congress and is well recognized in the academic literature.

The case for retaining a coverage formula that met needs on the ground was therefore solid. Congress might have been charged with rigidity had it afforded covered jurisdictions no way out or ignored jurisdictions that needed superintendence. Congress, however, responded to this concern. Critical components of the congressional design are the statutory provisions allowing jurisdictions to "bail out" of preclearance, and for court-ordered "bail ins." The VRA permits a jurisdiction to bail out by showing that it has complied with the Act for ten years, and has engaged in efforts to eliminate intimidation and harassment of voters. It also authorizes a court to subject a noncovered jurisdiction to federal preclearance upon finding that violations of the Fourteenth and Fifteenth Amendments have occurred there.

Congress was satisfied that the VRA's bailout mechanism provided an effective means of adjusting the VRA's coverage over time. Nearly 200 jurisdictions have successfully bailed out of the preclearance requirement, and DOJ has consented to every bailout application filed by an eligible jurisdiction since the current bailout procedure became effective in 1984. The bail-in mechanism has also worked. Several jurisdictions have been subject to federal preclearance by court orders, including the States of New Mexico and Arkansas.

This experience exposes the inaccuracy of the Court's portrayal of the Act as static, unchanged since 1965. Congress designed the VRA to be a dynamic statute, capable of adjusting to changing conditions. True, many covered jurisdictions have not been able to bail out due to recent acts of noncompliance with the VRA, but that truth reinforces the congressional judgment that these jurisdictions were rightfully subject to preclearance, and ought to remain under that regime.

IV

Congress approached the 2006 reauthorization of the VRA with great care and seriousness. The same cannot be said of the Court's opinion today. The Court makes no genuine attempt to engage with the massive legislative record that Congress assembled. Instead, it relies on increases in voter registration and turnout as if that were the whole story. Without even identifying a standard of review, the Court dismissively brushes off arguments based on "data from the record," and declines to enter the "debate [about] what [the] record shows." One would expect more from an opinion striking at the heart of the Nation's signal piece of civil-rights legislation. I note the most disturbing lapses. First, by what right, given its usual restraint, does the Court even address Shelby County's facial challenge to the VRA? Second, the Court veers away from controlling precedent regarding the "equal sovereignty" doctrine without even acknowledging that it is doing so. Third, hardly showing the respect ordinarily paid when Congress acts to implement the Civil War Amendments, and as just stressed, the Court does not even deign to grapple with the legislative record.

A

Shelby County launched a purely facial challenge to the VRA's 2006 reauthorization. "A facial challenge to a legislative Act," the Court has other times said, "is, of course, the most difficult challenge to mount successfully, since the challenger must establish that no set of circumstances exists under which the Act would be valid."

"Under our constitutional system, courts are not roving commissions assigned to pass judgment on the validity of the Nation's laws." Instead, the "judicial Power" is limited to deciding particular "Cases" and "Controversies." U.S. Const., Art. III, §2. "Embedded in the traditional rules governing constitutional adjudication is the principle that a person to whom a statute may constitutionally be applied will not be heard to challenge that statute on the ground that it may conceivably be applied unconstitutionally to others, in other situations not before the Court." Yet the Court's opinion in this case contains not a word explaining why Congress lacks the power to subject to preclearance the particular plaintiff that initiated this lawsuit—Shelby County, Alabama. The reason for the Court's silence is apparent, for as applied to Shelby County, the VRA's preclearance requirement is hardly contestable.

Alabama is home to Selma, site of the "Bloody Sunday" beatings of civil-rights demonstrators that served as the catalyst for the VRA's enactment. Following those events, Martin Luther King, Jr., led a march from Selma to Montgomery, Alabama's capital, where he called for passage of the VRA. If the Act passed, he foresaw, progress could be made even in Alabama, but there had to be a steadfast national commitment to see the task through to completion. In King's words, "the arc of the moral universe is long, but it bends toward justice."

History has proved King right. Although circumstances in Alabama have changed, serious concerns remain. Between 1982 and 2005, Alabama had one of the highest rates of successful §2 suits, second only to its VRA-covered neighbor Mississippi. In other words, even while subject to the restraining effect of §5, Alabama was found to have "denied or abridged" voting rights "on account of race or color" more frequently than nearly all other States in the Union. This fact prompted the dissenting judge below to concede that "a more narrowly tailored coverage formula" capturing Alabama and a handful of other jurisdictions with an established track record of racial discrimination in voting "might be defensible." That is an understatement. Alabama's sorry history of §2 violations alone provides sufficient justification for Congress' determination in 2006 that the State should remain subject to §5's preclearance requirement.*

A few examples suffice to demonstrate that, at least in Alabama, the "current burdens" imposed by §5's preclearance requirement are "justified by current needs." In the interim between the VRA's 1982 and 2006 reauthorizations, this Court twice confronted purposeful racial discrimination in Alabama. In *Pleasant Grove v. United States*, 479 U.S. 462 (1987), the Court held that Pleasant Grove—a city in Jefferson County, Shelby County's neighbor—engaged in purposeful discrimination by annexing all-white areas while rejecting the annexation request of an adjacent black neighborhood. The city had "shown unambiguous opposition to racial integration, both before and after the passage of the federal civil rights laws," and its strategic

---

* This lawsuit was filed by Shelby County, a political subdivision of Alabama, rather than by the State itself. Nevertheless, it is appropriate to judge Shelby County's constitutional challenge in light of instances of discrimination statewide because Shelby County is subject to §5's preclearance requirement by virtue of Alabama's designation as a covered jurisdiction under §4(b) of the VRA. In any event, Shelby County's recent record of employing an at-large electoral system tainted by intentional racial discrimination is by itself sufficient to justify subjecting the county to §5's preclearance mandate.

annexations appeared to be an attempt "to provide for the growth of a monolithic white voting block" for "the impermissible purpose of minimizing future black voting strength."

Two years before *Pleasant Grove*, the Court in *Hunter v. Underwood*, 471 U.S. 222 (1985), struck down a provision of the Alabama Constitution that prohibited individuals convicted of misdemeanor offenses "involving moral turpitude" from voting. The provision violated the Fourteenth Amendment's Equal Protection Clause, the Court unanimously concluded, because "its original enactment was motivated by a desire to discriminate against blacks on account of race, and the [provision] continues to this day to have that effect."

Pleasant Grove and *Hunter* were not anomalies. In 1986, a Federal District Judge concluded that the at-large election systems in several Alabama counties violated §2. *Dillard v. Crenshaw Cty.*, 640 F. Supp. 1347 (MD Ala. 1986). Summarizing its findings, the court stated that "from the late 1800's through the present, [Alabama] has consistently erected barriers to keep black persons from full and equal participation in the social, economic, and political life of the state."

The *Dillard* litigation ultimately expanded to include 183 cities, counties, and school boards employing discriminatory at-large election systems. One of those defendants was Shelby County, which eventually signed a consent decree to resolve the claims against it.

Although the *Dillard* litigation resulted in overhauls of numerous electoral systems tainted by racial discrimination, concerns about backsliding persist. In 2008, for example, the city of Calera, located in Shelby County, requested preclearance of a redistricting plan that "would have eliminated the city's sole majority-black district, which had been created pursuant to the consent decree in *Dillard*." Although DOJ objected to the plan, Calera forged ahead with elections based on the unprecleared voting changes, resulting in the defeat of the incumbent African-American councilman who represented the former majority-black district. The city's defiance required DOJ to bring a §5 enforcement action that ultimately yielded appropriate redress, including restoration of the majority-black district.

A recent FBI investigation provides a further window into the persistence of racial discrimination in state politics. Recording devices worn by state legislators cooperating with the FBI's investigation captured conversations between members of the state legislature and their political allies. The recorded conversations are shocking. Members of the state Senate derisively refer to African-Americans as "Aborigines" and talk openly of their aim to quash a particular gambling-related referendum because the referendum, if placed on the ballot, might increase African-American voter turnout. These conversations occurred not in the 1870's, or even in the 1960's, they took place in 2010. The District Judge presiding over the criminal trial at which the recorded conversations were introduced commented that the "recordings represent compelling evidence that political exclusion through racism remains a real and enduring problem" in Alabama. Racist sentiments, the judge observed, "remain regrettably entrenched in the high echelons of state government."

These recent episodes forcefully demonstrate that §5's preclearance requirement is constitutional as applied to Alabama and its political subdivisions.* And under our case law, that conclusion should suffice to resolve this case.

This Court has consistently rejected constitutional challenges to legislation enacted pursuant to Congress' enforcement powers under the Civil War Amendments upon finding that the legislation was constitutional as applied to the particular set of circumstances before the Court. A similar approach is warranted here.†

The VRA's exceptionally broad severability provision makes it particularly inappropriate for the Court to allow Shelby County to mount a facial challenge to §§4(b) and 5 of the VRA, even though application of those provisions to the county falls well within the bounds of Congress' legislative authority. The severability provision states:

> "If any provision of [this Act] or the application thereof to any person or circumstances is held invalid, the remainder of [the Act] and the application of the provision to other persons not similarly

---

* Congress continued preclearance over Alabama, including Shelby County, after considering evidence of current barriers there to minority voting clout. Shelby County, thus, is no "redhead" caught up in an arbitrary scheme.

† The Court does not contest that Alabama's history of racial discrimination provides a sufficient basis for Congress to require Alabama and its political subdivisions to preclear electoral changes. Nevertheless, the Court asserts that Shelby County may prevail on its facial challenge to §4's coverage formula because it is subject to §5's preclearance requirement by virtue of that formula. ("The county was selected [for preclearance] based on the [coverage] formula.") This misses the reality that Congress decided to subject Alabama to preclearance based on evidence of continuing constitutional violations in that State.

situated or to other circumstances shall not be affected thereby."
42 U.S.C. §1973p.

In other words, even if the VRA could not constitutionally be applied to
certain States—e.g., Arizona and Alaska—§1973p calls for those unconstitutional applications to be severed, leaving the Act in place for jurisdictions
as to which its application does not transgress constitutional limits.

Nevertheless, the Court suggests that limiting the jurisdictional scope
of the VRA in an appropriate case would be "to try our hand at updating
the statute." Just last Term, however, the Court rejected this very argument
when addressing a materially identical severability provision, explaining that
such a provision is "Congress' explicit textual instruction to leave unaffected
the remainder of [the Act]" if any particular "application is unconstitutional."
Leaping to resolve Shelby County's facial challenge without considering
whether application of the VRA to Shelby County is constitutional, or even
addressing the VRA's severability provision, the Court's opinion can hardly
be described as an exemplar of restrained and moderate decision-making.
Quite the opposite. Hubris is a fit word for today's demolition of the VRA.

B

The Court stops any application of §5 by holding that §4(b)'s coverage
formula is unconstitutional. It pins this result, in large measure, to "the fundamental principle of equal sovereignty." In *Katzenbach*, however, the Court
held, in no uncertain terms, that the principle "applies only to the terms
upon which States are admitted to the Union, and not to the remedies for
local evils which have subsequently appeared."

Katzenbach, the Court acknowledges, "rejected the notion that the
[equal sovereignty] principle operates as a bar on differential treatment outside [the] context [of the admission of new States]." But the Court clouds
that once clear understanding by citing dictum from *Northwest Austin* to
convey that the principle of equal sovereignty "remains highly pertinent in
assessing subsequent disparate treatment of States." If the Court is suggesting
that dictum in *Northwest Austin* silently overruled *Katzenbach*'s limitation of
the equal sovereignty doctrine to "the admission of new States," the suggestion is untenable. *Northwest Austin* cited *Katzenbach*'s holding in the course
of declining to decide whether the VRA was constitutional or even what
standard of review applied to the question. In today's decision, the Court

ratchets up what was pure dictum in *Northwest Austin*, attributing breadth to the equal sovereignty principle in flat contradiction of *Katzenbach*. The Court does so with nary an explanation of why it finds *Katzenbach* wrong, let alone any discussion of whether stare decisis nonetheless counsels adherence to *Katzenbach*'s ruling on the limited "significance" of the equal sovereignty principle.

Today's unprecedented extension of the equal sovereignty principle outside its proper domain—the admission of new States—is capable of much mischief. Federal statutes that treat States disparately are hardly novelties. Do such provisions remain safe given the Court's expansion of equal sovereignty's sway?

Of gravest concern, Congress relied on our path-marking *Katzenbach* decision in each reauthorization of the VRA. It had every reason to believe that the Act's limited geographical scope would weigh in favor of, not against, the Act's constitutionality. Congress could hardly have foreseen that the VRA's limited geographic reach would render the Act constitutionally suspect.

In the Court's conception, it appears, defenders of the VRA could not prevail upon showing what the record overwhelmingly bears out, i.e., that there is a need for continuing the preclearance regime in covered States. In addition, the defenders would have to disprove the existence of a comparable need elsewhere. I am aware of no precedent for imposing such a double burden on defenders of legislation.

C

The Court has time and again declined to upset legislation of this genre unless there was no or almost no evidence of unconstitutional action by States. No such claim can be made about the congressional record for the 2006 VRA reauthorization. Given a record replete with examples of denial or abridgment of a paramount federal right, the Court should have left the matter where it belongs: in Congress' bailiwick.

Instead, the Court strikes §4(b)'s coverage provision because, in its view, the provision is not based on "current conditions." It discounts, however, that one such condition was the preclearance remedy in place in the covered jurisdictions, a remedy Congress designed both to catch discrimination before it causes harm, and to guard against return to old ways. Volumes of evidence supported Congress' determination that the prospect of retrogression was real. Throwing out preclearance when it has worked and is continuing to work to stop discriminatory changes is like throwing away your umbrella in a rainstorm because you are not getting wet.

But, the Court insists, the coverage formula is no good; it is based on "decades-old data and eradicated practices." Even if the legislative record shows, as engaging with it would reveal, that the formula accurately identifies the jurisdictions with the worst conditions of voting discrimination, that is of no moment, as the Court sees it. Congress, the Court decrees, must "start from scratch." I do not see why that should be so.

Congress' chore was different in 1965 than it was in 2006. In 1965, there were a "small number of States . . . which in most instances were familiar to Congress by name," on which Congress fixed its attention. In drafting the coverage formula, "Congress began work with reliable evidence of actual voting discrimination in a great majority of the States" it sought to target. "The formula [Congress] eventually evolved to describe these areas" also captured a few States that had not been the subject of congressional factfinding. Nevertheless, the Court upheld the formula in its entirety, finding it fair "to infer a significant danger of the evil" in all places the formula covered.

The situation Congress faced in 2006, when it took up reauthorization of the coverage formula, was not the same. By then, the formula had been in effect for many years, and all of the jurisdictions covered by it were "familiar to Congress by name." The question before Congress: Was there still a sufficient basis to support continued application of the preclearance remedy in each of those already-identified places? There was at that point no chance that the formula might inadvertently sweep in new areas that were not the subject of congressional findings. And Congress could determine from the record whether the jurisdictions captured by the coverage formula still belonged under the preclearance regime. If they did, there was no need to alter the formula. That is why the Court, in addressing prior reauthorizations of the VRA, did not question the continuing "relevance" of the formula.

Consider once again the components of the record before Congress in 2006. The coverage provision identified a known list of places with an undisputed history of serious problems with racial discrimination in voting. Recent evidence relating to Alabama and its counties was there for all to see. Multiple Supreme Court decisions had upheld the coverage provision, most recently in 1999. There was extensive evidence that, due to the preclearance mechanism, conditions in the covered jurisdictions had notably improved. And there was evidence that preclearance was still having a substantial real-world effect, having stopped hundreds of discriminatory voting changes in the covered jurisdictions since the last reauthorization. In addition, there was evidence that racial polarization in voting was higher in covered jurisdictions than elsewhere, increasing the vulnerability of minority citizens in those jurisdictions. And countless witnesses, reports, and case studies documented continuing problems with voting discrimination in those jurisdictions. In light of this record, Congress had more than a reasonable basis to conclude that the existing coverage formula was not out of sync with conditions on the ground in covered areas. And certainly Shelby County was no candidate for release through the mechanism Congress provided.

The Court holds §4(b) invalid on the ground that it is "irrational to base coverage on the use of voting tests 40 years ago, when such tests have been illegal since that time." But the Court disregards what Congress set about to do in enacting the VRA. That extraordinary legislation scarcely stopped at the particular tests and devices that happened to exist in 1965. The grand aim of the Act is to secure to all in our polity equal citizenship stature, a voice in our democracy undiluted by race. As the record for the 2006 reauthorization makes abundantly clear, second-generation barriers to minority voting rights have emerged in the covered jurisdictions as attempted substitutes for the first-generation barriers that originally triggered preclearance in those jurisdictions.

The sad irony of today's decision lies in its utter failure to grasp why the VRA has proven effective. The Court appears to believe that the VRA's success in eliminating the specific devices extant in 1965 means that preclearance is no longer needed. With that belief, and the argument derived from it, history repeats itself. The same assumption—that the problem could be solved when particular methods of voting discrimination are identified and eliminated—was indulged and proved wrong repeatedly prior to the VRA's enactment. Unlike prior statutes, which singled out particular tests or devices, the VRA is grounded in Congress' recognition of the "variety and persistence" of measures designed to impair minority voting rights. In truth, the evolution of voting discrimination into more subtle second-generation barriers is powerful evidence that a remedy as effective as preclearance remains vital to protect minority voting rights and prevent backsliding.

Beyond question, the VRA is no ordinary legislation. It is extraordinary because Congress embarked on a mission long delayed and of extraordinary importance: to realize the purpose and promise of the Fifteenth Amendment. For a half century, a concerted effort has been made to end racial discrimination in voting. Thanks to the Voting Rights Act, progress once the subject of a dream has been achieved and continues to be made.

The record supporting the 2006 reauthorization of the VRA is also extraordinary. It was described by the Chairman of the House Judiciary Committee as "one of the most extensive considerations of any piece of legislation that the United States Congress has dealt with in the 27½ years" he had served in the House (July 13, 2006) (statement of Rep. Sensenbrenner).

After exhaustive evidence-gathering and deliberative process, Congress reauthorized the VRA, including the coverage provision, with overwhelming bipartisan support. It was the judgment of Congress that "40 years has not been a sufficient amount of time to eliminate the vestiges of discrimination following nearly 100 years of disregard for the dictates of the 15th amendment and to ensure that the right of all citizens to vote is protected as guaranteed by the Constitution." That determination of the body empowered to enforce the Civil War Amendments "by appropriate legislation" merits this Court's utmost respect. In my judgment, the Court errs egregiously by overriding Congress' decision.

★ ★ ★

For the reasons stated, I would affirm the judgment of the Court of Appeals.

ꙮ "Your Right to Swing Your Arms Ends": *Burwell v. Hobby Lobby Stores*

U nder the Affordable Care Act (ACA) of 2010, health insurance plans are required to cover birth control. The owners of two privately owned companies—cabinet manufacturer Conestoga Wood Specialties and Hobby Lobby Stores, a national chain of craft stores—claimed that their Christian religious beliefs prohibited them from providing access to birth control coverage for their employees. The owners sued the secretary of the U.S. Department of Health and Human Services (HHS) to block enforcement of this ACA provision. They claimed that the ACA's requirement violated the Religious Freedom Restoration Act (RFRA) of 1993, which prohibits the federal government from taking any action that substantially burdens the exercise of religion unless that action constitutes the least restrictive means of serving a compelling government interest.

Writing for the majority in the case, Justice Samuel Alito's opinion held that for-profit private corporations were to be treated no differently from sole proprietorships or partnerships with respect to assessing the corporations' "sincerely held religious beliefs" under RFRA. Justice Alito wrote that penalizing the owners under the ACA for their religious objections to contraceptives that the owners considered to be abortifacients amounted to a substantial burden on the owners' exercise of their religion under RFRA. HHS could extend to for-profit private corporations a system it had implemented that enabled employees of religious nonprofits to have access to contraceptives as required under the ACA without involving the religious employers, Alito reasoned.

In dissent, Justice Ginsburg noted that although solicitude had been extended to religious nonprofits in the past, allowing them to opt out of legislative provisions that conflicted with religious beliefs, never before had the Court extended such solicitude to for-profit commercial entities. She pointed out that religious opt-outs impose costs on others. Alito's solution of "letting the government pay" to make up for the owners' refusal to provide coverage for contraceptives had no logical stopping point: What about an employer whose sincere religious beliefs precluded paying employees the minimum wage? "A cosmopolitan nation is made up of people of almost every conceivable religious preference," she said. She invoked a famous description of the First Amendment's free speech clause: "Your right to swing your arms ends just where the other person's nose begins."

BURWELL, SECRETARY OF HEALTH AND HUMAN SERVICES, ET AL. V. HOBBY LOBBY STORES, INC., ET AL.

CERTIORARI TO THE UNITED STATES COURT OF APPEALS FOR THE TENTH CIRCUIT

573 U.S. ___ (June 30, 2014)*

*Together with No. 13–356, Conestoga Wood Specialties Corp. et al. v. Burwell, Secretary of Health and Human Services, et al., on certiorari to the United States Court of Appeals for the Third Circuit.

Dissent Announcement

Samuel Alito: Justice Ginsburg has filed a dissenting opinion in which Justice Sotomayor joins and in which Justices Breyer and Kagan join as to all but Part III-C-1.

Ruth Bader Ginsburg: Under the Affordable Care Act, employers with health plans must provide women with access to contraceptives at no cost to the insured employee.

The Court holds today that commercial enterprises employing workers of diverse faiths can opt out of contraceptive coverage if contraceptive use is incompatible with the employer's religious beliefs.

When an employer's religious practice detrimentally affects others, however, the First Amendment's Free Exercise Clause does not require accommodation to that practice.

Because precedent to that effect is well established, the Court does not rest its decision on the Free Exercise Clause, as Justice Alito announced, but solely on the Religious Freedom Restoration Act or RFRA. Justices Breyer, Sotomayor, Kagan and I find in that act no design to permit the opt-outs in question.

RFRA targeted this Court's decision in a particular case—one holding that native Americans could be denied unemployment benefits because they had ingested peyote as an essential part of a religious ceremony.

Congress sought to override that decision and to restore by statute the respect for religious exercise as it existed before the sacramental peyote decision was rendered, and nothing more.

Reading the act expansively, as the Court does, raises a host of me-too questions.

Can an employer in business for profit opt out of coverage for blood transfusions, vaccinations, anti-depressants, or medications derived from pigs based on the employer's sincerely held religious beliefs opposing those medical practices?

What of the employer whose religious faith teaches that it is sinful to employ a single woman without her father's consent or a married woman without her husband's consent? Can those employers opt out of Title VII's ban on gender discrimination in employment?

Those examples, by the way, are not hypothetical.

A wise legal scholar famously said of the First Amendment's Free Speech Clause, "your right to swing your arms ends just where the other person's nose begins."

The senators [in an amicus brief filed by 19 Democratic senators led by Senator Patty Murray of Washington] believe the same is true of the Free Exercise Clause and that Congress meant RFRA to be interpreted in line with that principle.

The genesis of the contraceptive coverage regulations should have enlightened the Court's decision.

The ability of women to participate equally in the economic and social life of the nation, this court appreciated over two decades ago, has been facilitated by their ability to control their reproductive lives.

Congress acted on that understanding when it called for coverage of preventive care responsive to women's needs as part of the Affordable Care Act, a nationwide insurance program intended to be comprehensive.

Carrying out Congress's direction, the Department of Heath and Human Services promulgated regulations requiring group health plans to cover without cost sharing all contraceptives approved by the Food and Drug Administration.

The scientific studies informing the HHS regulations demonstrate compellingly the benefits to public health and to women's well-being attending improved contraceptive access.

Notably, the Court assumes that contraceptive coverage under the Affordable Care Act does further compelling interests.

The Courts' reasoning, however, subordinates those interests, nor is subordination limited to the four contraceptives Hobby Lobby and Conestoga object to.

At oral argument, counsel for Hobby Lobby forthrightly acknowledged that his argument would apply just as well if an employer's religion ruled out use of every one of the 20 contraceptives the FDA has approved.

As a threshold issue, the parties dispute whether RFRA, which speaks of a person's exercise of religion, even applies to for-profit corporations, for they are not flesh-and-blood persons, they are artificial entities created by law.

True or not, the First Amendment's Free Exercise protections and RFRA's safeguards shelter not only natural persons, they shield as well churches and other non-profit religion-based organizations.

Yes, this Court's decisions have accorded special solicitude to religious institutions, but until today, no similar solicitude has ever been extended to for-profit commercial entities.

The reason why is not obscure. Religious organizations exist to foster the interest of persons subscribing to the same religious faith—not so for-profit corporations. Workers who sustain the operations of for-profit corporations commonly are not drawn from one religious community.

Indeed, by law, no religion-based criterion can restrict the workforce of for-profit corporations.

The difference between a community of believers in the same religion and a business embracing persons of diverse beliefs is slighted in today's decision.

Justice Sotomayor and I would hold that for-profit corporations should not be equated to non-profits existing to serve a religious community and would place them outside RFRA's domain.

Justices Breyer and Kagan have not endorsed the Court's reasoning on this point. They simply would not decide the threshold question whether for-profit corporations or their owners can bring RFRA claims.

All four of us, however, agree in unison that RFRA gives Hobby Lobby and Conestoga no right to opt out of contraceptive coverage.

The Court objects to the contraceptive coverage requirement on the ground that it fails to meet RFRA's least restrictive means test, but the Government shows that there is no less restrictive, equally effective means that would both satisfy the challengers' religious objections and ensure that women employees receive, at no cost to them, the preventive care needed to safeguard their health and well-being.

The Court's opinion does suggest first, "Well, let the Government pay for the contraceptives rather than the employees who do not share their employer's faith."

The Affordable Care Act, however, requires coverage of preventive services through existing employer-based systems of health insurance, not through substitution of the Government—in effect, of the general public....

And where is the stopping point to the "let the Government pay" solution?

Suppose it offends an employer's religious belief to pay the minimum wage or to accord women equal pay for substantially similar work.

Such claims in fact had been made, and in ruling on them, the courts have accepted such beliefs as sincere.

Is it right as a less restrictive alternative to require the Government to provide the pay to which the employer has a religion based objection?

Perhaps because those questions are not so easily answered, the Court rests on a different solution, extending to commercial enterprises the accommodation already afforded to non-profit religious-based organizations.

That extension solution was barely addressed in the parties' briefs.

Asked about it at oral argument, Hobby Lobby's counsel responded, "We haven't been offered that accommodation so we haven't had to decide what kind of objection, if any, we would make to that."

Ultimately, the Court hedges.

It declines to decide whether the extension solution [will] work for purposes of all religious claims.

The fatal flaw in any event bears reiteration.

The extension cure would equate to dissimilar categories, on the one hand, commercial businesses like Hobby Lobby and Conestoga whose workforces are open to persons of all faiths and, on the other, non-profit organizations designed to further the mission of a particular community of believers.

A pathmarking 1982 decision, a decision that RFRA preserved, is highly instructive in this regard, *United States v. Lee.*

Lee rejected the exemption claim of an Amish entrepreneur whose religious tenets were offended by the payment of Social Security taxes.

Tax cases are in a discrete category, today's Court suggests.

But *Lee* made two key points that cannot be confined to tax cases.

First, when followers of a particular sect entered into commercial activity as a matter of choice, the Lee Court observed, the limits they accept on their own conduct as a matter of conscience and faith are not to be superimposed on statutory schemes binding on others in that activity.

Second, the *Lee* Court said, allowing a religion-based exemption to a commercial employer would operate to impose the employer's religious faith on the employees.

Working for Hobby Lobby or Conestoga, in other words, should not deprive employees holding different beliefs of the employer-ensured preventive care available to workers at the shop next door.

Hobby Lobby and Conestoga, as shown by the real cases I described, hardly stand alone as commercial enterprises seeking religion-based exemptions from generally applicable laws—among them, ones prohibiting discrimination in the workplace.

How is the Court to divine when a religious belief is feigned to escape legal sanction or which genuine beliefs are worthy of accommodation and which are not?

Those questions are all the more perplexing given the majority opinion's repeated insistence that courts may not presume to determine the plausibility of a religious claim.

In sum, today's potentially sweeping decision minimizes the Government's compelling interest in uniform compliance with laws governing workplaces, in particular the Affordable Care Act, and discounts the disadvantages religion-based opt-outs imposed on others, in particular employees who do not share their employer's religious beliefs.

A cosmopolitan nation is made up of people of almost every conceivable religious preference.

In passing RFRA, Congress did not alter a tradition in which one person's right to free exercise of her religion must be kept in harmony with the rights of her fellow citizens and with the common good.

For the reasons I summarized, all of them, and others developed in the dissent and opinion, I would reverse the judgment of the Tenth Circuit and affirm the judgment of the Third Circuit.

DISSENT

Many citations and footnotes have been omitted, as well as some punctuation (including brackets and internal quotation marks).

Justice Ginsburg, with whom Justice Sotomayor joins, and with whom Justice Breyer and Justice Kagan join as to all but Part III–C–1, dissenting.

In a decision of startling breadth, the Court holds that commercial enterprises, including corporations, along with partnerships and sole proprietorships, can opt out of any law (saving only tax laws) they judge incompatible with their sincerely held religious beliefs. Compelling governmental interests in uniform compliance with the law, and disadvantages that religion-based optouts impose on others, hold no sway, the Court decides, at least when there is a "less restrictive alternative." And such an alternative, the Court suggests, there always will be whenever, in lieu of tolling an enterprise claiming a religion-based exemption, the government, i.e., the general public, can pick up the tab.*

The Court does not pretend that the First Amendment's Free Exercise Clause demands religion-based accommodations so extreme, for our decisions leave no doubt on that score. Instead, the Court holds that Congress, in the Religious Freedom Restoration Act of 1993 (RFRA), 42 U.S.C. §2000bb et seq., dictated the extraordinary religion-based exemptions today's decision endorses. In the Court's view, RFRA demands accommodation of a for-profit corporation's religious beliefs no matter the impact that accommodation may have on third parties who do not share the corporation owners' religious faith—in these cases, thousands of women employed by Hobby Lobby and Conestoga or dependents of persons those corporations employ. Persuaded that Congress enacted RFRA to serve a far less radical purpose, and mindful of the havoc the Court's judgment can introduce, I dissent.

---

* The Court insists it has held none of these things, for another less restrictive alternative is at hand: extending an existing accommodation, currently limited to religious nonprofit organizations, to encompass commercial enterprises. With that accommodation extended, the Court asserts, "women would still be entitled to all [Food and Drug Administration]-approved contraceptives without cost sharing." In the end, however, the Court is not so sure. In stark contrast to the Court's initial emphasis on this accommodation, it ultimately declines to decide whether the highlighted accommodation is even lawful.

I

"The ability of women to participate equally in the economic and social life of the Nation has been facilitated by their ability to control their reproductive lives." *Planned Parenthood of Southeastern Pa. v. Casey*, 505 U.S. 833, 856 (1992). Congress acted on that understanding when, as part of a nationwide insurance program intended to be comprehensive, it called for coverage of preventive care responsive to women's needs. Carrying out Congress' direction, the Department of Health and Human Services (HHS), in consultation with public health experts, promulgated regulations requiring group health plans to cover all forms of contraception approved by the Food and Drug Administration (FDA). The genesis of this coverage should enlighten the Court's resolution of these cases.

A

The Affordable Care Act (ACA), in its initial form, specified three categories of preventive care that health plans must cover at no added cost to the plan participant or beneficiary. Particular services were to be recommended by the U.S. Preventive Services Task Force, an independent panel of experts. The scheme had a large gap, however; it left out preventive services that "many women's health advocates and medical professionals believe are critically important." To correct this oversight, Senator Barbara Mikulski introduced the Women's Health Amendment, which added to the ACA's minimum coverage requirements a new category of preventive services specific to women's health. Women paid significantly more than men for preventive care, the amendment's proponents noted; in fact, cost barriers operated to block many women from obtaining needed care at all. And increased access to contraceptive services, the sponsors comprehended, would yield important public health gains.

As altered by the Women's Health Amendment's passage, the ACA requires new insurance plans to include coverage without cost sharing of "such additional preventive care and screenings . . . as provided for in comprehensive guidelines supported by the Health Resources and Services Administration [(HRSA)]," a unit of HHS. Thus charged, the HRSA developed recommendations in consultation with the Institute of Medicine (IOM).* The IOM convened a group of independent experts, including "specialists in disease

---

* The IOM is an arm of the National Academy of Sciences, an organization Congress established "for the explicit purpose of furnishing advice to the Government."

prevention [and] women's health"; those experts prepared a report evaluating the efficacy of a number of preventive services. Consistent with the findings of "numerous health professional associations" and other organizations, the IOM experts determined that preventive coverage should include the "full range" of FDA-approved contraceptive methods.

In making that recommendation, the IOM's report expressed concerns similar to those voiced by congressional proponents of the Women's Health Amendment. The report noted the disproportionate burden women carried for comprehensive health services and the adverse health consequences of excluding contraception from preventive care available to employees without cost sharing.

In line with the IOM's suggestions, the HRSA adopted guidelines recommending coverage of "all [FDA-]approved contraceptive methods, sterilization procedures, and patient education and counseling for all women with reproductive capacity." Thereafter, HHS, the Department of Labor, and the Department of Treasury promulgated regulations requiring group health plans to include coverage of the contraceptive services recommended in the HRSA guidelines, subject to certain exceptions, described infra. This opinion refers to these regulations as the contraceptive coverage requirement.

B

While the Women's Health Amendment succeeded, a countermove proved unavailing. The Senate voted down the so-called "conscience amendment," which would have enabled any employer or insurance provider to deny coverage based on its asserted "religious beliefs or moral convictions."* That amendment, Senator Mikulski observed, would have "put the personal opinion of employers and insurers over the practice of medicine" (Feb. 29, 2012). Rejecting the "conscience amendment," Congress left health care decisions—including the choice among contraceptive methods—in the hands of women, with the aid of their health care providers.

II

Any First Amendment Free Exercise Clause claim Hobby Lobby or Conestoga might assert is foreclosed by this Court's decision in *Employment Div., Dept. of Human Resources of Ore. v. Smith*, 494 U.S. 872 (1990). In *Smith*,

---

* Separating moral convictions from religious beliefs would be of questionable legitimacy.

two members of the Native American Church were dismissed from their jobs and denied unemployment benefits because they ingested peyote at, and as an essential element of, a religious ceremony. Oregon law forbade the consumption of peyote, and this Court, relying on that prohibition, rejected the employees' claim that the denial of unemployment benefits violated their free exercise rights. The First Amendment is not offended, *Smith* held, when "prohibiting the exercise of religion . . . is not the object of [governmental regulation] but merely the incidental effect of a generally applicable and otherwise valid provision." The ACA's contraceptive coverage requirement applies generally, it is "otherwise valid," it trains on women's well being, not on the exercise of religion, and any effect it has on such exercise is incidental.

Even if *Smith* did not control, the Free Exercise Clause would not require the exemption Hobby Lobby and Conestoga seek. Accommodations to religious beliefs or observances, the Court has clarified, must not significantly impinge on the interests of third parties.*

The exemption sought by Hobby Lobby and Conestoga would override significant interests of the corporations' employees and covered dependents. It would deny legions of women who do not hold their employers' beliefs access to contraceptive coverage that the ACA would otherwise secure. In sum, with respect to free exercise claims no less than free speech claims, "your right to swing your arms ends just where the other man's nose begins." Chafee, Freedom of Speech in War Time, 32 Harv. L. Rev. 932, 957 (1919).

III

A

Lacking a tenable claim under the Free Exercise Clause, Hobby Lobby and Conestoga rely on RFRA, a statute instructing that "government shall not substantially burden a person's exercise of religion even if the burden results from a rule of general applicability" unless the government shows that application of the burden is "the least restrictive means" to further a "compelling governmental interest." In RFRA, Congress "adopted a statutory rule comparable to the constitutional rule rejected in *Smith*."

RFRA's purpose is specific and written into the statute itself. The Act was crafted to "restore the compelling interest test as set forth in *Sherbert v.*

---

*. . . A balanced approach is all the more in order when the Free Exercise Clause itself is at stake, not a statute designed to promote accommodation to religious beliefs and practices.

Verner, 374 U.S. 398 (1963) and *Wisconsin v. Yoder,* 406 U.S. 205 (1972) and to guarantee its application in all cases where free exercise of religion is substantially burdened."*

The legislative history is correspondingly emphatic on RFRA's aim. In line with this restorative purpose, Congress expected courts considering RFRA claims to "look to free exercise cases decided prior to *Smith* for guidance." In short, the Act reinstates the law as it was prior to *Smith,* without "creating... new rights for any religious practice or for any potential litigant." Given the Act's moderate purpose, it is hardly surprising that RFRA's enactment in 1993 provoked little controversy.

B

Despite these authoritative indications, the Court sees RFRA as a bold initiative departing from, rather than restoring, pre-*Smith* jurisprudence. To support its conception of RFRA as a measure detached from this Court's decisions, one that sets a new course, the Court points first to the Religious Land Use and Institutionalized Persons Act of 2000 (RLUIPA), 42 U.S.C. §2000cc et seq., which altered RFRA's definition of the term "exercise of religion." RFRA, as originally enacted, defined that term to mean "the exercise of religion under the First Amendment to the Constitution." As amended by RLUIPA, RFRA's definition now includes "any exercise of religion, whether or not compelled by, or central to, a system of religious belief." That definitional change, according to the Court, reflects "an obvious effort to effect a complete separation from First Amendment case law." The Court's reading is not plausible. RLUIPA's alteration clarifies that courts should not question the centrality of a particular religious exercise. But the amendment in no way suggests that Congress meant to expand the class of entities qualified to mount religious accommodation claims, nor does it relieve courts of the obligation to inquire whether a government action substantially burdens a religious exercise.†

---

* Under *Sherbert* and *Yoder,* the Court "required the government to justify any substantial burden on religiously motivated conduct by a compelling state interest and by means narrowly tailored to achieve that interest."

† RLUIPA, the Court notes, includes a provision directing that "this chapter [i.e., RLUIPA] shall be construed in favor of a broad protection of religious exercise, to the maximum extent permitted by the terms of [the Act] and the Constitution." RFRA incorporates RLUIPA's definition of "exercise of religion," as RLUIPA does, but contains no omnibus rule of construction governing the statute in its entirety.

Next, the Court highlights RFRA's requirement that the government, if its action substantially burdens a person's religious observance, must demonstrate that it chose the least restrictive means for furthering a compelling interest. "By imposing a least-restrictive-means test," the Court suggests, RFRA "went beyond what was required by our pre-*Smith* decisions." But as RFRA's statements of purpose and legislative history make clear, Congress intended only to restore, not to scrap or alter, the balancing test as this Court has applied it pre-*Smith*.

The Congress that passed RFRA correctly read this Court's pre-*Smith* case law as including within the "compelling interest test" a "least restrictive means" requirement. And the view that the pre-*Smith* test included a "least restrictive means" requirement had been aired in testimony before the Senate Judiciary Committee by experts on religious freedom.

Our decision in *City of Boerne*, it is true, states that the least restrictive means requirement "was not used in the pre-*Smith* jurisprudence RFRA purported to codify." As just indicated, however, that statement does not accurately convey the Court's pre-*Smith* jurisprudence.*

C

With RFRA's restorative purpose in mind, I turn to the Act's application to the instant lawsuits. That task, in view of the positions taken by the Court, requires consideration of several questions, each potentially dispositive of Hobby Lobby's and Conestoga's claims: Do for-profit corporations rank among "persons" who "exercise...religion"? Assuming that they do, does the contraceptive coverage requirement "substantially burden" their religious exercise? If so, is the requirement "in furtherance of a compelling government interest"? And last, does the requirement represent the least restrictive means for furthering that interest?

Misguided by its errant premise that RFRA moved beyond the pre-*Smith* case law, the Court falters at each step of its analysis.

---

* The Court points out that I joined the majority opinion in *City of Boerne* and did not then question the statement that "least restrictive means...was not used [pre-*Smith*]." Concerning that observation, I remind my colleagues of Justice Jackson's sage comment: "I see no reason why I should be consciously wrong today because I was unconsciously wrong yesterday." *Massachusetts v. United States*, 333 U.S. 611, 639–640 (1948) (dissenting opinion).

1

RFRA's compelling interest test, as noted, applies to government actions that "substantially burden a person's exercise of religion." This reference, the Court submits, incorporates the definition of "person" found in the Dictionary Act, 1 U.S.C. §1, which extends to "corporations, companies, associations, firms, partnerships, societies, and joint stock companies, as well as individuals." The Dictionary Act's definition, however, controls only where "context" does not "indicate otherwise." Here, context does so indicate. RFRA speaks of "a person's exercise of religion."* Whether a corporation qualifies as a "person" capable of exercising religion is an inquiry one cannot answer without reference to the "full body" of pre-*Smith* "free-exercise case law." There is in that case law no support for the notion that free exercise rights pertain to for-profit corporations.

Until this litigation, no decision of this Court recognized a for-profit corporation's qualification for a religious exemption from a generally applicable law, whether under the Free Exercise Clause or RFRA. The absence of such precedent is just what one would expect, for the exercise of religion is characteristic of natural persons, not artificial legal entities. As Chief Justice Marshall observed nearly two centuries ago, a corporation is "an artificial being, invisible, intangible, and existing only in contemplation of law." *Trustees of Dartmouth College v. Woodward*, 4 Wheat. 518, 636 (1819). Corporations, Justice Stevens more recently reminded, "have no consciences, no beliefs, no feelings, no thoughts, no desires." *Citizens United v. Federal Election Comm'n*, 558 U.S. 310, 466 (2010) (opinion concurring in part and dissenting in part).

The First Amendment's free exercise protections, the Court has indeed recognized, shelter churches and other nonprofit religion-based organizations. "For many individuals, religious activity derives meaning in large measure from participation in a larger religious community," and "furtherance of the autonomy of religious organizations often furthers individual religious freedom as well." The Court's "special solicitude to the rights of religious organizations," however, is just that. No such solicitude is traditional for commercial

---

* As earlier explained, RLUIPA's amendment of the definition of "exercise of religion" does not bear the weight the Court places on it. Moreover, it is passing strange to attribute to RLUIPA any purpose to cover entities other than "religious assemblies or institutions." That law applies to land-use regulation. To permit commercial enterprises to challenge zoning and other land-use regulations under RLUIPA would "dramatically expand the statute's reach" and deeply intrude on local prerogatives, contrary to Congress' intent.

organizations.* Indeed, until today, religious exemptions had never been extended to any entity operating in "the commercial, profit-making world."

The reason why is hardly obscure. Religious organizations exist to foster the interests of persons subscribing to the same religious faith. Not so of for-profit corporations. Workers who sustain the operations of those corporations commonly are not drawn from one religious community. Indeed, by law, no religion-based criterion can restrict the work force of for-profit corporations. The distinction between a community made up of believers in the same religion and one embracing persons of diverse beliefs, clear as it is, constantly escapes the Court's attention.† One can only wonder why the Court shuts this key difference from sight.

Reading RFRA, as the Court does, to require extension of religion-based exemptions to for-profit corporations surely is not grounded in the pre-*Smith* precedent Congress sought to preserve. Had Congress intended RFRA to initiate a change so huge, a clarion statement to that effect likely would have been made in the legislation. The text of RFRA makes no such statement and the legislative history does not so much as mention for-profit corporations.

The Court notes that for-profit corporations may support charitable causes and use their funds for religious ends, and therefore questions the

---

* Typically, Congress has accorded to organizations religious in character religion-based exemptions from statutes of general application. It can scarcely be maintained that RFRA enlarges these exemptions to allow Hobby Lobby and Conestoga to hire only persons who share the religious beliefs of the Greens or Hahns. Nor does the Court suggest otherwise.

The Court does identify two statutory exemptions it reads to cover for-profit corporations, 42 U.S.C. §§300a-7(b)(2) and 238n(a), and infers from them that "Congress speaks with specificity when it intends a religious accommodation not to extend to for-profit corporations." The Court's inference is unwarranted. The exemptions the Court cites cover certain medical personnel who object to performing or assisting with abortions. Notably, the Court does not assert that these exemptions have in fact been afforded to for-profit corporations. These provisions are revealing in a way that detracts from one of the Court's main arguments. They show that Congress is not content to rest on the Dictionary Act when it wishes to ensure that particular entities are among those eligible for a religious accommodation. Moreover, the exemption codified in §238n(a) was not enacted until three years after RFRA's passage. If, as the Court believes, RFRA opened all statutory schemes to religion-based challenges by for-profit corporations, there would be no need for a statute-specific, post-RFRA exemption of this sort.

† I part ways with Justice Kennedy on the context relevant here. He sees it as the employers' "exercise [of] their religious beliefs within the context of their own closely held, for-profit corporations." I see as the relevant context the employers' asserted right to exercise religion within a nationwide program designed to protect against health hazards employees who do not subscribe to their employers' religious beliefs.

distinction between such corporations and religious nonprofit organizations.* Again, the Court forgets that religious organizations exist to serve a community of believers. For-profit corporations do not fit that bill. Moreover, history is not on the Court's side. Recognition of the discrete characters of "ecclesiastical and lay" corporations dates back to Blackstone, *Commentaries on the Laws of England* (1765), and was reiterated by this Court centuries before the enactment of the Internal Revenue Code. To reiterate, "for-profit corporations are different from religious non-profits in that they use labor to make a profit, rather than to perpetuate [the] religious values [shared by a community of believers]."

Citing *Braunfeld v. Brown*, 366 U.S. 599 (1961), the Court questions why, if "a sole proprietorship that seeks to make a profit may assert a free-exercise claim, [Hobby Lobby and Conestoga] can't...do the same?" But even accepting, arguendo, the premise that unincorporated business enterprises may gain religious accommodations under the Free Exercise Clause, the Court's conclusion is unsound. In a sole proprietorship, the business and its owner are one and the same. By incorporating a business, however, an individual separates herself from the entity and escapes personal responsibility for the entity's obligations. One might ask why the separation should hold only when it serves the interest of those who control the corporation. In any event, *Braunfeld* is hardly impressive authority for the entitlement Hobby Lobby and Conestoga seek. The free exercise claim asserted there was promptly rejected on the merits.

The Court's determination that RFRA extends to for-profit corporations is bound to have untoward effects. Although the Court attempts to cabin its language to closely held corporations, its logic extends to corporations of any size, public or private.† Little doubt that RFRA claims will proliferate, for the

---

* According to the Court, the Government "concedes" that "non-profit corporations" are protected by RFRA. That is not an accurate description of the Government's position, which encompasses only "churches," "religious institutions," and "religious non-profits."

† The Court does not even begin to explain how one might go about ascertaining the religious scruples of a corporation where shares are sold to the public. No need to speculate on that, the Court says, for "it seems unlikely" that large corporations "will often assert RFRA claims." Perhaps so, but as Hobby Lobby's case demonstrates, such claims are indeed pursued by large corporations, employing thousands of persons of different faiths, whose ownership is not diffuse. "Closely held" is not synonymous with "small." Hobby Lobby is hardly the only enterprise of sizable scale that is family owned or closely held. For example, the family-owned candy giant Mars, Inc., takes in $33 billion in revenues and has some 72,000 employees, and closely held Cargill, Inc., takes in more than $136 billion in revenues and employs some 140,000 persons. Nor does the Court offer any instruction on how to

Court's expansive notion of corporate personhood—combined with its other errors in construing RFRA—invites for-profit entities to seek religion-based exemptions from regulations they deem offensive to their faith.

2

Even if Hobby Lobby and Conestoga were deemed RFRA "persons," to gain an exemption, they must demonstrate that the contraceptive coverage requirement "substantially burden[s] [their] exercise of religion." Congress no doubt meant the modifier "substantially" to carry weight. In the original draft of RFRA, the word "burden" appeared unmodified. The word "substantially" was inserted pursuant to a clarifying amendment offered by Senators Kennedy and Hatch. In proposing the amendment, Senator Kennedy stated that RFRA, in accord with the Court's pre-*Smith* case law, "does not require the Government to justify every action that has some effect on religious exercise."

The Court barely pauses to inquire whether any burden imposed by the contraceptive coverage requirement is substantial. Instead, it rests on the Greens' and Hahns' "belief that providing the coverage demanded by the HHS regulations is connected to the destruction of an embryo in a way that is sufficient to make it immoral for them to provide the coverage."* I agree with the Court that the Green and Hahn families' religious convictions regarding contraception are sincerely held.† But those beliefs, however deeply held, do not suffice to sustain an RFRA claim. RFRA, properly understood, distinguishes between "factual allegations that [plaintiffs'] beliefs are sincere

resolve the disputes that may crop up among corporate owners over religious values and accommodations. The Court is satisfied that "state corporate law provides a ready means for resolving any conflicts," but the authorities cited in support of that proposition are hardly helpful. And even if a dispute settlement mechanism is in place, how is the arbiter of a religion-based intracorporate controversy to resolve the disagreement, given this Court's instruction that "courts have no business addressing [whether an asserted religious belief] is substantial"?

* The Court dismisses the argument, advanced by some amici, that the $2,000-per-employee tax charged to certain employers that fail to provide health insurance is less than the average cost of offering health insurance, noting that the Government has not provided the statistics that could support such an argument. The Court overlooks, however, that it is not the Government's obligation to prove that an asserted burden is insubstantial. Instead, it is incumbent upon plaintiffs to demonstrate, in support of a RFRA claim, the substantiality of the alleged burden.

† The Court levels a criticism that is as wrongheaded as can be. In no way does the dissent "tell the plaintiffs that their beliefs are flawed." Right or wrong in this domain is a judgment no Member of this Court, or any civil court, is authorized or equipped to make.

and of a religious nature," which a court must accept as true, and the "legal conclusion…that [plaintiffs'] religious exercise is substantially burdened," an inquiry the court must undertake.

That distinction is a facet of the pre-*Smith* jurisprudence RFRA incorporates. *Bowen v. Roy*, 476 U.S. 693 (1986), is instructive. There, the Court rejected a free exercise challenge to the Government's use of a Native American child's Social Security number for purposes of administering benefit programs. Without questioning the sincerity of the father's religious belief that "use of [his daughter's Social Security] number may harm [her] spirit," the Court concluded that the Government's internal uses of that number "placed [no] restriction on what [the father] may believe or what he may do." Recognizing that the father's "religious views may not accept" the position that the challenged uses concerned only the Government's internal affairs, the Court explained that "for the adjudication of a constitutional claim, the Constitution, rather than an individual's religion, must supply the frame of reference." Inattentive to this guidance, today's decision elides entirely the distinction between the sincerity of a challenger's religious belief and the substantiality of the burden placed on the challenger.

Undertaking the inquiry that the Court forgoes, I would conclude that the connection between the families' religious objections and the contraceptive coverage requirement is too attenuated to rank as substantial. The requirement carries no command that Hobby Lobby or Conestoga purchase or provide the contraceptives they find objectionable. Instead, it calls on the companies covered by the requirement to direct money into undifferentiated funds that finance a wide variety of benefits under comprehensive health plans. Those plans, in order to comply with the ACA, must offer contraceptive coverage without cost sharing, just as they must cover an array of other preventive services.

Importantly, the decisions whether to claim benefits under the plans are made not by Hobby Lobby or Conestoga, but by the covered employees and dependents, in consultation with their health care providers. Should an employee of Hobby Lobby or Conestoga share the religious beliefs of the Greens and Hahns, she is of course under no compulsion to use the contraceptives in

What the Court must decide is not "the plausibility of a religious claim," but whether accommodating that claim risks depriving others of rights accorded them by the laws of the United States.

question. But "no individual decision by an employee and her physician—be it to use contraception, treat an infection, or have a hip replaced—is in any meaningful sense [her employer's] decision or action." It is doubtful that Congress, when it specified that burdens must be "substantial," had in mind a linkage thus interrupted by independent decision makers (the woman and her health counselor) standing between the challenged government action and the religious exercise claimed to be infringed. Any decision to use contraceptives made by a woman covered under Hobby Lobby's or Conestoga's plan will not be propelled by the Government, it will be the woman's autonomous choice, informed by the physician she consults.

3

Even if one were to conclude that Hobby Lobby and Conestoga meet the substantial burden requirement, the Government has shown that the contraceptive coverage for which the ACA provides furthers compelling interests in public health and women's well being. Those interests are concrete, specific, and demonstrated by a wealth of empirical evidence. To recapitulate, the mandated contraception coverage enables women to avoid the health problems unintended pregnancies may visit on them and their children. The coverage helps safeguard the health of women for whom pregnancy may be hazardous, even life threatening. And the mandate secures benefits wholly unrelated to pregnancy, preventing certain cancers, menstrual disorders, and pelvic pain.

That Hobby Lobby and Conestoga resist coverage for only 4 of the 20 FDA-approved contraceptives does not lessen these compelling interests. Notably, the corporations exclude intrauterine devices (IUDs), devices significantly more effective, and significantly more expensive than other contraceptive methods.* Moreover, the Court's reasoning appears to permit commercial enterprises like Hobby Lobby and Conestoga to exclude from their group health plans all forms of contraceptives.

Perhaps the gravity of the interests at stake has led the Court to assume, for purposes of its RFRA analysis, that the compelling interest criterion is met in these cases.† It bears note in this regard that the cost of an IUD is nearly

---

* IUDs, which are among the most reliable forms of contraception, generally cost women more than $1,000 when the expenses of the office visit and insertion procedure are taken into account.

† Although the Court's opinion makes this assumption grudgingly, one Member of the majority recognizes, without reservation, that "the [contraceptive coverage] mandate

equivalent to a month's full-time pay for workers earning the minimum wage; that almost one-third of women would change their contraceptive method if costs were not a factor; and that only one-fourth of women who request an IUD actually have one inserted after finding out how expensive it would be.

Stepping back from its assumption that compelling interests support the contraceptive coverage requirement, the Court notes that small employers and grandfathered plans are not subject to the requirement. If there is a compelling interest in contraceptive coverage, the Court suggests, Congress would not have created these exclusions.

Federal statutes often include exemptions for small employers, and such provisions have never been held to undermine the interests served by these statutes.

The ACA's grandfathering provision, 42 U.S.C. §18011, allows a phasing-in period for compliance with a number of the Act's requirements (not just the contraceptive coverage or other preventive services provisions). Once specified changes are made, grandfathered status ceases. Hobby Lobby's own situation is illustrative. By the time this litigation commenced, Hobby Lobby did not have grandfathered status. Asked why by the District Court, Hobby Lobby's counsel explained that the "grandfathering requirements mean that you can't make a whole menu of changes to your plan that involve things like the amount of co-pays, the amount of coinsurance, deductibles, that sort of thing." Counsel acknowledged that, "just because of economic realities, our plan has to shift over time. I mean, insurance plans, as everyone knows, shift over time."* The percentage of employees in grandfathered plans is steadily declining, having dropped from 56% in 2011 to 48% in 2012 to 36% in 2013. In short, far from ranking as a categorical exemption, the grandfathering provision is "temporary, intended to be a means for gradually transitioning employers into mandatory coverage."

The Court ultimately acknowledges a critical point: RFRA's application "must take adequate account of the burdens a requested accommodation may impose on nonbeneficiaries." No tradition, and no prior decision under

---

serves the Government's compelling interest in providing insurance coverage that is necessary to protect the health of female employees."

* Hobby Lobby's amicus National Religious Broadcasters similarly states that, "given the nature of employers' needs to meet changing economic and staffing circumstances, and to adjust insurance coverage accordingly, the actual benefit of the 'grandfather' exclusion is de minimis and transitory at best."

RFRA, allows a religion-based exemption when the accommodation would be harmful to others—here, the very persons the contraceptive coverage requirement was designed to protect.

4

After assuming the existence of compelling government interests, the Court holds that the contraceptive coverage requirement fails to satisfy RFRA's least restrictive means test. But the Government has shown that there is no less restrictive, equally effective means that would both (1) satisfy the challengers' religious objections to providing insurance coverage for certain contraceptives (which they believe cause abortions); and (2) carry out the objective of the ACA's contraceptive coverage requirement, to ensure that women employees receive, at no cost to them, the preventive care needed to safeguard their health and well-being. A "least restrictive means" cannot require employees to relinquish benefits accorded them by federal law in order to ensure that their commercial employers can adhere unreservedly to their religious tenets.*

Then let the government pay (rather than the employees who do not share their employer's faith), the Court suggests. "The most straightforward [alternative]," the Court asserts, "would be for the Government to assume the cost of providing...contraceptives...to any women who are unable to obtain them under their health-insurance policies due to their employers' religious objections." The ACA, however, requires coverage of preventive services through the existing employer-based system of health insurance "so that [employees] face minimal logistical and administrative obstacles." Impeding women's receipt of benefits "by requiring them to take steps to learn about, and to sign up for, a new [government funded and administered] health benefit" was scarcely what Congress contemplated. Moreover, Title X of the Public Health Service Act, 42 U.S.C. §300 et seq., "is the nation's only dedicated source of federal funding for safety net family planning services." "Safety net programs like Title X are not designed to absorb the unmet needs of...insured individuals."

---

* As the Court made clear in *Cutter*, the government's license to grant religion-based exemptions from generally applicable laws is constrained by the Establishment Clause. "We are a cosmopolitan nation made up of people of almost every conceivable religious preference," a "rich mosaic of religious faiths." Consequently, one person's right to free exercise must be kept in harmony with the rights of her fellow citizens, and "some religious practices [must] yield to the common good."

Note, too, that Congress declined to write into law the preferential treatment Hobby Lobby and Conestoga describe as a less restrictive alternative.

And where is the stopping point to the "let the government pay" alternative? Suppose an employer's sincerely held religious belief is offended by health coverage of vaccines, or paying the minimum wage, or according women equal pay for substantially similar work? Does it rank as a less restrictive alternative to require the government to provide the money or benefit to which the employer has a religion-based objection? Because the Court cannot easily answer that question, it proposes something else: Extension to commercial enterprises of the accommodation already afforded to nonprofit religion-based organizations. "At a minimum," according to the Court, such an approach would not "impinge on [Hobby Lobby's and Conestoga's] religious belief." I have already discussed the "special solicitude" generally accorded nonprofit religion-based organizations that exist to serve a community of believers, solicitude never before accorded to commercial enterprises comprising employees of diverse faiths.

Ultimately, the Court hedges on its proposal to align for-profit enterprises with nonprofit religion-based organizations. "We do not decide today whether [the] approach [the opinion advances] complies with RFRA for purposes of all religious claims." Counsel for Hobby Lobby was similarly noncommittal. Asked at oral argument whether the Court-proposed alternative was acceptable,* counsel responded: "We haven't been offered that accommodation, so we haven't had to decide what kind of objection, if any, we would make to that."

Conestoga suggests that, if its employees had to acquire and pay for the contraceptives (to which the corporation objects) on their own, a tax credit

---

* On brief, Hobby Lobby and Conestoga barely addressed the extension solution, which would bracket commercial enterprises with nonprofit religion-based organizations for religious accommodations purposes. The hesitation is understandable, for challenges to the adequacy of the accommodation accorded religious nonprofit organizations are currently sub judice. At another point in today's decision, the Court refuses to consider an argument neither "raised below [nor] advanced in this Court by any party," giving Hobby Lobby and Conestoga "[no] opportunity to respond to [that] novel claim." Yet the Court is content to decide this case (and this case only) on the ground that HHS could make an accommodation never suggested in the parties' presentations. RFRA cannot sensibly be read to "require the government to...refute each and every conceivable alternative regulation," especially where the alternative on which the Court seizes was not pressed by any challenger.

would qualify as a less restrictive alternative. A tax credit, of course, is one variety of "let the government pay." In addition to departing from the existing employer-based system of health insurance, Conestoga's alternative would require a woman to reach into her own pocket in the first instance, and it would do nothing for the woman too poor to be aided by a tax credit. In sum, in view of what Congress sought to accomplish, i.e., comprehensive preventive care for women furnished through employer-based health plans, none of the proffered alternatives would satisfactorily serve the compelling interests to which Congress responded.

IV

Among the pathmarking pre-*Smith* decisions RFRA preserved is *United States v. Lee*, 455 U.S. 252 (1982). Lee, a sole proprietor engaged in farming and carpentry, was a member of the Old Order Amish. He sincerely believed that withholding Social Security taxes from his employees or paying the employer's share of such taxes would violate the Amish faith. This Court held that, although the obligations imposed by the Social Security system conflicted with Lee's religious beliefs, the burden was not unconstitutional.* The Government urges that *Lee* should control the challenges brought by Hobby Lobby and Conestoga. In contrast, today's Court dismisses *Lee* as a tax case. Indeed, it was a tax case and the Court in *Lee* homed in on "the difficulty in attempting to accommodate religious beliefs in the area of taxation." But the *Lee* Court made two key points one cannot confine to tax cases. "When followers of a particular sect enter into commercial activity as a matter of choice," the Court observed, "the limits they accept on their own conduct as a matter of conscience and faith are not to be superimposed on statutory schemes which are binding on others in that activity." The statutory scheme of employer-based comprehensive health coverage involved in these cases is surely binding on others engaged in the same trade or business as the corporate challengers here, Hobby Lobby and Conestoga. Further, the Court recognized in *Lee* that allowing a religion-based exemption to a commercial employer would "operate to impose the employer's religious faith on the employees."† No doubt the

---

* As a sole proprietor, Lee was subject to personal liability for violating the law of general application he opposed. His claim to a religion-based exemption would have been even thinner had he conducted his business as a corporation, thus avoiding personal liability.

† Congress amended the Social Security Act in response to *Lee*. The amended statute permits Amish sole proprietors and partnerships (but not Amish-owned corporations) to

Greens and Hahns and all who share their beliefs may decline to acquire for themselves the contraceptives in question. But that choice may not be imposed on employees who hold other beliefs. Working for Hobby Lobby or Conestoga, in other words, should not deprive employees of the preventive care available to workers at the shop next door, at least in the absence of directions from the Legislature or Administration to do so.

Why should decisions of this order be made by Congress or the regulatory authority, and not this Court? Hobby Lobby and Conestoga surely do not stand alone as commercial enterprises seeking exemptions from generally applicable laws on the basis of their religious beliefs. See, e.g., *Newman v. Piggie Park Enterprises, Inc.*, 256 F. Supp. 941, 945 (S.C. 1966) (owner of restaurant chain refused to serve black patrons based on his religious beliefs opposing racial integration), 390 U.S. 400 (1968); *In re Minnesota ex rel. McClure*, 370 N. W. 2d 844, 847 (Minn. 1985) (born-again Christians who owned closely held, for-profit health clubs believed that the Bible proscribed hiring or retaining an "individual living with but not married to a person of the opposite sex," "a young, single woman working without her father's consent or a married woman working without her husband's consent," and any person "antagonistic to the Bible," including "fornicators and homosexuals," 478 U.S. 1015 (1986); *Elane Photography, LLC v. Willock*, ___ N.M. ___, (for-profit photography business owned by a husband and wife refused to photograph a lesbian couple's commitment ceremony based on the religious beliefs of the company's owners), 572 U.S. ___ (2014). Would RFRA require exemptions in cases of this ilk? And if not, how does the Court divine which religious beliefs are worthy of accommodation, and which are not? Isn't the Court disarmed from making such a judgment given its recognition that "courts must not presume to determine...the plausibility of a religious claim"?

Would the exemption the Court holds RFRA demands for employers with religiously grounded objections to the use of certain contraceptives extend to employers with religiously grounded objections to blood transfusions (Jehovah's Witnesses); antidepressants (Scientologists); medications derived

obtain an exemption from the obligation to pay Social Security taxes only for employees who are coreligionists and who likewise seek an exemption and agree to give up their Social Security benefits. Thus, employers with sincere religious beliefs have no right to a religion-based exemption that would deprive employees of Social Security benefits without the employee's consent—an exemption analogous to the one Hobby Lobby and Conestoga seek here.

from pigs, including anesthesia, intravenous fluids, and pills coated with gelatin (certain Muslims, Jews, and Hindus); and vaccinations (Christian Scientists, among others)?* According to counsel for Hobby Lobby, "each one of these cases...would have to be evaluated on its own...applying the compelling interest–least restrictive alternative test." Not much help there for the lower courts bound by today's decision.

The Court, however, sees nothing to worry about. Today's cases, the Court concludes, are "concerned solely with the contraceptive mandate. Our decision should not be understood to hold that an insurance-coverage mandate must necessarily fall if it conflicts with an employer's religious beliefs. Other coverage requirements, such as immunizations, may be supported by different interests (for example, the need to combat the spread of infectious diseases) and may involve different arguments about the least restrictive means of providing them." But the Court has assumed, for RFRA purposes, that the interest in women's health and well being is compelling and has come up with no means adequate to serve that interest, the one motivating Congress to adopt the Women's Health Amendment.

There is an overriding interest, I believe, in keeping the courts "out of the business of evaluating the relative merits of differing religious claims," or the sincerity with which an asserted religious belief is held. Indeed, approving some religious claims while deeming others unworthy of accommodation could be "perceived as favoring one religion over another," the very "risk the Establishment Clause was designed to preclude." The Court, I fear, has ventured into a minefield by its immoderate reading of RFRA. I would confine religious exemptions under that Act to organizations formed "for a religious purpose," "engaged primarily in carrying out that religious purpose," and not "engaged... substantially in the exchange of goods or services for money beyond nominal amounts."

★ ★ ★

For the reasons stated, I would reverse the judgment of the Court of Appeals for the Tenth Circuit and affirm the judgment of the Court of Appeals for the Third Circuit.

* Religious objections to immunization programs are not hypothetical.

⚬ "Women in Desperate Circumstances"
⚬ *Whole Woman's Health et al. v. Hellerstedt*

Justice Ginsburg had the opportunity to revisit abortion restrictions in her concurrence to Justice Stephen Breyer's majority opinion holding unconstitutional a Texas abortion law (House Bill 2, or H. B. 2) enacted in 2013. The law required physicians who perform abortions to have admitting privileges at a hospital within thirty miles, and abortion facilities to meet standards equivalent to those for ambulatory surgical centers.

A group of Texas abortion providers challenged the law as applied to physicians at two abortion facilities, including Whole Woman's Health. The federal district court found that the surgical center requirement imposed an undue burden on the right of Texas women to seek a pre-viability abortion. The law effectively cut in half the number of abortion providers in the state, doubling the number of women of reproductive age who lived more than fifty miles from an abortion clinic. The U.S. Court of Appeals for the Fifth Circuit reversed that decision, and the abortion providers appealed to the U.S. Supreme Court, where six justices voted that the law was unconstitutional.

Justice Breyer's opinion held that the Fifth Circuit had mistakenly applied too lenient a standard of judicial review to the Texas law. Breyer reasoned that the surgical center requirement provided few if any health benefits; other laws already required abortion facilities to meet numerous health and safety requirements. Moreover, the additional requirements imposed were not required at facilities where other procedures, less safe than abortion, were performed. Three justices, Alito, Roberts, and Thomas, dissented.

Justice Ginsburg joined Justice Breyer's opinion but also wrote a separate concurrence to underscore the importance of access to safe abortion for the health of women facing real-life difficulties: "Women in desperate circumstances may resort to unlicensed rogue practitioners...at great risk to their health and safety."

WHOLE WOMAN'S HEALTH ET AL. V. HELLERSTEDT, COMMISSIONER, TEXAS DEPARTMENT OF STATE HEALTH SERVICES, ET AL.

CERTIORARI TO THE UNITED STATES COURT OF APPEALS
FOR THE FIFTH CIRCUIT
573 U.S. ___ (June 27, 2016)

CONCURRENCE

Justice Ginsburg, concurring.

The Texas law called H. B. 2 inevitably will reduce the number of clinics and doctors allowed to provide abortion services. Texas argues that H. B. 2's restrictions are constitutional because they protect the health of women who experience complications from abortions. In truth, "complications from an abortion are both rare and rarely dangerous." See Brief for American College of Obstetricians and Gynecologists et al. as Amici Curiae 6–10 (collecting studies and concluding "abortion is one of the safest medical procedures performed in the United States"); Brief for Social Science Researchers as Amici Curiae 5–9 (compiling studies that show "complication rates from abortion are very low"). Many medical procedures, including childbirth, are far more dangerous to patients, yet are not subject to ambulatory-surgical-center or hospital admitting-privileges requirements. See Brief for Social Science Researchers 9–11 (comparing statistics on risks for abortion with tonsillectomy, colonoscopy, and in-office dental surgery); Brief for American Civil Liberties Union et al. as Amici Curiae 7 (all District Courts to consider admitting privileges requirements found abortion "is at least as safe as other medical procedures routinely performed in outpatient settings"). Given those realities, it is beyond rational belief that H. B. 2 could genuinely protect the health of women, and certain that the law "would simply make it more difficult for them to obtain abortions." When a State severely limits access to safe and legal procedures, women in desperate circumstances may resort to unlicensed rogue practitioners, *faute de mieux* [for want of a better alternative], at great risk to their health and safety. So long as this Court adheres to *Roe v. Wade*, 410 U.S. 113 (1973), and *Planned Parenthood of Southeastern Pa. v. Casey*, 505 U.S. 833 (1992), Targeted Regulation of Abortion Providers laws like H. B. 2 that "do little or nothing for health, but rather strew impediments to abortion" cannot survive judicial inspection.

⚞ "A Vexing Issue"
Sessions v. Morales-Santana

Luis Ramón Morales-Santana was born in 1962 in the Dominican Republic to an unmarried couple, a father who was a U.S. citizen and a Dominican mother. The government sought to deport Morales-Santana as an alien after he was convicted of several crimes. Morales-Santana claimed that he should be treated as a citizen because the birthright citizenship law, which made it easier for unwed U.S. citizen mothers to confer citizenship on their offspring than for unwed U.S. citizen fathers to do so, violated equal protection.

Equal Protection, Equal Residency Requirements?

Under the law, a child born out of the country to an unwed U.S. citizen mother obtained U.S. citizenship if the mother had previously resided in the United States continuously for one year. For an unwed U.S. citizen father, the continuous residency requirement was ten years, with five of those years after age fourteen. Morales-Santana's father had missed meeting the residency requirement by only about twenty days when he left Puerto Rico as an eighteen-year-old to work in the Dominican Republic.

An immigration judge ruled that Morales-Santana should be deported. The U.S. Court of Appeals for the Second Circuit reversed that ruling, holding that the birthright citizenship law's discrimination between unwed fathers and unwed mothers violated equal protection. As a remedy, the Second Circuit held that Morales-Santana derived citizenship from his father.

The Problem of a Remedy

The federal government appealed this decision. Justice Ginsburg's opinion, holding that the birthright citizenship law as written violated equal protection, carried the majority, but part of the reason was likely that the opinion provided a different remedy from the Second Circuit. On this "vexing issue," the majority ruled that the law should be interpreted to equalize the treatment of the sexes by requiring the mother to meet the more difficult residency requirement imposed on the father in order to confer citizenship on a child—not by allowing the father to meet the mother's more lenient requirement.

In cases involving the equal extension of benefits to both sexes that Ginsburg had argued in her work with the ACLU, the remedy was generally to create equal treatment by extending equally generous benefits to both sexes rather than taking away an advantage that a law had reserved for one or the other. But these are different times, and a different Court. Justice Clarence Thomas, who was joined by Justice Samuel Alito in concurring only in part of the Court's decision in the case, noted that he was voting with the majority only because the result was that Morales-Santana would be deported.

JEFFERSON B. SESSIONS, III, ATTORNEY GENERAL, PETITIONER V. LUIS RAMÓN MORALES-SANTANA
CERTIORARI TO THE UNITED STATES COURT OF APPEALS
FOR THE SECOND CIRCUIT
582 U.S. ___ (June 12, 2017)

Opinion Announcement

Ruth Bader Ginsburg: This case concerns a birthright citizenship statute that treats unwed U.S. citizen mothers more favorably than unwed U.S. citizen fathers.

A child born abroad to an unwed U.S. citizen mother becomes a citizen at birth if her mother previously resided in the United States for a continuous period of one year.

Unwed U.S. citizen fathers, however, are subject to a longer residency requirement.

In 1962, when respondent Luis Ramón Morales-Santana was born, that more onerous requirement was 10 years' U.S. residency before the child's birth, five of those years after age 14.

Today the requirement is five years, two after age 14.

Morales-Santana had lived in the United States since age 13.

His father, Jose Morales, was a U.S. citizen.

Jose left the country just 20 days short of his 19th birthday to work in the Dominican Republic, where he met the Dominican woman who gave birth to Morales-Santana.

Jose accepted parental responsibility, living with and later marrying Morales-Santana's mother.

In 2000, the government sought to remove Morales-Santana after he served time on several criminal convictions.

He ranked as an alien, the government maintained, because at the time of his birth in the Dominican Republic, his father Jose Morales had not resided in the United States for five years after age 14.

An immigration judge ordered Morales-Santana's removal, and the Board of Immigration Appeals upheld the removal.

The Second Circuit reversed.

The statute's differential treatment of unwed mothers and fathers, the Court of Appeals held, violates the Constitution's equal protection guarantee.

To cure the infirmity, the Second Circuit held that Morales-Santana derived citizenship through his father just as he would had his mother been the U.S. citizen.

We granted review to resolve a matter on which we divided equally six years ago.

We now hold that the gender line Congress drew is incompatible with the Constitution's guarantee of the equal protection of the laws to all persons.

Legislative classifications on the basis of gender are today subject to heightened scrutiny, which means they fail unless supported by an exceedingly persuasive justification.

When enacting the statute here at issue in the mid 20th century, Congress codified the stereotype that an unwed mother is the sole guardian of a non-marital child.

Unwed U.S. citizen fathers needed a longer period of U.S. residency, on this view, as it was assumed most men cared little about their non-marital children.

An unwed citizen mother needed no such prophylactic, it was thought, because the alien father would not be around to be a foreign influence on the child.

We discern no exceedingly persuasive reason for laws resting on these gender-based stereotypes.

The government suggests that Congress's aim was to reduce the risk of statelessness for the foreign born child of a U.S. citizen.

In fact, however, the risk of parenting stateless children abroad was and remains substantial for unmarried U.S. citizen fathers, a risk perhaps greater than for unmarried U.S. citizen mothers.

Because the statute's prescription of different physical presence requirements for unwed mothers and fathers violates the Constitution's equal protection guarantee, we turn next to a vexing issue.

What is the appropriate remedy?

To answer that question, we must ask, what solution would Congress have preferred had it been aware of the statute's unconstitutionality?

Ordinarily, extension of statutory benefits to the left-out class is the right disposition.

But here, Congress has bracketed unwed fathers with married couples—one spouse, male or female, a citizen and the other an alien.

Unwed mothers are the exception to the main rule.

If the one-year dispensation were extended to unwed citizen fathers, would it not be irrational to retain the longer term when the U.S. citizen parent is married?

Although I just said the preferred route in a typical case is to extend favorable treatment, this is hardly the typical case.

The extension here would render the special treatment Congress prescribed—the one-year physical presence requirement for unwed U.S. citizen mothers—the general rule no longer the exception.

The longer physical presence requirement applicable to a substantial majority of children born abroad to one U.S. citizen parent and one foreign citizen parent, therefore, must hold sway.

Going forward, Congress may address the issue and settle on a uniform prescription that neither favors nor disadvantages any person on the basis of gender.

In the interim, the Government must ensure that the laws in question are administered with an even hand.

With provisions stated more elaborately in the Court's opinion, we affirm the judgment of the Second Circuit in part, reverse in part and remand.

OPINION

Most citations and footnotes have been omitted, as well as some punctuation (including brackets and internal quotation marks).

Justice Ginsburg delivered the opinion of the Court.

This case concerns a gender-based differential in the law governing acquisition of U.S. citizenship by a child born abroad, when one parent is a U.S. citizen, the other, a citizen of another nation. The main rule appears in 8 U.S.C. §1401(a)(7), now §1401(g). Applicable to married couples, §1401(a)(7) requires a period of physical presence in the United States for the U.S.-citizen parent. The requirement, as initially prescribed, was ten years' physical presence prior to the child's birth; currently, the requirement is five years pre-birth. That main rule is rendered applicable to unwed U.S.-citizen fathers by §1409(a). Congress ordered an exception, however, for unwed U.S.-citizen mothers. Contained in §1409(c), the exception allows an unwed mother to transmit her citizenship to a child born abroad if she has lived in the United States for just one year prior to the child's birth.

The respondent in this case, Luis Ramón Morales-Santana, was born in the Dominican Republic when his father was just 20 days short of meeting §1401(a)(7)'s physical-presence requirement. Opposing removal to the Dominican Republic, Morales-Santana asserts that the equal protection principle implicit in the Fifth Amendment* entitles him to citizenship stature. We hold that the gender line Congress drew is incompatible with the requirement that the Government accord to all persons "the equal protection of the laws." Nevertheless, we cannot convert §1409(c)'s exception for unwed mothers into the main rule displacing §1401(a)(7) (covering married couples) and §1409(a) (covering unwed fathers). We must therefore leave it to Congress to select, going forward, a physical-presence requirement (ten years, one year, or some other period) uniformly applicable to all children born abroad with one U.S.-citizen and one alien parent, wed or unwed. In the interim, the Government must ensure that the laws in question are administered in a manner free from gender-based discrimination.

I

A

We first describe in greater detail the regime Congress constructed. The general rules for acquiring U.S. citizenship are found in 8 U.S.C. §1401, the first section in Chapter 1 of Title III of the Immigration and Nationality Act (1952 Act or INA), §301. Section 1401 sets forth the INA's rules for determining who "shall be nationals and citizens of the United States at birth" by establishing a range of residency and physical-presence requirements calibrated primarily to the parents' nationality and the child's place of birth. The primacy of §1401 in the statutory scheme is evident. Comprehensive in coverage, §1401 provides the general framework for the acquisition of citizenship at birth. In particular, at the time relevant here, §1401(a)(7) provided for the U.S. citizenship of

"a person born outside the geographical limits of the United States and its outlying possessions of parents one of whom is an alien,

---

* As this case involves federal, not state, legislation, the applicable equality guarantee is not the Fourteenth Amendment's explicit Equal Protection Clause, it is the guarantee implicit in the Fifth Amendment's Due Process Clause. See *Weinberger v. Wiesenfeld*, 420

and the other a citizen of the United States who, prior to the birth of such person, was physically present in the United States or its outlying possessions for a period or periods totaling not less than ten years, at least five of which were after attaining the age of fourteen years: Provided, That any periods of honorable service in the Armed Forces of the United States by such citizen parent may be included in computing the physical presence requirements of this paragraph."

Congress has since reduced the duration requirement to five years, two after age 14. §1401(g) (2012 ed.).

Section 1409 pertains specifically to children with unmarried parents. Its first subsection, §1409(a), incorporates by reference the physical-presence requirements of §1401, thereby allowing an acknowledged unwed citizen parent to transmit U.S. citizenship to a foreign-born child under the same terms as a married citizen parent. Section 1409(c)—a provision applicable only to unwed U.S.-citizen mothers—states an exception to the physical-presence requirements of §§1401 and 1409(a). Under §1409(c)'s exception, only one year of continuous physical presence is required before unwed mothers may pass citizenship to their children born abroad.

B

Respondent Luis Ramón Morales-Santana moved to the United States at age thirteen, and has resided in this country most of his life. Now facing deportation, he asserts U.S. citizenship at birth based on the citizenship of his biological father, José Morales, who accepted parental responsibility and included Morales-Santana in his household. José Morales was born in Guánica, Puerto Rico, on March 19, 1900. Puerto Rico was then, as it is now, part of the United States, and José became a U.S. citizen under the Organic Act of Puerto Rico. After living in Puerto Rico for nearly two decades, José left his childhood home on February 27, 1919, twenty days short of his nineteenth birthday, therefore failing to satisfy §1401(a)(7)'s requirement of five years' physical presence after age fourteen. He did so to take up employment as a

U.S. 636, 638, n. 2 (1975) ("While the Fifth Amendment contains no equal protection clause, it does forbid discrimination that is so unjustifiable as to be violative of due process. This Court's approach to Fifth Amendment equal protection claims has always been precisely the same as to equal protection claims under the Fourteenth Amendment.")

builder-mechanic for a U.S. company in the then-U.S.-occupied Dominican Republic.

By 1959, José attested in a June 21, 1971 affidavit presented to the U.S. Embassy in the Dominican Republic, he was living with Yrma Santana Montilla, a Dominican woman he would eventually marry. In 1962, Yrma gave birth to their child, respondent Luis Morales-Santana. While the record before us reveals little about Morales-Santana's childhood, the Dominican archives disclose that Yrma and José married in 1970, and that José was then added to Morales-Santana's birth certificate as his father. José also related in the same affidavit that he was then saving money "for the sustenance of [his] family" in anticipation of undergoing surgery in Puerto Rico, where members of his family still resided. In 1975, when Morales-Santana was 13, he moved to Puerto Rico, and by 1976, the year his father died, he was attending public school in the Bronx, a New York City borough.

C

In 2000, the Government placed Morales-Santana in removal proceedings based on several convictions for offenses under New York State Penal Law, all of them rendered on May 17, 1995. Morales-Santana ranked as an alien despite the many years he lived in the United States, because, at the time of his birth, his father did not satisfy the requirement of five years' physical presence after age 14. An immigration judge rejected Morales-Santana's claim to citizenship derived from the U.S. citizenship of his father, and ordered Morales-Santana's removal to the Dominican Republic. In 2010, Morales-Santana moved to reopen the proceedings, asserting that the Government's refusal to recognize that he derived citizenship from his U.S.-citizen father violated the Constitution's equal protection guarantee. The Board of Immigration Appeals (BIA) denied the motion.

The United States Court of Appeals for the Second Circuit reversed the BIA's decision. Relying on this Court's post-1970 construction of the equal protection principle as it bears on gender-based classifications, the court held unconstitutional the differential treatment of unwed mothers and fathers. To cure the constitutional flaw, the court further held that Morales-Santana derived citizenship through his father, just as he would were his mother the U.S. citizen. In so ruling, the Second Circuit declined to follow the conflicting decision of the Ninth Circuit in *United States v. Flores-Villar*, 536 F. 3d 990 (2008). We granted certiorari in *Flores-Villar*, but ultimately affirmed by an equally divided Court. Taking up Morales-Santana's request for review, we consider the matter anew.

II

Because §1409 treats sons and daughters alike, Morales-Santana does not suffer discrimination on the basis of his gender. He complains, instead, of gender-based discrimination against his father, who was unwed at the time of Morales-Santana's birth and was not accorded the right an unwed U.S.-citizen mother would have to transmit citizenship to her child. Although the Government does not contend otherwise, we briefly explain why Morales-Santana may seek to vindicate his father's right to the equal protection of the laws.

Ordinarily, a party "must assert his own legal rights" and "cannot rest his claim to relief on the legal rights...of third parties." But we recognize an exception where, as here, "the party asserting the right has a close relationship with the person who possesses the right [and] there is a hindrance to the possessor's ability to protect his own interests." José Morales' ability to pass citizenship to his son, respondent Morales-Santana, easily satisfies the "close relationship" requirement. So, too, is the "hindrance" requirement well met. José Morales' failure to assert a claim in his own right "stems from disability," not "disinterest," for José died in 1976, many years before the current controversy arose. Morales-Santana is thus the "obvious claimant," the "best available proponent," of his father's right to equal protection.

III

Sections 1401 and 1409, we note, date from an era when the lawbooks of our Nation were rife with overbroad generalizations about the way men and women are. Today, laws of this kind are subject to review under the heightened scrutiny that now attends "all gender-based classifications." See, e.g., *United States v. Virginia*, 518 U.S. 515, 555–556 (1996) (state-maintained military academy may not deny admission to qualified women).

Laws granting or denying benefits "on the basis of the sex of the qualifying parent," our post-1970 decisions affirm, differentiate on the basis of gender, and therefore attract heightened review under the Constitution's equal protection guarantee.

Prescribing one rule for mothers, another for fathers, §1409 is of the same genre as the classifications we declared unconstitutional in *Reed,*

Frontiero, Wiesenfeld, Goldfarb, and *Westcott.* As in those cases, heightened scrutiny is in order. Successful defense of legislation that differentiates on the basis of gender, we have reiterated, requires an "exceedingly persuasive justification."

A

The defender of legislation that differentiates on the basis of gender must show "at least that the [challenged] classification serves important governmental objectives and that the discriminatory means employed are substantially related to the achievement of those objectives." Moreover, the classification must substantially serve an important governmental interest today, for "in interpreting the equal protection [guarantee], [we have] recognized that new insights and societal understandings can reveal unjustified inequality...that once passed unnoticed and unchallenged." Here, the Government has supplied no "exceedingly persuasive justification," for §1409(a) and (c)'s "gender-based" and "gender biased" disparity.

1

History reveals what lurks behind §1409. Enacted in the Nationality Act of 1940 (1940 Act), §1409 ended a century and a half of congressional silence on the citizenship of children born abroad to unwed parents. During this era, two once habitual, but now untenable, assumptions pervaded our Nation's citizenship laws and underpinned judicial and administrative rulings: In marriage, husband is dominant, wife subordinate; unwed mother is the natural and sole guardian of a non–marital child.

Under the once entrenched principle of male dominance in marriage, the husband controlled both wife and child. "Dominance [of] the husband," this Court observed in 1915, "is an ancient principle of our jurisprudence." *Mackenzie v. Hare,* 239 U.S. 299, 311 (1915). Through the early 20th century, a male citizen automatically conferred U.S. citizenship on his alien wife. A female citizen, however, was incapable of conferring citizenship on her husband; indeed, she was subject to expatriation if she married an alien. The family of a citizen or a lawfully admitted permanent resident enjoyed statutory exemptions from entry requirements, but only if the citizen or resident was male. And from 1790 until 1934, the foreign-born child of a married couple gained U.S. citizenship only through the father.

For unwed parents, the father-controls tradition never held sway. Instead, the mother was regarded as the child's natural and sole guardian. At common law, the mother, and only the mother, was "bound to maintain [a nonmarital child] as its natural guardian." In line with that understanding, in the early 20th century, the State Department sometimes permitted unwed mothers to pass citizenship to their children, despite the absence of any statutory authority for the practice.

In the 1940 Act, Congress discarded the father-controls assumption concerning married parents, but codified the mother-as-sole-guardian perception regarding unmarried parents. The Roosevelt administration, which proposed §1409, explained: "The mother [of a nonmarital child] stands in the place of the father..., has a right to the custody and control of such a child as against the putative father, and is bound to maintain it as its natural guardian."

This unwed-mother-as-natural-guardian notion renders §1409's gender-based residency rules understandable. Fearing that a foreign-born child could turn out "more alien than American in character," the administration believed that a citizen parent with lengthy ties to the United States would counteract the influence of the alien parent. Concern about the attachment of foreign-born children to the United States explains the treatment of unwed citizen fathers, who, according to the familiar stereotype, would care little about, and have scant contact with, their nonmarital children. For unwed citizen mothers, however, there was no need for a prolonged residency prophylactic: The alien father, who might transmit foreign ways, was presumptively out of the picture.

2

For close to a half century, as earlier observed, this Court has viewed with suspicion laws that rely on "overbroad generalizations about the different talents, capacities, or preferences of males and females." In particular, we have recognized that if a "statutory objective is to exclude or 'protect' members of one gender" in reliance on "fixed notions concerning [that gender's] roles and abilities," the "objective itself is illegitimate." In accord with this eventual understanding, the Court has held that no "important [governmental] interest" is served by laws grounded, as §1409(a) and (c) are, in the obsolescing view that "unwed fathers [are] invariably less qualified and entitled than mothers" to take responsibility for nonmarital children. Overbroad generalizations of that order, the Court has come to comprehend, have a constraining impact,

descriptive though they may be of the way many people still order their lives.*
Laws according or denying benefits in reliance on "stereotypes about women's
domestic roles," the Court has observed, may "create a self-fulfilling cycle of
discrimination that forces women to continue to assume the role of primary
family caregiver." Correspondingly, such laws may disserve men who exercise responsibility for raising their children. In light of the equal protection
jurisprudence this Court has developed since 1971, §1409(a) and (c)'s discrete
duration-of-residence requirements for unwed mothers and fathers who have
accepted parental responsibility is stunningly anachronistic.

B

In urging this Court nevertheless to reject Morales-Santana's equal
protection plea, the Government cites three decisions of this Court: *Fiallo
v. Bell*, 430 U.S. 787 (1977); *Miller v. Albright*, 523 U.S. 420; and *Nguyen v.
INS*, 533 U.S. 53. None controls this case. The 1952 Act provision at issue
in *Fiallo* gave special immigration preferences to alien children of citizen (or
lawful-permanent-resident) mothers, and to alien unwed mothers of citizen
(or lawful-permanent-resident) children. Unwed fathers and their children,
asserting their right to equal protection, sought the same preferences. Applying minimal scrutiny (rational-basis review), the Court upheld the provision,
relying on Congress' "exceptionally broad power" to admit or exclude aliens.
This case, however, involves no entry preference for aliens. Morales-Santana
claims he is, and since birth has been, a U.S. citizen. Examining a claim of
that order, the Court has not disclaimed, as it did in *Fiallo*, the application of
an exacting standard of review.

The provision challenged in *Miller* and *Nguyen* as violative of equal
protection requires unwed U.S.-citizen fathers, but not mothers, to formally
acknowledge parenthood of their foreign-born children in order to transmit
their U.S. citizenship to those children. After *Miller* produced no opinion for
the Court, we took up the issue anew in *Nguyen*. There, the Court held that
imposing a paternal-acknowledgment requirement on fathers was a justifiable, easily met means of ensuring the existence of a biological parent-child
relationship, which the mother establishes by giving birth. Morales-Santana's
challenge does not renew the contest over §1409's paternal-acknowledgment

---

* Even if stereotypes frozen into legislation have "statistical support," our decisions reject
measures that classify unnecessarily and overbroadly by gender when more accurate
and impartial lines can be drawn. In fact, unwed fathers assume responsibility for their
children in numbers already large and notably increasing....

requirement (whether the current version or that in effect in 1970), and the Government does not dispute that Morales-Santana's father, by marrying Morales-Santana's mother, satisfied that requirement.

Unlike the paternal-acknowledgment requirement at issue in *Nguyen* and *Miller*, the physical-presence requirements now before us relate solely to the duration of the parent's prebirth residency in the United States, not to the parent's filial tie to the child. As the Court of Appeals observed in this case, a man needs no more time in the United States than a woman "in order to have assimilated citizenship-related values to transmit to [his] child." And unlike *Nguyen*'s parental-acknowledgment requirement, §1409(a)'s age-calibrated physical-presence requirements cannot fairly be described as "minimal."

C

Notwithstanding §1409(a) and (c)'s provenance in traditional notions of the way women and men are, the Government maintains that the statute serves two important objectives: (1) ensuring a connection between the child to become a citizen and the United States and (2) preventing "statelessness," i.e., a child's possession of no citizenship at all. Even indulging the assumption that Congress intended §1409 to serve these interests, neither rationale survives heightened scrutiny.

1

We take up first the Government's assertion that §1409(a) and (c)'s gender-based differential ensures that a child born abroad has a connection to the United States of sufficient strength to warrant conferral of citizenship at birth. The Government does not contend, nor could it, that unmarried men take more time to absorb U.S. values than unmarried women do. Instead, it presents a novel argument, one it did not advance in *Flores-Villar*.

An unwed mother, the Government urges, is the child's only "legally recognized" parent at the time of childbirth. An unwed citizen father enters the scene later, as a second parent. A longer physical connection to the United States is warranted for the unwed father, the Government maintains, because of the "competing national influence" of the alien mother. Congress, the Government suggests, designed the statute to bracket an unwed U.S.-citizen mother with a married couple in which both parents are U.S. citizens, and to align an unwed U.S.-citizen father with a married couple, one spouse a citizen, the other, an alien.

Underlying this apparent design is the assumption that the alien father of a nonmarital child born abroad to a U.S.-citizen mother will not accept parental responsibility. For an actual affiliation between alien father and nonmarital child would create the "competing national influence" that, according to the Government, justifies imposing on unwed U.S.-citizen fathers, but not unwed U.S.-citizen mothers, lengthy physical-presence requirements. Hardly gender neutral, that assumption conforms to the long-held view that unwed fathers care little about, indeed are strangers to, their children. Lump characterization of that kind, however, no longer passes equal protection inspection.

Accepting, arguendo, that Congress intended the diverse physical-presence prescriptions to serve an interest in ensuring a connection between the foreign-born nonmarital child and the United States, the gender-based means scarcely serve the posited end. The scheme permits the transmission of citizenship to children who have no tie to the United States so long as their mother was a U.S. citizen continuously present in the United States for one year at any point in her life prior to the child's birth. The transmission holds even if the mother marries the child's alien father immediately after the child's birth and never returns with the child to the United States. At the same time, the legislation precludes citizenship transmission by a U.S.-citizen father who falls a few days short of meeting §1401(a)(7)'s longer physical-presence requirements, even if the father acknowledges paternity on the day of the child's birth and raises the child in the United States. One cannot see in this driven-by-gender scheme the close means–end fit required to survive heightened scrutiny.

2

The Government maintains that Congress established the gender-based residency differential in §1409(a) and (c) to reduce the risk that a foreign-born child of a U.S. citizen would be born stateless. This risk, according to the Government, was substantially greater for the foreign-born child of an unwed U.S.-citizen mother than it was for the foreign-born child of an unwed U.S.-citizen father. But there is little reason to believe that a statelessness concern prompted the diverse physical-presence requirements. Nor has the Government shown that the risk of statelessness disproportionately endangered the children of unwed mothers.

As the Court of Appeals pointed out, with one exception, nothing in the congressional hearings and reports on the 1940 and 1952 Acts "refers to the problem of statelessness for children born abroad." Reducing the incidence of statelessness was the express goal of other sections of the 1940 Act. The justification for §1409's gender-based dichotomy, however, was not the child's plight, it was the mother's role as the "natural guardian" of a nonmarital child. It will not do to "hypothesize or invent" governmental purposes for gender classifications "post hoc in response to litigation."

Infecting the Government's risk-of-statelessness argument is an assumption without foundation. "Foreign laws that would put the child of the U.S.-citizen mother at risk of statelessness (by not providing for the child to acquire the father's citizenship at birth)," the Government asserts, "would protect the child of the U.S.-citizen father against statelessness by providing that the child would take his mother's citizenship." The Government, however, neglected to expose this supposed "protection" to a reality check. Had it done so, it would have recognized the formidable impediments placed by foreign laws on an unwed mother's transmission of citizenship to her child.

Experts who have studied the issue report that, at the time relevant here, in "at least thirty countries," citizen mothers generally could not transmit their citizenship to nonmarital children born within the mother's country. "As many as forty-five countries," they further report, "did not permit their female citizens to assign nationality to a nonmarital child born outside the subject country with a foreign father." In still other countries, they also observed, there was no legislation in point, leaving the nationality of nonmarital children uncertain. Taking account of the foreign laws actually in force, these experts concluded, "the risk of parenting stateless children abroad was, as of [1940 and 1952], and remains today, substantial for unmarried U.S. fathers, a risk perhaps greater than that for unmarried U.S. mothers." One can hardly characterize as gender neutral a scheme allegedly attending to the risk of statelessness for children of unwed U.S. citizen mothers while ignoring the same risk for children of unwed U.S.-citizen fathers.

In 2014, the United Nations High Commissioner for Refugees (UNHCR) undertook a ten-year project to eliminate statelessness by 2024. Cognizant that discrimination against either mothers or fathers in citizenship and nationality laws is a major cause of statelessness, the Commissioner has made a key component of its project the elimination of gender discrimination in such laws. In this light, we cannot countenance risk of statelessness as a reason to uphold, rather than strike out, differential treatment of unmarried women and men with regard to transmission of citizenship to their children.

In sum, the Government has advanced no "exceedingly persuasive" justification for §1409(a) and (c)'s gender-specific residency and age criteria. Those disparate criteria, we hold, cannot withstand inspection under a Constitution that requires the Government to respect the equal dignity and stature of its male and female citizens.

IV

While the equal protection infirmity in retaining a longer physical-presence requirement for unwed fathers than for unwed mothers is clear, this Court is not equipped to grant the relief Morales-Santana seeks, i.e., extending to his father (and, derivatively, to him) the benefit of the one-year physical-presence term §1409(c) reserves for unwed mothers. There are "two remedial alternatives," our decisions instruct, when a statute benefits one class (in this case, unwed mothers and their children), as §1409(c) does, and excludes another from the benefit (here, unwed fathers and their children). "A court may either declare [the statute] a nullity and order that its benefits not extend to the class that the legislature intended to benefit, or it may extend the coverage of the statute to include those who are aggrieved by exclusion."

"When the 'right invoked is that to equal treatment,' the appropriate remedy is a mandate of equal treatment, a result that can be accomplished by withdrawal of benefits from the favored class as well as by extension of benefits to the excluded class." "How equality is accomplished...is a matter on which the Constitution is silent."

The choice between these outcomes is governed by the legislature's intent, as revealed by the statute at hand.

Ordinarily, we have reiterated, "extension, rather than nullification, is the proper course." Illustratively, in a series of cases involving federal financial assistance benefits, the Court struck discriminatory exceptions denying benefits to discrete groups, which meant benefits previously denied were extended.

Here, however, the discriminatory exception consists of favorable treatment for a discrete group (a shorter physical-presence requirement for unwed U.S.-citizen mothers giving birth abroad). Following the same approach as in those benefits cases—striking the discriminatory exception—leads here to extending the general rule of longer physical-presence requirements to cover the previously favored group.

The Court has looked to Justice Harlan's concurring opinion in *Welsh v. United States*, 398 U.S., at 361–367, in considering whether the legislature would have struck an exception and applied the general rule equally to all, or instead, would have broadened the exception to cure the equal protection violation. In making this assessment, a court should "measure the intensity of commitment to the residual policy"—the main rule, not the exception—"and consider the degree of potential disruption of the statutory scheme that would occur by extension as opposed to abrogation."

The residual policy here, the longer physical-presence requirement stated in §§1401(a)(7) and 1409, evidences Congress' recognition of "the importance of residence in this country as the talisman of dedicated attachment." And the potential for "disruption of the statutory scheme" is large. For if §1409(c)'s one-year dispensation were extended to unwed citizen fathers, would it not be irrational to retain the longer term when the U.S.-citizen parent is married? Disadvantageous treatment of marital children in comparison to nonmarital children is scarcely a purpose one can sensibly attribute to Congress.*

Although extension of benefits is customary in federal benefit cases, all indicators in this case point in the opposite direction. Put to the choice, Congress, we believe, would have abrogated §1409(c)'s exception, preferring preservation of the general rule.†

V

The gender-based distinction infecting §§1401(a)(7) and 1409(a) and (c), we hold, violates the equal protection principle, as the Court of Appeals correctly ruled. For the reasons stated, however, we must adopt the remedial course Congress likely would have chosen "had it been apprised of the constitutional infirmity." Although the preferred rule in the typical case is to extend favorable treatment, this is hardly the typical case.‡ Extension here would render the special treatment Congress prescribed in §1409(c), the

---

* Distinctions based on parents' marital status, we have said, are subject to the same heightened scrutiny as distinctions based on gender.

† Compare with the remedial issue presented here suits under Title VII of the Civil Rights Act of 1964 challenging laws prescribing terms and conditions of employment applicable to women only, e.g., minimum wage, premium pay, rest breaks, or lunch breaks. Most courts, perhaps mindful of the mixed motives implicated in passage of such legislation (some conceiving the laws as protecting women, others, as discouraging employers from hiring women), and, taking into account the economic burdens extension would impose on employers, have invalidated the provisions.

‡ The Court of Appeals found the remedial issue "the most vexing problem in this case."

one-year physical-presence requirement for U.S.-citizen mothers, the general rule, no longer an exception. Section 1401(a)(7)'s longer physical-presence requirement, applicable to a substantial majority of children born abroad to one U.S.-citizen parent and one foreign-citizen parent, therefore, must hold sway.* Going forward, Congress may address the issue and settle on a uniform prescription that neither favors nor disadvantages any person on the basis of gender. In the interim, as the Government suggests, §1401(a)(7)'s now-five-year requirement should apply, prospectively, to children born to unwed U.S.-citizen mothers.

The judgment of the Court of Appeals for the Second Circuit is affirmed in part and reversed in part, and the case is remanded for further proceedings consistent with this opinion.

It is so ordered.

---

* That Morales-Santana did not seek this outcome does not restrain the Court's judgment. The issue turns on what the legislature would have willed. "The relief the complaining party requests does not circumscribe this inquiry."

"There Is Strength in Numbers"
Epic Systems Corp. v. Lewis

Employees of Epic Systems Corporation and Ernst & Young were required to sign arbitration agreements banning them from taking part in any collective judicial or arbitration proceedings of any kind. The employees claimed that they had been underpaid in violation of the Fair Labor Standards Act and state laws, and they filed suit against the employers collectively, allowing them to share attorney and other fees. The employers responded that the arbitration agreements required employees to litigate their wage and hour claims individually rather than collectively or in a class action.

Federal Arbitration Act or National Labor Relations Act?

The Federal Arbitration Act, enacted in 1925, provides that arbitration agreements "shall be valid, irrevocable, and enforceable, save upon such grounds as exist at law or in equity for the revocation of any contract." The employees argued that the "saving clause" ("save upon such grounds as exist at law or in equity for the revocation of any contract") in the Arbitration Act permitted invalidation of the collective litigation provision in the arbitration agreement if that provision violated some other federal law. The employees argued that requiring them to litigate their wage claims one by one, rather than collectively, violated the National Labor Relations Act (NLRA), which protected "concerted activities" by workers. In 2012, the National Labor Relations Board ruled that the NLRA nullifies the Arbitration Act in such cases.

In a majority opinion written by Justice Neal Gorsuch, the Court ruled that the Arbitration Act required enforcement of the arbitration agreements the employees had signed. The Court reasoned that Congress did not intend that the NLRA's protection of "concerted activities" by employees would extend to class and collective lawsuits, which had not been provided for by court rules at the time the NLRA was enacted in 1935. The Court ruled that the Federal Arbitration Act took precedence in this situation.

The Yellow Dog Contract Revisited

In dissent, Justice Ginsburg called the majority's ruling "egregiously wrong." She pointed out how little bargaining power employees had when signing the arbitration agreements required by the employers. The arbitration agreement provision barring collective litigation was similar to a "yellow dog contract," or a contract requiring workers to pledge not to join a labor union. Such contracts were outlawed in 1932 by the forerunner of the NLRA, the Norris-LaGuardia Act.

Justice Ginsburg argued that Congress recognized that "there is strength in numbers" for workers challenging workplace abuses and that collective litigation was one of the "concerted activities" protected under the NLRA. For each individual employee, small amounts of wages were involved. Cutting the expense of litigation and the risk of retaliation by joining forces was probably the only realistic way these employees could try to obtain their claimed lost wages.

Ginsburg's dissent warned that there would likely be widespread under-enforcement of laws protecting workers in the wake of the Court's decision. She called for congressional action to make it clear that the NLRA took precedence over the Arbitration Act in cases such as these. So far, no such action has been forthcoming. The majority's ruling has been called "a vivid illustration of the declining power of workers in the U.S. political system."[1]

EPIC SYSTEMS CORPORATION, PETITIONER V. JACOB LEWIS;
ON WRIT OF CERTIORARI TO THE UNITED STATES COURT OF APPEALS FOR THE SEVENTH CIRCUIT

ERNST & YOUNG LLP, ET AL., PETITIONERS V. STEPHEN MORRIS, ET AL.; AND
ON WRIT OF CERTIORARI TO THE UNITED STATES COURT OF APPEALS FOR THE NINTH CIRCUIT

NATIONAL LABOR RELATIONS BOARD, PETITIONER V. MURPHY OIL USA, INC., ET AL.
ON WRIT OF CERTIORARI TO THE UNITED STATES COURT OF APPEALS FOR THE FIFTH CIRCUIT

584 U.S. ___ (2018) [May 21, 2018]

Dissent Announcement

Ruth Bader Ginsburg: The employees in these cases complain that their employers have underpaid them in violation of the Fair Labor Standards Act and similar state laws.

Individually their claims are small.

The expenses entailed in seeking redress and the risk of employer retaliation would likely dissuade most workers from seeking redress alone.

But by joining their claims together in collective judicial or arbitral proceedings, the employees can spread the costs of litigation, lessen the risk of retaliation, and gain effective redress for wage underpayments all too often experienced.

To block employees from acting in concert, their employers required them to sign arbitration agreements banning collective judicial and arbitral proceedings of any kind.

The Court today holds enforceable these arm-twisted, take-it-or-leave-it contracts including the provisions requiring employees to litigate wage and hour claims only one by one.

Federal labor law does not countenance such isolation of employees.

Over 80 years ago, Congress recognized that for workers striving to gain from their employers decent terms and conditions of employment, there is strength in numbers.

In accord with that reality, Congress passed two statutes, the Norris-LaGuardia Act and the National Labor Relations Act, to protect workers' right to band together when confronting employers about working conditions.

Both statutes declare that employees have a fundamental right to engage in concerted activities for their mutual aid or protection.

These laws make it unlawful for employers to interfere with employees' concerted activities and stop courts from enforcing contractual provisions that require employees to refrain from engaging in such activities.

Justices Breyer, Sotomayor, Kagan and I would hold that the Norris-LaGuardia Act and the National Labor Relations Act rendered the employer-dictated collective-litigation bans unlawful and therefore unenforceable.

Suits to enforce workplace rights collectively fit comfortably within the ordinary meaning of the statutory terms "concerted activities for employees' mutual aid or protection."

Safeguarding employees from employer interference when they seek to litigate work-related claims in concert is firmly rooted in Congress's express will to protect workers' right to join forces in pursuit of better working conditions.

For over 75 years, the agency responsible for administering the National Labor Relations Act, the National Labor Relations Board, has consistently held that suits to enforce workplace rights collectively rank as protected activities with which employers may not interfere.

Lower courts too have taken that view.

The Court today rules otherwise. It concludes that the Norris-LaGuardia Act and the National Labor Relations Act are about forming unions and engaging in collective bargaining and do not safeguard employees' ability to litigate shared legal claims in collective proceedings.

In the Court's view, not even two workers could join in a complaint.

That cramped interpretation of the Labor Act's protections shuts from sight this clear understanding.

To repeat, when workers charge their employers with unlawful conduct—in this case, violations of laws governing wages earned and hours worked—there is strength in numbers.

Today's decision is driven not by the Court's finding in the Arbitration Act an emphatic command to enforce the employer-imposed take-it-or-leave-it arbitration agreements according to the terms, including the provision confining employees to solo proceedings.

The Arbitration Act was adopted in 1925 to enable merchants of roughly equal bargaining power to enter into binding agreements to arbitrate commercial disputes.

In recent decades, this Court's decisions have stretched the Arbitration Act far beyond that intended scope.

But even accepting this Court's Arbitration Act decisions as they are, nothing compels the destructive result the Court reaches today.

The Arbitration Act includes an equal treatment rule for arbitration agreements falling within its reach.

Congress said in so many words that agreements falling within the compass of the Arbitration Act are as enforceable as other contracts, but not more so. Congress accordingly included a saving clause pursuant to which arbitration provisions may be invalidated based on generally applicable contract defenses.

Illegality is such a defense. Properly assessed under federal labor law, the employer-dictated collective-litigation stoppers should be recognized as unlawful.

Declining to enforce them would put them on the same footing as any other contract provision incompatible with controlling federal law.

The Arbitration Act thus can and should be applied in harmony with federal labor policy.

Even if the saving clause is not construed to accommodate federal labor policy, the Norris-LaGuardia Act and the National Labor Relations Act should prevail over the Arbitration Act for reasons stated in written opinion.

The inevitable result of today's decision: there will be huge underenforcement of federal and state statutes designed to advance the well-being of vulnerable workers.

Congressional action is urgently in order to correct the Court's elevation of the Arbitration Act over workers' right to act in concert.

DISSENT

Most citations and footnotes have been omitted, as well as some punctuation (including brackets and internal quotation marks).

Justice Ginsburg, with whom Justice Breyer, Justice Sotomayor, and Justice Kagan join, dissenting.

The employees in these cases complain that their employers have underpaid them in violation of the wage and hours prescriptions of the Fair Labor Standards Act of 1938 (FLSA) and analogous state laws. Individually, their claims are small, scarcely of a size warranting the expense of seeking redress alone. See Ruan, What's Left To Remedy Wage Theft? How Arbitration Mandates That Bar Class Actions Impact Low-Wage Workers, 2012 Mich. St. L. Rev. 1103, 1118–1119 (Ruan). But by joining together with others similarly circumstanced, employees can gain effective redress for wage underpayment commonly experienced. To block such concerted action, their employers required them to sign, as a condition of employment, arbitration agreements banning collective judicial and arbitral proceedings of any kind. The question presented: Does the Federal Arbitration Act (Arbitration Act or FAA) permit employers to insist that their employees, whenever seeking redress for commonly experienced wage loss, go it alone, never mind the right secured to employees by the National Labor Relations Act (NLRA) "to engage in...concerted activities" for their "mutual aid or protection"? The answer should be a resounding "No."

In the NLRA and its forerunner, the Norris-LaGuardia Act (NLGA), Congress acted on an acute awareness: For workers striving to gain from their employers decent terms and conditions of employment, there is strength in numbers. A single employee, Congress understood, is disarmed in dealing with an employer. The Court today subordinates employee-protective labor legislation to the Arbitration Act. In so doing, the Court forgets the labor market imbalance that gave rise to the NLGA and the NLRA, and ignores the destructive consequences of diminishing the right of employees "to band together in confronting an employer." Congressional correction of the Court's elevation of the FAA over workers' rights to act in concert is urgently in order.

To explain why the Court's decision is egregiously wrong, I first refer to the extreme imbalance once prevalent in our Nation's workplaces, and

Congress' aim in the NLGA and the NLRA to place employers and employees on a more equal footing. I then explain why the Arbitration Act, sensibly read, does not shrink the NLRA's protective sphere.

I

It was once the dominant view of this Court that "the right of a person to sell his labor upon such terms as he deems proper is...the same as the right of the purchaser of labor to prescribe [working] conditions." *Adair v. United States*, 208 U.S. 161, 174 (1908) (invalidating federal law prohibiting interstate railroad employers from discharging or discriminating against employees based on their membership in labor organizations).

The NLGA and the NLRA operate on a different premise, that employees must have the capacity to act collectively in order to match their employers' clout in setting terms and conditions of employment. For decades, the Court's decisions have reflected that understanding.

A

The end of the 19th century and beginning of the 20th was a tumultuous era in the history of our Nation's labor relations. Under economic conditions then prevailing, workers often had to accept employment on whatever terms employers dictated. Aiming to secure better pay, shorter workdays, and safer workplaces, workers increasingly sought to band together to make their demands effective.

Employers, in turn, engaged in a variety of tactics to hinder workers' efforts to act in concert for their mutual benefit. Notable among such devices was the "yellow-dog contract." Such agreements, which employers required employees to sign as a condition of employment, typically commanded employees to abstain from joining labor unions. Many of the employer-designed agreements cast an even wider net, "proscribing all manner of concerted activities." As a prominent United States Senator observed, contracts of the yellow-dog genre rendered the "laboring man...absolutely helpless" by "waiving his right...to free association" and by requiring that he "singly present any grievance he has."

Early legislative efforts to protect workers' rights to band together were unavailing. Courts, including this one, invalidated the legislation based on then-ascendant notions about employers' and employees' constitutional right to "liberty of contract." While stating that legislatures could curtail contractual "liberty" in the interest of public health, safety, and the general welfare, courts placed outside those bounds legislative action to redress the bargaining power imbalance workers faced.

In the 1930's, legislative efforts to safeguard vulnerable workers found more receptive audiences. As the Great Depression shifted political winds further in favor of worker-protective laws, Congress passed two statutes aimed at protecting employees' associational rights. First, in 1932, Congress passed the NLGA, which regulates the employer-employee relationship indirectly. Section 2 of the Act declares:

"Whereas...the individual unorganized worker is commonly helpless to exercise actual liberty of contract and to protect his freedom of labor,...it is necessary that he have full freedom of association, self-organization, and designation of representatives of his own choosing,...and that he shall be free from the interference, restraint, or coercion of employers...in the designation of such representatives or in self-organization or in other concerted activities for the purpose of collective bargaining or other mutual aid or protection."

Section 3 provides that federal courts shall not enforce "any...undertaking or promise in conflict with the public policy declared in [§2]." In adopting these provisions, Congress sought to render ineffective employer-imposed contracts proscribing employees' concerted activity of any and every kind. While banning court enforcement of contracts proscribing concerted action by employees, the NLGA did not directly prohibit coercive employer practices.

But Congress did so three years later, in 1935, when it enacted the NLRA. Relevant here, §7 of the NLRA guarantees employees "the right to self-organization, to form, join, or assist labor organizations, to bargain collectively through representatives of their own choosing, and to engage in other concerted activities for the purpose of collective bargaining or other mutual aid or protection." Section 8(a)(1) safeguards those rights by making it an "unfair labor practice" for an employer to "interfere with, restrain, or coerce employees in the exercise of the rights guaranteed in [§7]." To oversee the Act's guarantees, the Act established the National Labor Relations Board (Board or NLRB), an independent regulatory agency empowered to administer "labor policy for the Nation."

Unlike earlier legislative efforts, the NLGA and the NLRA had staying power. When a case challenging the NLRA's constitutionality made its way here, the Court, in retreat from its *Lochner*-era contractual-"liberty" decisions, upheld the Act as a permissible exercise of legislative authority. The Court recognized that employees have a "fundamental right" to join together to advance their common interests and that Congress, in lieu of "ignoring" that right, had elected to "safeguard" it.

B

Despite the NLRA's prohibitions, the employers in the cases now before the Court required their employees to sign contracts stipulating to submission of wage and hours claims to binding arbitration, and to do so only one-by-one.* When employees subsequently filed wage and hours claims in federal court and sought to invoke the collective-litigation procedures provided for in the FLSA and Federal Rules of Civil Procedure,† the employers moved to compel individual arbitration. The Arbitration Act, in their view, requires courts to enforce their take-it-or-leave-it arbitration agreements as written, including the collective-litigation abstinence demanded therein.

In resisting enforcement of the group-action foreclosures, the employees involved in this litigation do not urge that they must have access to a judicial forum. They argue only that the NLRA prohibits their employers from denying them the right to pursue work-related claims in concert in any forum. If they may be stopped by employer-dictated terms from pursuing

---

* The Court's opinion opens with the question: "Should employees and employers be allowed to agree that any disputes between them will be resolved through one-on-one arbitration?" Were the "agreements" genuinely bilateral? Petitioner Epic Systems Corporation e-mailed its employees an arbitration agreement requiring resolution of wage and hours claims by individual arbitration. The agreement provided that if the employees "continued to work at Epic," they would "be deemed to have accepted the Agreement." Ernst & Young similarly e-mailed its employees an arbitration agreement, which stated that the employees' continued employment would indicate their assent to the agreement's terms. Epic's and Ernst & Young's employees thus faced a Hobson's choice: accept arbitration on their employer's terms or give up their jobs.

† The FLSA establishes an opt-in collective-litigation procedure for employees seeking to recover unpaid wages and overtime pay. In particular, it authorizes "one or more employees" to maintain an action "in behalf of himself or themselves and other employees similarly situated." "Similarly situated" employees may become parties to an FLSA collective action (and may share in the recovery) only if they file written notices of consent to be joined as parties. The Federal Rules of Civil Procedure provide two collective-litigation procedures relevant here. First, Rule 20(a) permits individuals to join as plaintiffs in a single action if they assert claims arising out of the same transaction or occurrence and their claims involve common questions of law or fact. Second, Rule 23 establishes an opt-out class-action procedure, pursuant to which "one or more members of a class" may bring an action on behalf of the entire class if specified prerequisites are met.

collective procedures in court, they maintain, they must at least have access to similar procedures in an arbitral forum.

C

Although the NLRA safeguards, first and foremost, workers' rights to join unions and to engage in collective bargaining, the statute speaks more embracively. In addition to protecting employees' rights "to form, join, or assist labor organizations" and "to bargain collectively through representatives of their own choosing," the Act protects employees' rights "to engage in other concerted activities for the purpose of…mutual aid or protection."

Suits to enforce workplace rights collectively fit comfortably under the umbrella "concerted activities for the purpose of…mutual aid or protection." "Concerted" means "planned or accomplished together; combined." "Mutual" means "reciprocal." When employees meet the requirements for litigation of shared legal claims in joint, collective, and class proceedings, the litigation of their claims is undoubtedly "accomplished together." By joining hands in litigation, workers can spread the costs of litigation and reduce the risk of employer retaliation.

Recognizing employees' right to engage in collective employment litigation and shielding that right from employer blockage are firmly rooted in the NLRA's design. Congress expressed its intent, when it enacted the NLRA, to "protect the exercise by workers of full freedom of association," thereby remedying "the inequality of bargaining power" workers faced. There can be no serious doubt that collective litigation is one way workers may associate with one another to improve their lot.

Since the Act's earliest days, the Board and federal courts have understood §7's "concerted activities" clause to protect myriad ways in which employees may join together to advance their shared interests. For example, the Board and federal courts have affirmed that the Act shields employees from employer interference when they participate in concerted appeals to the media, legislative bodies, and government agencies. "The 74th Congress," this Court has noted, "knew well enough that labor's cause often is advanced on fronts other than collective bargaining and grievance settlement within the immediate employment context."

Crucially important here, for over 75 years, the Board has held that the NLRA safeguards employees from employer interference when they pursue joint, collective, and class suits related to the terms and conditions of their employment. For decades, federal courts have endorsed the Board's view, comprehending that "the filing of a labor related civil action by a group of employees is ordinarily a concerted activity protected by §7." The Court pays scant heed to this longstanding line of decisions.*

D

In face of the NLRA's text, history, purposes, and longstanding construction, the Court nevertheless concludes that collective proceedings do not fall within the scope of §7. None of the Court's reasons for diminishing §7 should carry the day.

1

The Court relies principally on the ejusdem generis [of the same kind] canon. Observing that §7's "other concerted activities" clause "appears at the end of a detailed list of activities," the Court says the clause should be read to "embrace" only activities "similar in nature" to those set forth first in the list, i.e., "self-organization, forming, joining, or assisting labor organizations," and "bargaining collectively." The Court concludes that §7 should, therefore, be read to protect "things employees 'just do' for themselves." It is far from apparent why joining hands in litigation would not qualify as "things employees just do for themselves." In any event, there is no sound reason to employ the ejusdem generis canon to narrow §7's protections in the manner the Court suggests.

The ejusdem generis canon may serve as a useful guide where it is doubtful Congress intended statutory words or phrases to have the broad scope their ordinary meaning conveys. Courts must take care, however, not to deploy the canon to undermine Congress' efforts to draft encompassing legislation. Nothing suggests that Congress envisioned a cramped construction of the NLRA. Quite the opposite, Congress expressed an embracive purpose in enacting the legislation, i.e., to "protect the exercise by workers of full freedom of association."

---

* In 2012, the Board held that employer-imposed contracts barring group litigation in any forum—arbitral or judicial—are unlawful. D. R. Horton, 357 N.L.R.B. 2277. In so ruling, the Board simply applied its precedents recognizing that (1) employees have a §7 right to engage in collective employment litigation and (2) employers cannot lawfully require employees to sign away their §7 rights. It broke no new ground.

2

In search of a statutory hook to support its application of the ejusdem generis canon, the Court turns to the NLRA's "structure." Citing a handful of provisions that touch upon unionization, collective bargaining, picketing, and strikes, the Court asserts that the NLRA "establishes a regulatory regime" governing each of the activities protected by §7. That regime, the Court says, offers "specific guidance" and "rules" regulating each protected activity. Observing that none of the NLRA's provisions explicitly regulates employees' resort to collective litigation, the Court insists that "it is hard to fathom why Congress would take such care to regulate all the other matters mentioned in [§7] yet remain mute about this matter alone—unless, of course, [§7] doesn't speak to class and collective action procedures in the first place."

This argument is conspicuously flawed. When Congress enacted the NLRA in 1935, the only §7 activity Congress addressed with any specificity was employees' selection of collective-bargaining representatives. The Act did not offer "specific guidance" about employees' rights to "form, join, or assist labor organizations." Nor did it set forth "specific guidance" for any activity falling within §7's "other concerted activities" clause. The only provision that touched upon an activity falling within that clause stated: "Nothing in this Act shall be construed so as to interfere with or impede or diminish in any way the right to strike." That provision hardly offered "specific guidance" regarding employees' right to strike.

Without much in the original Act to support its "structure" argument, the Court cites several provisions that Congress added later, in response to particular concerns. It is difficult to comprehend why Congress' later inclusion of specific guidance regarding some of the activities protected by §7 sheds any light on Congress' initial conception of §7's scope.

But even if each of the provisions the Court cites had been included in the original Act, they still would provide little support for the Court's conclusion. For going on 80 years now, the Board and federal courts—including this one—have understood §7 to protect numerous activities for which the Act provides no "specific" regulatory guidance.

3

In a related argument, the Court maintains that the NLRA does not "even whisper" about the "rules [that] should govern the adjudication of class or collective actions in court or arbitration." The employees here involved, of course, do not look to the NLRA for the procedures enabling them to vindicate their employment rights in arbitral or judicial forums. They assert that the Act establishes their right to act in concert using existing, generally available procedures, and to do so free from employer interference. The FLSA and the Federal Rules on joinder and class actions provide the procedures pursuant to which the employees may ally to pursue shared legal claims. Their employers cannot lawfully cut off their access to those procedures, they urge, without according them access to similar procedures in arbitral forums.

To the employees' argument, the Court replies: If the employees "really take existing class and collective action rules as they find them, they surely take them subject to the limitations inherent in those rules—including the principle that parties may (as here) contract to depart from them in favor of individualized arbitration procedures." The freedom to depart asserted by the Court, as already underscored, is entirely one sided. Once again, the Court ignores the reality that sparked the NLRA's passage: Forced to face their employers without company, employees ordinarily are no match for the enterprise that hires them. Employees gain strength, however, if they can deal with their employers in numbers. That is the very reason why the NLRA secures against employer interference employees' right to act in concert for their "mutual aid or protection."

4

Further attempting to sow doubt about §7's scope, the Court asserts that class and collective procedures were "hardly known when the NLRA was adopted in 1935." In particular, the Court notes, the FLSA's collective-litigation procedure postdated §7 "by years" and Rule 23 "didn't create the modern class action until 1966."

First, one may ask, is there any reason to suppose that Congress intended to protect employees' right to act in concert using only those procedures and forums available in 1935? Congress framed §7 in broad terms, "entrusting" the Board with "responsibility to adapt the Act to changing patterns of industrial life." With fidelity to Congress' aim, the Board and federal courts have recognized that the NLRA shields employees from employer interference when they, e.g., join together to file complaints with administrative agencies, even if those agencies did not exist in 1935.

Moreover, the Court paints an ahistorical picture. As Judge Wood, writing for the Seventh Circuit, cogently explained, the FLSA's collective-litigation procedure and the modern class action were "not written on a clean slate." By 1935, permissive joinder was scarcely uncommon in courts of equity. Nor were representative and class suits novelties. Indeed, their origins trace back to medieval times. And beyond question, "class suits long have been a part of American jurisprudence." Early instances of joint proceedings include cases in which employees allied to sue an employer. It takes no imagination, then, to comprehend that Congress, when it enacted the NLRA, likely meant to protect employees' joining together to engage in collective litigation.*

E

Because I would hold that employees' §7 rights include the right to pursue collective litigation regarding their wages and hours, I would further hold that the employer-dictated collective-litigation stoppers, i.e., "waivers," are unlawful. As earlier recounted, §8(a)(1) makes it an "unfair labor practice" for an employer to "interfere with, restrain, or coerce" employees in the exercise of their §7 rights. Beyond genuine dispute, an employer "interferes with" and "restrains" employees in the exercise of their §7 rights by mandating that they prospectively renounce those rights in individual employment agreements. The law could hardly be otherwise: Employees' rights to band together to meet their employers' superior strength would be worth precious little if employers could condition employment on workers signing away those rights. Properly assessed, then, the "waivers" rank as unfair labor practices outlawed by the NLRA, and therefore unenforceable in court.

II

Today's decision rests largely on the Court's finding in the Arbitration Act "emphatic directions" to enforce arbitration agreements according to their terms, including collective-litigation prohibitions. Nothing in the FAA or this Court's case law, however, requires subordination of the NLRA's protections. Before addressing the interaction between the two laws, I briefly recall the FAA's history and the domain for which that Act was designed.

---

* The Court additionally suggests that something must be amiss because the employees turn to the NLRA, rather than the FLSA, to resist enforcement of the collective-litigation waivers. But the employees' reliance on the NLRA is hardly a reason to "raise a judicial eyebrow." The NLRA's guiding purpose is to protect employees' rights to work together when addressing shared workplace grievances of whatever kind.

A

1

Prior to 1925, American courts routinely declined to order specific performance of arbitration agreements. Growing backlogs in the courts, which delayed the resolution of commercial disputes, prompted the business community to seek legislation enabling merchants to enter into binding arbitration agreements. The business community's aim was to secure to merchants an expeditious, economical means of resolving their disputes. The American Bar Association's Committee on Commerce, Trade and Commercial Law took up the reins in 1921, drafting the legislation Congress enacted, with relatively few changes, four years later.

The legislative hearings and debate leading up to the FAA's passage evidence Congress' aim to enable merchants of roughly equal bargaining power to enter into binding agreements to arbitrate commercial disputes.*

The FAA's legislative history also shows that Congress did not intend the statute to apply to arbitration provisions in employment contracts. In brief, when the legislation was introduced, organized labor voiced concern. Herbert Hoover, then Secretary of Commerce, suggested that if there were "objections" to including "workers' contracts in the law's scheme," Congress could amend the legislation to say: "but nothing herein contained shall apply to contracts of employment of seamen, railroad employees, or any other class of workers engaged in interstate or foreign commerce." Congress adopted Secretary Hoover's suggestion virtually verbatim in §1 of the Act.

Congress, it bears repetition, envisioned application of the Arbitration Act to voluntary, negotiated agreements. Congress never endorsed a policy favoring arbitration where one party sets the terms of an agreement while the other is left to "take it or leave it."

---

* American Bar Association member Julius H. Cohen, credited with drafting the legislation, wrote shortly after the FAA's passage that the law was designed to provide a means of dispute resolution "particularly adapted to the settlement of commercial disputes." Arbitration, he and a colleague explained, is "peculiarly suited to the disposition of the ordinary disputes between merchants as to questions of fact—quantity, quality, time of delivery, compliance with terms of payment, excuses for non-performance, and the like." "It has a place also," they noted, "in the determination of the simpler questions of law" that "arise out of the daily relations between merchants, [for example,] the passage of title, [and] the existence of warranties."

2

In recent decades, this Court has veered away from Congress' intent simply to afford merchants a speedy and economical means of resolving commercial disputes. In 1983, the Court declared, for the first time in the FAA's then 58-year history, that the FAA evinces a "liberal federal policy favoring arbitration." Soon thereafter, the Court ruled, in a series of cases, that the FAA requires enforcement of agreements to arbitrate not only contract claims, but statutory claims as well. Further, in 1991, the Court concluded in *Gilmer v. Interstate/Johnson Lane Corp.*, 500 U.S. 20, 23 (1991), that the FAA requires enforcement of agreements to arbitrate claims arising under the Age Discrimination in Employment Act of 1967, a workplace antidiscrimination statute. Then, in 2001, the Court ruled in *Circuit City Stores, Inc. v. Adams*, 532 U.S. 105, 109 (2001), that the Arbitration Act's exemption for employment contracts should be construed narrowly, to exclude from the Act's scope only transportation workers' contracts.

Employers have availed themselves of the opportunity opened by court decisions expansively interpreting the Arbitration Act. Few employers imposed arbitration agreements on their employees in the early 1990's. After *Gilmer* and *Circuit City*, however, employers' exaction of arbitration clauses in employment contracts grew steadily. See, e.g., Economic Policy Institute (EPI), A. Colvin, The Growing Use of Mandatory Arbitration 1–2, 4 (Sept. 27, 2017) (data indicate only 2.1% of nonunionized companies imposed mandatory arbitration agreements on their employees in 1992, but 53.9% do today). Moreover, in response to subsequent decisions addressing class arbitration,* employers have increasingly included in their arbitration agreements express group-action waivers. ([Estimates are] that 23.1% of nonunionized employees are now subject to express class-action waivers in mandatory arbitration agreements.) It is, therefore, this Court's exorbitant application of the FAA—stretching it far beyond contractual disputes between merchants—that

---

* In *Green Tree Financial Corp. v. Bazzle*, 539 U.S. 444 (2003), a plurality suggested arbitration might proceed on a class basis where not expressly precluded by an agreement. After *Bazzle*, companies increasingly placed explicit collective-litigation waivers in consumer and employee arbitration agreements. In *AT&T Mobility LLC v. Concepcion*, 563 U.S. 333 (2011), and *American Express Co. v. Italian Colors Restaurant*, 570 U.S. 228 (2013), the Court held enforceable class-action waivers in the arbitration agreements at issue in those cases. No surprise, the number of companies incorporating express class-action waivers in consumer and employee arbitration agreements spiked. See 2017 Carlton Fields Class Action Survey: Best Practices in Reducing Cost and Managing Risk in Class Action Litigation 29 (2017), available at https://www.classactionsurvey.com/pdf/2017-class-

led the NLRB to confront, for the first time in 2012, the precise question whether employers can use arbitration agreements to insulate themselves from collective employment litigation.

As I see it, in relatively recent years, the Court's Arbitration Act decisions have taken many wrong turns. Yet, even accepting the Court's decisions as they are, nothing compels the destructive result the Court reaches today. Cf. R. Bork, The Tempting of America 169 (1990) ("Judges...live on the slippery slope of analogies; they are not supposed to ski it to the bottom.").

B

Through the Arbitration Act, Congress sought "to make arbitration agreements as enforceable as other contracts, but not more so." Congress thus provided in §2 of the FAA that the terms of a written arbitration agreement "shall be valid, irrevocable, and enforceable, save upon such grounds as exist at law or in equity for the revocation of any contract." Pursuant to this "saving clause," arbitration agreements and terms may be invalidated based on "generally applicable contract defenses, such as fraud, duress, or unconscionability."

Illegality is a traditional, generally applicable contract defense. "Authorities from the earliest time to the present unanimously hold that no court will lend its assistance in any way towards carrying out the terms of an illegal contract." *Kaiser Steel*, 455 U.S., at 77 (quoting *McMullen v. Hoffman*, 174 U.S. 639, 654 (1899)). For the reasons stated, I would hold that the arbitration agreements' employer-dictated collective-litigation waivers are unlawful. By declining to enforce those adhesive waivers, courts would place them on the same footing as any other contract provision incompatible with controlling federal law. The FAA's saving clause can thus achieve harmonization of the FAA and the NLRA without undermining federal labor policy.

The Court urges that our case law—most forcibly, *AT&T Mobility LLC v. Concepcion*, 563 U.S. 333 (2011)—rules out reconciliation of the NLRA and the FAA through the latter's saving clause. I disagree. True, the Court's Arbitration Act decisions establish that the saving clause "offers no refuge" for defenses that discriminate against arbitration, "either by name or by more subtle methods." The Court, therefore, has rejected saving clause salvage where state courts have invoked generally applicable contract defenses to discriminate

---

action-survey.pdf (reporting that 16.1% of surveyed companies' arbitration agreements expressly precluded class actions in 2012, but 30.2% did so in 2016).

"covertly" against arbitration. In *Concepcion*, the Court held that the saving clause did not spare the California Supreme Court's invocation of unconscionability doctrine to establish a rule blocking enforcement of class-action waivers in adhesive consumer contracts. Class proceedings, the Court said, would "sacrifice the principal advantage of arbitration—its informality—and make the process slower, more costly, and more likely to generate procedural morass than final judgment." Accordingly, the Court concluded, the California Supreme Court's rule, though derived from unconscionability doctrine, impermissibly disfavored arbitration, and therefore could not stand.

Here, however, the Court is not asked to apply a generally applicable contract defense to generate a rule discriminating against arbitration. At issue is application of the ordinarily superseding rule that "illegal promises will not be enforced," to invalidate arbitration provisions at odds with the NLRA, a pathmarking federal statute. That statute neither discriminates against arbitration on its face, nor by covert operation. It requires invalidation of all employer-imposed contractual provisions prospectively waiving employees' §7 rights.

C

Even assuming that the FAA and the NLRA were inharmonious, the NLRA should control. Enacted later in time, the NLRA should qualify as "an implied repeal" of the FAA, to the extent of any genuine conflict. Moreover, the NLRA should prevail as the more pinpointed, subject-matter specific legislation, given that it speaks directly to group action by employees to improve the terms and conditions of their employment.*

Citing statutory examples, the Court asserts that when Congress wants to override the FAA, it does so expressly. The statutes the Court cites, however, are of recent vintage. Each was enacted during the time this Court's decisions increasingly alerted Congress that it would be wise to leave not the slightest room for doubt if it wants to secure access to a judicial forum or to provide a green light for group litigation before an arbitrator or court. The Congress that drafted the NLRA in 1935 was scarcely on similar alert.

---

* Enacted, as was the NLRA, after passage of the FAA, the NLGA also qualifies as a statute more specific than the FAA. Indeed, the NLGA expressly addresses the enforceability of contract provisions that interfere with employees' ability to engage in concerted activities. Moreover, the NLGA contains an express repeal provision, which provides that "all acts and parts of acts in conflict with [the Act's] provisions…are repealed."

III

The inevitable result of today's decision will be the underenforcement of federal and state statutes designed to advance the well-being of vulnerable workers.

The probable impact on wage and hours claims of the kind asserted in the cases now before the Court is all too evident. Violations of minimum-wage and overtime laws are widespread. One study estimated that in Chicago, Los Angeles, and New York City alone, low-wage workers lose nearly $3 billion in legally owed wages each year. The U.S. Department of Labor, state labor departments, and state attorneys general can uncover and obtain recoveries for some violations. Because of their limited resources, however, government agencies must rely on private parties to take a lead role in enforcing wage and hours laws.

If employers can stave off collective employment litigation aimed at obtaining redress for wage and hours infractions, the enforcement gap is almost certain to widen. Expenses entailed in mounting individual claims will often far outweigh potential recoveries.*

Fear of retaliation may also deter potential claimants from seeking redress alone. Further inhibiting single-file claims is the slim relief obtainable, even of the injunctive kind. The upshot: Employers, aware that employees will be disinclined to pursue small-value claims when confined to proceeding one-by-one, will no doubt perceive that the cost-benefit balance of underpaying workers tips heavily in favor of skirting legal obligations.

In stark contrast to today's decision,† the Court has repeatedly recognized the centrality of group action to the effective enforcement of antidiscrimination statutes. With Court approbation, concerted legal actions have played a critical role in enforcing prohibitions against workplace discrimination based on race, sex, and other protected characteristics. In this context, the Court has comprehended that government entities charged with enforcing antidiscrimination statutes are unlikely to be funded at levels that could even begin to compensate for a significant dropoff in private enforcement

---

* Based on a 2015 study, the Bureau of Consumer Financial Protection found that "predispute arbitration agreements are being widely used to prevent consumers from seeking relief from legal violations on a class basis, and that consumers rarely file individual lawsuits or arbitration cases to obtain such relief."

† The Court observes that class actions can be abused, but under its interpretation, even two employees would be stopped from proceeding together.

efforts. That reality, as just noted, holds true for enforcement of wage and hours laws.

I do not read the Court's opinion to place in jeopardy discrimination complaints asserting disparate-impact and pattern-or-practice claims that call for proof on a groupwide basis, which some courts have concluded cannot be maintained by solo complainants. It would be grossly exorbitant to read the FAA to devastate Title VII of the Civil Rights Act of 1964, and other laws enacted to eliminate, root and branch, class-based employment discrimination. With fidelity to the Legislature's will, the Court could hardly hold otherwise.

I note, finally, that individual arbitration of employee complaints can give rise to anomalous results. Arbitration agreements often include provisions requiring that outcomes be kept confidential or barring arbitrators from giving prior proceedings precedential effect. As a result, arbitrators may render conflicting awards in cases involving similarly situated employees—even employees working for the same employer. Arbitrators may resolve differently such questions as whether certain jobs are exempt from overtime laws. With confidentiality and no-precedential-value provisions operative, irreconcilable answers would remain unchecked.

If these untoward consequences stemmed from legislative choices, I would be obliged to accede to them. But the edict that employees with wage and hours claims may seek relief only one-by-one does not come from Congress. It is the result of take-it-or-leave-it labor contracts harking back to the type called "yellow dog," and of the readiness of this Court to enforce those unbargained-for agreements. The FAA demands no such suppression of the right of workers to take concerted action for their "mutual aid or protection." Accordingly, I would reverse the judgment of the Fifth Circuit in No. 16–307 and affirm the judgments of the Seventh and Ninth Circuits in Nos. 16–285 and 16–300.

❦ "Soldiers of All Faiths": *The American Legion v. American Humanist Assn.*

In Bladensburg, Maryland, a large cross, known as the "Peace Cross," had been erected in 1925 to honor soldiers from Prince George's County, Maryland, who were killed in World War I. The cross now stood in a traffic island in the middle of a busy intersection, owned and maintained by an agency of the state of Maryland.

The Establishment Clause of the First Amendment

Several non-Christian residents of the county, along with the American Humanist Association—a nonprofit that advocated for the separation of church and state—sued the state agency. They claimed that the state's display and maintenance of the Peace Cross violated the establishment clause of the First Amendment to the U.S. Constitution: "Congress shall make no law respecting an establishment of religion." These plaintiffs argued that the cross was an unambivalently Christian symbol and that the First Amendment prohibited Maryland from seeming to endorse Christianity over other religions or no religion.

On appeal from conflicting decisions by the lower courts, the U.S. Supreme Court held that the state's display and maintenance of the Peace Cross did not offend the establishment clause. Writing an opinion joined by the majority of justices only in part, Justice Samuel Alito reasoned that the cross had become a secular symbol, understood by viewers not as a religious symbol but as a more universal, secular mark of respect for war dead, like the crosses in Flanders Field. where many soldiers who died in World War I were buried.

Longstanding Monuments, Offended Observers

Four of the nine justices agreed with Justice Alito that "where monuments, symbols, and practices with a longstanding history follow in the tradition of the First Congress in respecting and tolerating different views, endeavoring to achieve inclusivity and nondiscrimination, and recognizing the important role religion plays in the lives of many Americans, they are likewise constitutional." Justices Neal Gorsuch and Clarence Thomas stated that an "offended observer," like the non-Christian residents or the

American Humanist Association, did not have standing to claim that the establishment clause was violated. Five justices filed separate concurrences, and Justice Ginsburg dissented, joined by Justice Sonia Sotomayor.

Her dissent in this case noted that the keynote speaker at the dedication of the monument and press at the time described the Peace Cross as a symbol of Calvary, where Jesus Christ was crucified. She argued that the cross is the preeminent symbol of Christianity and widely so understood and that it was never used to mark the grave of a soldier known to be non-Christian.

United by Love of Country, Not Religious Faith

Children's books about Justice Ginsburg's life recount a story about Ginsburg as a child: on a trip with her parents, they drove past a hotel that made it clear her Jewish family was unwelcome with the sign "No Dogs or Jews Allowed."[1] Justice Ginsburg saw the Peace Cross as sending the same message as that sign: "To non-Christians, nearly 30% of the population of the United States, the State's choice to display the cross on public buildings or spaces conveys a message of exclusion: It tells them they 'are outsiders, not full members of the political community.'" She continued, "Soldiers of all faiths are united by their love of country, not by their embrace of the meaning of the cross."

THE AMERICAN LEGION ET AL. V. AMERICAN HUMANIST ASSN. ET AL.

CERTIORARI TO THE UNITED STATES COURT OF APPEALS
FOR THE FOURTH CIRCUIT

588 U.S. ___ (June 20, 2019)

Dissent Announcement

Ruth Bader Ginsburg: This case, as you have just heard, concerns an immense Latin cross standing alone on a traffic island at the center of a busy three-way intersection in Bladensburg, Maryland.

Known as the Peace Cross, the monument was erected in 1925 to honor soldiers from the county who lost their lives in World War I.

Both the Peace Cross and the traffic island are owned and maintained by an agency of the State of Maryland.

Decades ago this Court recognized that the Establishment Clause of the First Amendment demands government neutrality among religious faiths and between religion and non-religion.

Today, the Court erodes that neutrality principle, diminishing precedent serving to preserve it.

I therefore dissent from the Court's decision.

The Latin cross is the foremost symbol of the Christian faith, embodying the central theological claim of Christianity that the son of God died on the cross, that he rose from the dead, and that his death and resurrection offer the possibility of eternal life.

The Latin cross is not emblematic of any other faith.

By maintaining the Peace Cross on a public highway, the state places Christianity above other faiths and conveys a message of exclusion to non-Christians, nearly 30% of the U.S. population, telling them they are outsiders, not full members of the political community.

In defense of the state's display, the Court refers to American cemeteries overseas established for soldiers who died in World War I.

Yes, one sees in those cemeteries row upon row of cross-shaped grave markers.

These grave markers, the Court asserts, gave to the Latin cross an added, largely secular meaning when used in World War I memorials.

The Court's attempt to secularize what is unquestionably a sacred symbol does not withstand rational inspection.

The Latin cross is a common marker for the graves of Christian soldiers precisely because it symbolizes the foundational tenets of Christianity.

In World War I and thereafter, the cross was never perceived as an appropriate headstone or memorial for soldiers who did not adhere to Christianity.

Even in Flanders Field, Stars of David marked the graves of eight American soldiers of Jewish faith, and the remains of soldiers who were neither Christian nor Jewish could be repatriated to the United States for burial under an appropriate headstone.

Because the Christian character of the Latin cross is inescapable, the overwhelming majority of public World War I memorials contain no religious symbols.

Instead, they display secular images, prominent among them the American doughboy, images that pay equal respect to all members of the armed forces who perished in the service of our country. Soldiers of all faiths are united by their love of country, not by their embrace of the meaning of the cross.

As every Court of Appeals to reach the question has recognized, making a Latin cross a war memorial does not make the cross secular.

Quite the contrary, the image of the cross makes the war memorial sectarian.

The Peace Cross is no exception, as was plain from the time it was erected.

At the dedication ceremony the keynote speaker compared the sacrifice of honored soldiers to that of Jesus Christ, calling the Peace Cross symbolic of Calvary, where Jesus was crucified.

Local reporters described the monument as a likeness of the cross of Calvary, as described in the Bible.

The character of the monument has not changed with the passage of time.

Memorializing the service of American soldiers is an admirable and unquestionably secular objective, but the state did not serve that objective by displaying a symbol that bears a starkly sectarian message.

If the aim of the Establishment Clause is genuinely to uncouple government from church, the clause does not permit a display of the character of the Bladensburg's Peace Cross.

Justice Sotomayor joins me in this dissent.

DISSENT

Many citations and footnotes have been omitted, as well as some punctuation (including brackets and internal quotation marks).

Justice Ginsburg, with whom Justice Sotomayor joins, dissenting.

An immense Latin cross stands on a traffic island at the center of a busy three-way intersection in Bladensburg, Maryland. "Monumental, clear, and bold" by day, the cross looms even larger illuminated against the night-time sky. Known as the Peace Cross, the monument was erected by private citizens in 1925 to honor local soldiers who lost their lives in World War I. "The town's most prominent symbol" was rededicated in 1985 and is now said to honor "the sacrifices made [in] all wars," by "all veterans." Both the Peace Cross and the traffic island are owned and maintained by the Maryland-National Capital Park and Planning Commission (Commission), an agency of the State of Maryland.

Decades ago, this Court recognized that the Establishment Clause of the First Amendment to the Constitution demands governmental neutrality among religious faiths, and between religion and nonreligion. Numerous times since, the Court has reaffirmed the Constitution's commitment to neutrality. Today the Court erodes that neutrality commitment, diminishing precedent designed to preserve individual liberty and civic harmony in favor of a "presumption of constitutionality for longstanding monuments, symbols, and practices."*

---

* Some of my colleagues suggest that the Court's new presumption extends to all governmental displays and practices, regardless of their age. See Kavanaugh, J., concurring; Thomas, J., concurring in judgment; Gorsuch, J., concurring in judgment. I read the Court's opinion to mean what it says: "Retaining established, religiously expressive monuments, symbols, and practices is quite different from erecting or adopting new ones," and, consequently, only "longstanding monuments, symbols, and practices" enjoy "a presumption of constitutionality."

The Latin cross is the foremost symbol of the Christian faith, embodying the "central theological claim of Christianity: that the son of God died on the cross, that he rose from the dead, and that his death and resurrection offer the possibility of eternal life." Precisely because the cross symbolizes these sectarian beliefs, it is a common marker for the graves of Christian soldiers. For the same reason, using the cross as a war memorial does not transform it into a secular symbol, as the Courts of Appeals have uniformly recognized. Just as a Star of David is not suitable to honor Christians who died serving their country, so a cross is not suitable to honor those of other faiths who died defending their nation. Soldiers of all faiths "are united by their love of country, but they are not united by the cross."

By maintaining the Peace Cross on a public highway, the Commission elevates Christianity over other faiths, and religion over nonreligion. Memorializing the service of American soldiers is an "admirable and unquestionably secular" objective. But the Commission does not serve that objective by displaying a symbol that bears "a starkly sectarian message."

I

A

The First Amendment commands that the government "shall make no law" either "respecting an establishment of religion" or "prohibiting the free exercise thereof." Adoption of these complementary provisions followed centuries of "turmoil, civil strife, and persecution, generated in large part by established sects determined to maintain their absolute political and religious supremacy." Mindful of that history, the fledgling Republic ratified the Establishment Clause, in the words of Thomas Jefferson, to "build a wall of separation between church and state."

This barrier "protects the integrity of individual conscience in religious matters." It guards against the "anguish, hardship and bitter strife" that can occur when "the government weighs in on one side of religious debate." And while the "union of government and religion tends to destroy government and to degrade religion," separating the two preserves the legitimacy of each.

The Establishment Clause essentially instructs: "The government may not favor one religion over another, or religion over irreligion." For, as James Madison observed, the government is not "a competent Judge of Religious Truth." When the government places its "power, prestige [or] financial support...behind a particular religious belief," the government's imprimatur "makes adherence to [that] religion relevant...to a person's standing in the political community." Correspondingly, "the indirect coercive pressure upon religious minorities to conform to the prevailing officially approved religion is plain." And by demanding neutrality between religious faith and the absence thereof, the Establishment Clause shores up an individual's "right to select any religious faith or none at all."

B

In cases challenging the government's display of a religious symbol, the Court has tested fidelity to the principle of neutrality by asking whether the display has the "effect of 'endorsing' religion." The display fails this requirement if it objectively "conveys a message that religion or a particular religious belief is favored or preferred."* To make that determination, a court must consider "the pertinent facts and circumstances surrounding the symbol and its placement."†

As I see it, when a cross is displayed on public property, the government may be presumed to endorse its religious content. The venue is surely associated with the State; the symbol and its meaning are just as surely associated exclusively with Christianity. "It certainly is not common for property owners to open up their property [to] monuments that convey a message with which they do not wish to be associated." To non-Christians, nearly 30% of the population of the United States, the State's choice to display the cross on public buildings or spaces conveys a message of exclusion: It tells them they "are outsiders, not full members of the political community."‡ A

---

* Justice Gorsuch's "no standing" opinion is startling in view of the many religious-display cases this Court has resolved on the merits. And, if Justice Gorsuch is right, three Members of the Court were out of line when they recognized that "the [Establishment] Clause forbids a city to permit the permanent erection of a large Latin cross on the roof of city hall," *Buono*, 559 U.S., at 715 (opinion of Kennedy, J., joined by Roberts, C.J., and Alito, J.), for no one, according to Justice Gorsuch, should be heard to complain about such a thing. But see Brief for Law Professors as Amici Curiae (explaining why offended observer standing is necessary and proper).

† This inquiry has been described by some Members of the Court as the "reasonable observer" standard.

‡ See also Jews and Christians Discussion Group in the Central Committee of German Catholics, A Convent and Cross in Auschwitz, in *The Continuing Agony: From the Carmelite Convent to the Crosses at Auschwitz* 231–232 (A. Berger, H. Cargas, & S. Nowak eds. 2004) ("We Christians must appreciate [that] throughout history many non-Christians, especially Jews, have experienced the Cross as a symbol of persecution, through the Crusades, the Inquisition and the compulsory baptisms.").

presumption of endorsement, of course, may be overcome. A display does not run afoul of the neutrality principle if its "setting...plausibly indicates" that the government has not sought "either to adopt [a] religious message or to urge its acceptance by others." The "typical museum setting," for example, "though not neutralizing the religious content of a religious painting, negates any message of endorsement of that content." Similarly, when a public school history teacher discusses the Protestant Reformation, the setting makes clear that the teacher's purpose is to educate, not to proselytize. The Peace Cross, however, is not of that genre.

II
A

"For nearly two millennia," the Latin cross has been the "defining symbol" of Christianity, evoking the foundational claims of that faith. Christianity teaches that Jesus Christ was "a divine Savior" who "illuminated a path toward salvation and redemption." Central to the religion are the beliefs that "the son of God," Jesus Christ, "died on the cross," that "he rose from the dead," and that "his death and resurrection offer the possibility of eternal life."* "From its earliest times," Christianity was known as "religio crucis—the religion of the cross." Christians wear crosses, not as an ecumenical symbol, but to proclaim their adherence to Christianity.

An exclusively Christian symbol, the Latin cross is not emblematic of any other faith.† The principal symbol of Christianity around the world should not loom over public thoroughfares, suggesting official recognition of that religion's paramountcy.

B

The Commission urges in defense of its monument that the Latin cross "is not merely a reaffirmation of Christian beliefs"; rather, "when used in the context of a war memorial," the cross becomes "a universal symbol of the sacrifices of those who fought and died."

* Under "one widespread reading of Christian scriptures," non-Christians are barred from eternal life and, instead, are condemned to hell. On this reading, the Latin cross symbolizes both the promise of salvation and the threat of damnation by "dividing the world between the saved and the damned."

† Christianity comprises numerous denominations. The term is here used to distinguish Christian sects from religions that do not embrace the defining tenets of Christianity.

The Commission's "attempts to secularize what is unquestionably a sacred [symbol] defy credibility and disserve people of faith." The asserted commemorative meaning of the cross rests on—and is inseparable from—its Christian meaning: "the crucifixion of Jesus Christ and the redeeming benefits of his passion and death," specifically, "the salvation of man."

Because of its sacred meaning, the Latin cross has been used to mark Christian deaths since at least the fourth century. The cross on a grave "says that a Christian is buried here," and "commemorates [that person's death] by evoking a conception of salvation and eternal life reserved for Christians." As a commemorative symbol, the Latin cross simply "makes no sense apart from the crucifixion, the resurrection, and Christianity's promise of eternal life."*

The cross affirms that, thanks to the soldier's embrace of Christianity, he will be rewarded with eternal life. "To say that the cross honors the Christian war dead does not identify a secular meaning of the cross; it merely identifies a common application of the religious meaning." Scarcely "a universal symbol of sacrifice," the cross is "the symbol of one particular sacrifice."†

Every Court of Appeals to confront the question has held that "making a…Latin cross a war memorial does not make the cross secular," it "makes the war memorial sectarian."

The Peace Cross is no exception. That was evident from the start. At the dedication ceremony, the keynote speaker analogized the sacrifice of the honored soldiers to that of Jesus Christ, calling the Peace Cross "symbolic of Calvary," where Jesus was crucified. Local reporters variously described the monument as "a mammoth cross, a likeness of the Cross of Calvary, as described in the Bible"; "a monster Calvary cross"; and "a huge sacrifice cross." The character of the monument has not changed with the passage of time.

---

* The Court sets out familiar uses of the Greek cross, including the Red Cross and the Navy Cross, and maintains that, today, they carry no religious message. But because the Latin cross has never shed its Christian character, its commemorative meaning is exclusive to Christians. The Court recognizes as much in suggesting that the Peace Cross features the Latin cross for the same reason "why Holocaust memorials invariably include Stars of David": those sectarian "symbols…signify what death meant for those who are memorialized."

† Christian soldiers have drawn parallels between their experiences in war and Jesus's suffering and sacrifice. This comparison has been portrayed by artists and documented by historians.

C

The Commission nonetheless urges that the Latin cross is a "well-established" secular symbol commemorating, in particular, "military valor and sacrifice [in] World War I." Calling up images of United States cemeteries overseas showing row upon row of cross-shaped grave markers, the Commission overlooks this reality: The cross was never perceived as an appropriate headstone or memorial for Jewish soldiers and others who did not adhere to Christianity.

1

A page of history is worth retelling. On November 11, 1918, the Great War ended. Bereaved families of American soldiers killed in the war sought to locate the bodies of their loved ones, and then to decide what to do with their remains. Once a soldier's body was identified, families could choose to have the remains repatriated to the United States or buried overseas in one of several American military cemeteries, yet to be established. Eventually, the remains of 46,000 soldiers were repatriated, and those of 30,000 soldiers were laid to rest in Europe.

While overseas cemeteries were under development, the graves of American soldiers in Europe were identified by one of two temporary wooden markers painted white. Christian soldiers were buried beneath the cross; the graves of Jewish soldiers were marked by the Star of David. The remains of soldiers who were neither Christian nor Jewish could be repatriated to the United States for burial under an appropriate headstone.*

When the War Department began preparing designs for permanent headstones in 1919, "no topic managed to stir more controversy than the use of religious symbolism." Everyone involved in the dispute, however, saw the Latin cross as a Christian symbol, not as a universal or secular one. To achieve uniformity, the War Department initially recommended replacing the temporary sectarian markers with plain marble slabs resembling "those designed for the national cemeteries in the United States."

---

* For unidentified soldiers buried overseas, the American Battle Monuments Commission (ABMC) used the cross and the Star of David markers "in 'proportion of known Jewish dead to known Christians.' " The ABMC later decided that "all unidentified graves would be marked with a cross." This change was prompted by "fear [that] a Star of David would be placed over an unknown Christian," not by the belief that the cross had become a universal symbol.

The War Department's recommendation angered prominent civil organizations, including the American Legion and the Gold Star associations: the United States, they urged, ought to retain both the cross and Star of David. In supporting sectarian markers, these groups were joined by the American Battle Monuments Commission (ABMC), a newly created independent agency charged with supervising the establishment of overseas cemeteries. Congress weighed in by directing the War Department to erect headstones "of such design and material as may be agreed upon by the Secretary of War and the American Battle Monuments Commission." In 1924, the War Department approved the ABMC's "designs for a Cross and Star of David."

Throughout the headstone debate, no one doubted that the Latin cross and the Star of David were sectarian grave markers, and therefore appropriate only for soldiers who adhered to those faiths. A committee convened by the War Department composed of representatives from "seven prominent war-time organizations" as well as "religious bodies, Protestant, Jewish, [and] Catholic" agreed "unanimously...that marble crosses be placed on the graves of all Christian American dead buried abroad, and that the graves of the Jewish American dead be marked by the six-pointed star." The Executive Director of the Jewish Welfare Board stated that "if any religious symbol is erected over the graves, then Judaism should have its symbol over the graves of its dead." Others expressing views described the Latin cross as the appropriate symbol to "mark the graves of the Christian heroes of the American forces." As stated by the National Catholic War Council, "the sentiment and desires of all Americans, Christians and Jews alike, are one": "They who served us in life should be honored, as they would have wished, in death."*

Far more crosses than Stars of David, as one would expect, line the grounds of American cemeteries overseas, for Jews composed only 3% of the United States population in 1917. Jews accounted for nearly 6% of U.S. forces in World War I (in numbers, 250,000), and 3,500 Jewish soldiers died in that war. Even in Flanders Field, with its "crosses, row on row," "Stars of David mark the graves of [eight American soldiers] of Jewish faith."

---

* As noted, the bodies of soldiers who were neither Christian nor Jewish could be repatriated to the United States and buried in a national cemetery (with a slab headstone) or in a private cemetery (with a headstone of the family's choosing).

2

Reiterating its argument that the Latin cross is a "universal symbol" of World War I sacrifice, the Commission states that "40 World War I monuments...built in the United States...bear the shape of a cross." This figure includes memorials that merely "incorporate" a cross* Moreover, the 40 monuments compose only 4% of the "948 outdoor sculptures commemorating the First World War." The Court lists just seven free-standing cross memorials, less than 1% of the total number of monuments to World War I in the United States. Cross memorials, in short, are outliers. The overwhelming majority of World War I memorials contain no Latin cross.

In fact, the "most popular and enduring memorial of the [post-World War I] decade" was "the mass-produced Spirit of the American Doughboy statue." That statue, depicting a U.S. infantryman, "met with widespread approval throughout American communities." Indeed, the first memorial to World War I erected in Prince George's County "depicts a doughboy." The Peace Cross, as Plaintiffs' expert historian observed, was an "aberration...even in the era [in which] it was built and dedicated."

Like cities and towns across the country, the United States military comprehended the importance of "paying equal respect to all members of the Armed Forces who perished in the service of our country," and therefore avoided incorporating the Latin cross into memorials. The construction of the Tomb of the Unknown Soldier is illustrative. When a proposal to place a cross on the Tomb was advanced, the Jewish Welfare Board objected; no cross appears on the Tomb. In sum, "there is simply 'no evidence...that the cross has been widely embraced by'—or even applied to—'non-Christians as a secular symbol of death' or of sacrifice in military service" in World War I or otherwise.

D

Holding the Commission's display of the Peace Cross unconstitutional would not, as the Commission fears, "inevitably require the destruction of other cross-shaped memorials throughout the country." When a religious symbol appears in a public cemetery—on a headstone, or as the headstone itself, or perhaps integrated into a larger memorial—the setting counters the inference that the government seeks "either to adopt the religious message

---

* No other monument in Bladensburg's Veterans Memorial Park displays the Latin cross.

or to urge its acceptance by others." In a cemetery, the "privately selected religious symbols on individual graves are best understood as the private speech of each veteran." Such displays are "linked to, and show respect for, the individual honoree's faith and beliefs." They do not suggest governmental endorsement of those faith and beliefs.

Recognizing that a Latin cross does not belong on a public highway or building does not mean the monument must be "torn down."* "Like the determination of the violation itself," the "proper remedy...is necessarily context specific." In some instances, the violation may be cured by relocating the monument to private land or by transferring ownership of the land and monument to a private party.

★ ★ ★

In 1790, President Washington visited Newport, Rhode Island, "a longtime bastion of religious liberty and the home of one of the first communities of American Jews." In a letter thanking the congregation for its warm welcome, Washington praised "the citizens of the United States of America" for "giving to mankind...a policy worthy of imitation": "All possess alike liberty of conscience and immunities of citizenship." As Washington and his contemporaries were aware, "some of them from bitter personal experience," religion is "too personal, too sacred, too holy, to permit its 'unhallowed perversion' by a civil magistrate." The Establishment Clause, which preserves the integrity of both church and state, guarantees that "however...individuals worship, they will count as full and equal American citizens." "If the aim of the Establishment Clause is genuinely to uncouple government from church," the Clause does "not permit...a display of the character" of Bladensburg's Peace Cross.

---

* The Court asserts that the Court of Appeals "entertained" the possibility of "amputating the arms of the cross." The appeals court, however, merely reported Plaintiffs' "desired injunctive relief," namely, "removal or demolition of the Cross, or removal of the arms from the Cross 'to form a non-religious slab or obelisk.'"

Notes

Introduction

1. For example, Irin Carmon and Shana Knizhnik, *Notorious RBG: The Life and Times of Ruth Bader Ginsburg* (New York: Dey Street/William Morrow, 2015); Antonia Felix and Mimi Leder, *The Unstoppable Ruth Bader Ginsburg: American Icon* (New York: Sterling, 2018), a pictorial retrospective of her life and career; Jane Sherron De Hart, *Ruth Bader Ginsburg: A Life* (New York: Knopf, 2019).

2. For example, Debbie Levy, *I Dissent: Ruth Bader Ginsburg Makes Her Mark*, illustrated by Elizabeth Baddeley (New York: Simon and Schuster Books for Young Readers, 2016); Jonah Winter, *Ruth Bader Ginsburg: The Case of R.B.G. vs. Inequality*, illustrated by Stacy Innerst (New York: Abrams Books for Young Readers, 2017).

3. For example, ABC's *Bless This Mess*, "Scare Night" (Season 2, Episode 5, aired October 29, 2019), featured actor Pam Grier dressed as RBG; NBC's *Superstore*, "Trick-or-Treat" (Season 5, Episode 6, aired October 31, 2019), featured actor America Ferrera dressed as Ginsburg.

4. *Craig v. Boren*, Brief Amicus Curiae for American Civil Liberties Union, filed February 26, 1976, 10.

5. Katy Steinmetz, "How Ruth Bader Ginsburg Found Her Voice: A New Study of the Supreme Court Justice's Accent Says Something About the Way We All Talk," *Time* (n.d.), https://time.com/ruth-bader-ginsburg-supreme-court/, accessed December 10, 2019.

6. Jeffrey Rosen, *Conversations with RBG: Ruth Bader Ginsburg on Life, Love, Liberty, and Law* (New York: Henry Holt, 2019), 42.

7. Carmon and Knizhnik, *Notorious RBG*, 103.

8. For example, Carmon and Knizhnik, "The Notorious RBG Workout," *Notorious RBG*, 158–159; Valentina Zarya, "If You Could Do as Many Push-ups as Ruth Bader Ginsburg, You Wouldn't Retire Either," *Fortune*, September 22, 2016; Ben Schreckinger, "I Did Ruth Bader Ginsburg's Workout: It Nearly Broke Me," *Politico*, February 27, 2017; Lauren Gambino, "Pistol Squats and Push-ups: How Ruth Bader Ginsburg Stays Fighting Fit," *Guardian*, October 29, 2017; Yohana Desta, "See Ruth Bader Ginsburg Barely Tolerate a Workout with Stephen Colbert," *Vanity Fair*, March 22, 2018. Ginsburg's personal trainer, Bryant Johnson, wrote a book, *The RBG Workout: How She Stays Strong... and You Can Too!* (New York: Houghton Mifflin Harcourt, 2017).

9. Jeffrey Toobin, "Heavyweight: How Ruth Bader Ginsburg Has Moved the Supreme Court," *New Yorker*, March 11, 2013.

10. Chloe Foussianes, "Ruth Bader Ginsburg's Newest Collar Was Sent to Her By a Fan," *Town and Country*, December 13, 2018.

11. De Hart, *Ruth Bader Ginsburg*, 3–4.

12. De Hart, *Ruth Bader Ginsburg*, 5.

13. De Hart, *Ruth Bader Ginsburg*, 23.

14. Carmon and Knizhnik, *Notorious RBG*, 28.

15. Rosen, *Conversations with RBG*, 37.

16. Carmon and Knizhnik, *Notorious RBG*, 32–33.

17. De Hart, *Ruth Bader Ginsburg*, 63–73.

18. Andrew Prokop, "Ruth Bader Ginsburg Works Out like a Canadian Air Force Pilot," *Vox*, September 30, 2014.

19. De Hart, *Ruth Bader Ginsburg*, 94.

20. Carmon and Knizhnik, *Notorious RBG*, 48–49.

21. De Hart, *Ruth Bader Ginsburg*, 133–134.

22. De Hart, *Ruth Bader Ginsburg*, 143.

23. Stephanie Garlock, "Ginsburg Discusses Justice and Advocacy at Radcliffe Day Celebration," *Harvard Magazine*, May 29, 2015.

24. Carmon and Knizhnik, *Notorious RBG*, 81.
25. Jill Lepore, "Ruth Bader Ginsburg's Unlikely Path to the Supreme Court," *New Yorker*, October 1, 2018.
26. "Ruth Bader Ginsburg, USSC nomination acceptance," June 14, 1993, White House Rose Garden, YouTube.com.
27. Carmon and Knizhnik, *Notorious RBG*, 113.
28. Toobin, "Heavyweight."
29. Carmon and Knizhnik, *Notorious RBG*, 114–115.
30. Toobin, "Heavyweight."
31. Ruth Bader Ginsburg, "Remarks for the Second Circuit Judicial Conference," June 7, 2019.
32. De Hart, *Ruth Bader Ginsburg*, 349.
33. De Hart, *Ruth Bader Ginsburg*, 411.
34. Rosen, *Conversations with RBG*, 41.
35. Nina Totenberg, "Justice Ruth Bader Ginsburg Again Treated for Cancer," *All Things Considered*, NPR, August 23, 2019.

"All I Ask": Briefs and Oral Argument from *Reed v. Reed* to *Craig v. Boren*

1. Wendy Webster Williams, "Ruth Bader Ginsburg's Equal Protection Clause: 1970–1980," *Columbia Journal of Gender and Law* 25 (2013), 41–49.
2. The Fourteenth Amendment states, in part: "No State shall make or enforce any law which shall abridge the privileges or immunities of citizens of the United States; nor shall any State deprive any person of life, liberty, or property, without due process of law; nor deny to any person within its jurisdiction the equal protection of the laws." (The Fifth Amendment applies these restrictions to the federal government.)
3. Jane Sherron De Hart, *Ruth Bader Ginsburg* (New York: Knopf, 2019), 147.
4. Jeffrey Rosen, *Conversations with RBG: Ruth Bader Ginsburg on Life, Love, Liberty, and Law* (New York: Henry Holt, 2019), 31.
5. Jennifer Cheeseman Day, "Number of Women Lawyers at Record High but Men Still Highest Earners," United States Census Bureau, May 8, 2018, https://www.census.gov/library/stories/2018/05/women-lawyers.html.
6. "History of the Equal Rights Amendment," Alice Paul Institute, equalrightsamendment.org, 2019, https://www.equalrightsamendment.org/history.
7. Jeffrey Toobin, "Heavyweight: How Ruth Bader Ginsburg Has Moved the Supreme Court," *New Yorker*, March 11, 2013, https://www.newyorker.com/magazine/2013/03/11/heavyweight-ruth-bader-ginsburg.
8. Rosen, *Conversations with RBG*, 26–27.
9. Rosen, *Conversations with RBG*, 34.

"The Way Women Are": *United States v. Virginia*

1. Ruth Bader Ginsburg, "Advocating the Elimination of Gender-Based Discrimination: The 1970s New Look at the Equality Principle," remarks made at Wake Forest Law School's summer program in Venice, Italy, in July 2008, in *In My Own Words* (New York: Simon and Schuster, 2016), 163.

"The Magnitude and Permanence of the Loss": *M.L.B. v. S.L.J.*

1. Jeffrey Rosen, *Conversations with RBG: Ruth Bader Ginsburg on Life, Love, Liberty, and Law* (New York: Henry Holt, 2019), 76.

Notes

"I Dissent": *Bush et al. v. Gore et al.*

1. Federal Election Commission, 2000 Presidential Electoral and Popular Vote (December 2001), https://transition.fec.gov/pubrec/fe2000/elecpop.htm; Lance de Haven Smith (ed.), *The Battle for Florida: An Annotated Compendium of Materials from the 2000 Presidential Election* (Gainesville, FL: United States: University Press of Florida).
2. Michael Levy, United States Presidential Election of 2000, *Encyclopaedia Brittanica*, https://www.britannica.com/event/United-States-presidential-election-of-2000.
3. Linda Greenhouse, "BUSH V. GORE: A Special Report; Election Case a Test and a Trauma for Justices," *New York Times*, February 20, 2001, https://www.nytimes.com/2001/02/20/us/bush-v-gore-a-special-report-election-case-a-test-and-a-trauma-for-justices.html.
4. Irin Carmon and Shana Knizhnik, *Notorious RBG: The Life and Times of Ruth Bader Ginsburg* (New York: Dey Street/William Morrow, 2015), quoting Jeffrey Toobin, *Too Close to Call: The Thirty-Day Battle to Decide the 2000 Election* (New York: Random House, 2001).
5. Carmon and Knizhnik, *Notorious RBG*, 128.
6. Associated Press, "Ginsburg Recalls Florida Recount Case," *New York Times*, February 4, 2001.

"Today's Decision Is Alarming": *Gonzales v. Carhart*

1. Jill Lepore, "Ruth Bader Ginsburg's Unlikely Path to the Supreme Court," *New Yorker*, October 1, 2018.
2. Ruth Bader Ginsburg, "Speaking in a Judicial Voice," 24th James Madison Lecture on Constitutional Law at New York University School of Law on March 9, 1993, *New York University Law Review* 67(6)(1992),1185–1209, 1198, https://www.law.nyu.edu/sites/default/files/ECM_PRO_059254.pdf; also included in Ginsburg's *In My Own Words* (New York: Simon and Schuster, 2016), 228.
3. Lepore, "Ruth Bader Ginsburg's Unlikely Path to the Supreme Court."
4. Ginsburg, "Speaking in a Judicial Voice," 1200–1205.
5. Lepore, "Ruth Bader Ginsburg's Unlikely Path to the Supreme Court."
6. Lepore, "Ruth Bader Ginsburg's Unlikely Path to the Supreme Court."
7. Jane Sherron De Hart, *Ruth Bader Ginsburg* (New York: Knopf, 2019), 386.

"The Ball Lies in Congress's Court": *Ledbetter v. Goodyear Tire and Rubber Company*

1. Note, however, that the record offered some evidence that Ledbetter knew several years earlier about the disparity between her pay and what men in the same job earned; see, for example, Hans Bader, "Misconceptions about Ledbetter v. Goodyear Tire & Rubber Co.," *Federalist Society* 13, 3 (October 2012), https://fedsoc.org/commentary/publications/misconceptions-about-ledbetter-v-goodyear-tire-rubber-co. Nevertheless, the majority's ruling apparently extended to cases in which the employee did not know about intentional discrimination leading to pay disparities until too much time had passed to sue under Title VII.
2. Justice Ginsburg included her bench announcement of her dissent—a simplified oral summary that she read from the bench on the day the decision in the *Ledbetter* case was handed down—in her best-selling book *In My Own Words: Ruth Bader Ginsburg* (with Mary Hartnett and Wendy W. Williams [New York: Simon & Schuster, 2016]). Justice Ginsburg wrote that this dissent was intended "to engage or energize the public and propel prompt legislative overruling of the Court's decision" (p. 284).
3. Garrett Epps, "Justice Alito's Inexcusable Rudeness," *Atlantic*, June 24, 2013, https://www.theatlantic.com/national/archive/2013/06/justice-alitos-inexcusable-rudeness/277163/.

Notes

"Throwing Away Your Umbrella in a Rainstorm"

1. Maggie Astor, "Seven Ways Alabama Has Made It Harder to Vote," *New York Times*, June 23, 2018; Vann R. Newkirk II, "How *Shelby County v. Holder* Broke America," *Atlantic*, July 10, 2018.
2. In *Husted v. A. Philip Randolph Institute*, 584 U.S. ___ (2018), involving the National Voter Registration Act of 1993, the Court approved Ohio's system of voter roll purges; Justice Ginsburg joined Justice Stephen Breyer's dissent. In *Abbot v. Perez*, 585 U.S. ___ (2018), the Court upheld Texas's redrawing of congressional and state legislative maps with districts drawn to minimize minority voting power; Justice Ginsburg joined Justice Sonia Sotomayor's 46-page dissent.

"There Is Strength in Numbers": *Epic Systems Corp. v. Lewis*

1. "Employment Law: *Epic Systems Corp. v. Lewis*," 132 *Harvard Law Review* 427, November 9, 2018, https://harvardlawreview.org/2018/11/epic-systems-corp-v-lewis/.

"Soldiers of All Faiths": *The American Legion v. American Humanist Assn.*

1. For example, Debbie Levy, *I Dissent: Ruth Bader Ginsburg Makes Her Mark*, illustrated by Elizabeth Baddeley (New York: Simon and Schuster Books for Young Readers, 2016), 7–8; Jonah Winter, *Ruth Bader Ginsburg: The Case of R.B.G. vs. Inequality*, illustrated by Stacy Innerst (New York: Abrams Books for Young Readers, 2017), 910.